Creation Through Wisdom

Creation
Through Wisdom

Theology and the New Biology

CELIA E. DEANE-DRUMMOND

T&T CLARK
EDINBURGH

T&T CLARK LTD
59 GEORGE STREET
EDINBURGH EH2 2LQ
SCOTLAND

www.tandtclark.co.uk

First published 2000

ISBN 0 567 08736 0

British Library Cataloguing-in-Publication Data.
A catalogue record for this book is available from the British Library.

Typeset by Waverley Typesetters, Galashiels
Printed in Great Britain by Bookcraft,
Midsomer Norton, Somerset

In memory of
Sergii Bulgakov (1871–1944)

Contents

Acknowledgements

I would like to acknowledge all those who, directly or indirectly, have helped me in the process of writing this book. This book would be far poorer were it not for their helpful advice, stimulating criticism and insightful wisdom. I would like to thank the Ecumenical Patriarchate for inviting me to the first international seminar on ecology and theology at Halki in 1994, where I first began thinking about the importance of wisdom for ecology. I am deeply grateful to Professor Daniel Hardy and Michael Walsh for giving me helpful comments and criticism on an early outline for this book. Others have given me helpful comments on specific themes. Dr Arthur Peacocke alerted me to the importance of the Revd Thomas Traherne, Professor Sarah Coakley gave me an important reference to Dr Barbara Meehan, Dr Robert Murray pointed me to Margaret Barker's work on *Enoch*, and Sion Cowell made some very helpful suggestions on the work of Pierre Teilhard de Chardin.

I am also grateful to my colleagues at Chester College. In particular, Dr Eric Christianson for most helpful comments on the sections on Old Testament wisdom literature, to Dr Lottie Hosie from the biology department for comments on the sections on ecology and Peter Cox, my PhD student, for insights on Matthew Fox and new social movement theory. Thanks also to Chester College for providing a term's sabbatical leave in which to finish writing this book. I am also privileged to have easy access to St Deiniol's library in

Hawarden, which provides a welcome sanctuary of quiet along with others on similar journeys of writing and research.

I am also grateful to my colleagues at the Centre for the Study of Environmental Change, Robin Grove White and Dr Bronislaw Szerszynski. In this book I refer to our joint work on public attitudes to genetic engineering which is sponsored by a grant from the Christendom Trust, to whom we are indebted. I am also grateful for the ongoing support of my peers, especially Professor Mary Grey, Dr Christopher Southgate and Dr Margaret Yee, who have always given me encouragement at times when I most needed it. Of course, special thanks are due to Stratford Caldecott, the commissioning editor for T&T Clark, for his constructive critical comments and encouragement. I would also like to thank Roger Ruston for his most helpful comments as copy-editor for T&T Clark. On a personal level I would like to thank my husband, Henry Curtis, who has shown me patience, and given me both understanding and encouragement as this work evolved through various stages to completion.

Some of the ideas for this book have already appeared in articles, or are in press or I have presented them as papers at conferences. I am grateful for all the anonymous reviewers of these works and conference participants for their helpful critical comments and suggestions. More specifically, some ideas for Chapters 3, 4 and 5 first appeared as 'Sophia: The Feminine Face of God as a Metaphor for an Ecotheology', *Feminist Theology* 16 (1997), 11–31. Some ideas for Chapters 1 and 5 are also in 'FutureNatural? A Future of Science Through the Lens of Wisdom', *The Heythrop Journal* 40 (1) (1999), 41–59. I have also drawn on an article due to be published in the Food issue of *Ecotheology* in 2000, entitled 'Come to the Banquet: Seeking Wisdom in a Genetically Engineered Earth'. Some of the ideas for a paper entitled 'Seeking Wisdom: The Church and the New Biology' presented at the Society of St Sergius and St Alban annual conference in August 1999 are incorporated into Chapter 3. Again, some of the ideas for Chapter 6 are drawn from a paper entitled 'Theology and the Culture of the Sciences' which I presented at the Catholic Theological Association of Great Britain in

September 1999. A shortened version of that paper is published in *New Blackfriars* 81 (947) (2000), 36–46. Finally, I have presented two papers at the Ian Ramsey Centre at Oxford University, the first at the John Templeton Workshop on Science and Religion in January 1999 and the second at the Ian Ramsey Seminar Series in October 1999. The first was entitled 'Wisdom: A Voice for Theology at the Boundary with Science' and the second 'Biotechnology, Ecology and Wisdom'. Ideas from the first paper are scattered throughout this book, and those for the second are mostly in Chapters 5, 6 and 7. The first paper will be published in the Science issue of *Ecotheology* in 2001.

Preface

The idea for this book first occurred to me while I was on the way to the first international Orthodox seminar in theology and ecology at Halki in June 1994. While on the journey, I had the opportunity to spend some time in Hagia Sophia Cathedral in Istanbul. This magnificent building, dedicated to Sophia, yet showing living mosaics of Christ as Pantocrator, Creator of the world, caught my imagination in a way that is hard to describe. Since that time I have made a more intellectual journey in search of wisdom and its relevance to issues in the new biology. In particular, I am indebted to the sophiological work of Sergii Bulgakov, to whom this book is dedicated.

I begin this book by addressing the context in which we find ourselves at the start of a new millennium, namely the rise in the new biology. The Human Genome Project, with the first draft published in June 2000, promises enormous benefits, but also unknown risks. As genetically engineered products enter the food chain, how do we know if such 'advances' in science will be used for human benefit or the wider common good of people and planet? The crisis that we face seems to be a crisis in knowledge, more specifically a crisis stemming from a translation of wisdom into information. Broader issues beyond the scientific ones come into view. However, it is important to recognise that science at its best also involves commitment. In other words science need not be as secular as it appears and champions of the new physics have even turned to the wisdom of the East. Yet in their search for concord, many of those engaged in debates in science and religion have tried to assimilate theology to science, wary of the perceived historical resistance of the Church to new advances in science.

I suggest that in order to give theology a clearer voice in the debate a deeper appreciation of the theological meaning of wisdom is both relevant and necessary. The way this voice comes to be expressed in a theology of creation is the main theme of this book. It is, above all, grounded in an under-standing of biblical wisdom in the Old Testament, where Wisdom is acknowledged as the artificer of creation. Yet wisdom is also broader than this and challenges readers to face situations of injustice wherever they occur in the community. Those early scientists who tried to use wisdom as a basis for a natural theology can best be understood as those who used wisdom for wonder, but not for confronting current practice.

In particular, the challenge of wisdom becomes sharper and more distinct once we begin to reflect on the wisdom of the cross, which I discuss in Chapter 2. Such an emphasis is an important critique to alternative visions of creation, such as Gaia or creation spirituality, where themes of redemption dis-appear in a romanticised theology of creation. Such a reaction is understandable in view of the long neglect of creation themes in Christian theology. In teasing out the relationship between Christ and Wisdom, a Wisdom Christology that is relevant for today comes into view.

Nonetheless, such a Wisdom Christology has had a long history in the early Eastern Christian traditions, culminating in the translation of all theological themes into wisdom cate-gories that we find in the magnificent sophiology of the Russian theologian Sergii Bulgakov, whose life spanned the turn of the last century. Pierre Teilhard de Chardin, who was one of the pioneers at the interface of science and religion, could not escape the allure of wisdom in his notion of the Eternal Feminine. I suggest that the use of wisdom as a practical basis for ethics in Thomas Aquinas complements the more mystical sophiologies of the Eastern tradition. The third chapter is an exploration of these strands of East and West and outlines how such a combination is an appropriate framework for a theology of creation.

Yet how might wisdom come to be expressed in a contemporary creation theology? I suggest in the fourth chapter that while Christology is the cornerstone, understanding wisdom narrowly in Christological terms is misleading. Contrary, perhaps, to expectations, wisdom is also characteristic of the Spirit, leading to a cosmic understanding of the work of the Holy Spirit. I suggest, further, that wisdom has a Trinitarian shape, one that includes all persons of the Trinity in such a way that Wisdom becomes the feminine face of God. Such a discussion has particular relevance to eco-feminist theology. It is through this dynamic of the Trinity that the relationship between God and creation can be best understood. Creation emerges in Love, but is through Wisdom. A creation theology understood in these terms has a bearing on theology's relationship with science, for now wisdom becomes the key underlying process, rather than simply information.

Theological reflections on the future of creation have often emerged in a way that excludes current scientific understanding. Yet a clear analysis of the future is necessary if we are going to assess the futures proposed by science and that emerging in the new genetics. In Chapter 5, I bring together the unlikely combination of wisdom and apocalyptic in order to show how biblical writers used wisdom in their discussions about the future. How far is this interpretation compatible with the projections of modern science? I suggest that an understanding of eschatology in cosmic categories is essential if theology is to take up the challenge offered by science. There is, as in all eschatology, the difficulty of relating creation, as we know it now, with the new creation yet to come. Yet I show that a wisdom theology does give us an outline for such a development. Furthermore, with Aquinas we can envisage the final end of creation as wisdom expressed through beauty. In the end any definitive understanding of the future of creation is bound to fail, though hints at a correction of such an attitude come from Hildegard de Bingen's mystical visions of wisdom.

How might this future image of creation be relevant for the practice of modern science? I take up this theme in the sixth chapter, where I suggest that we can only gain clues about the future of science if we start to understand the way science works, its particular culture. As we probe into an investigation of this culture, deeper philosophical issues come into view. Hence we return once again to a discussion of the philosophy of science with which I began this book. Yet on a practical level the future of science will be shaped by public attitudes. The response of the public to new genetic technologies shows a remarkable degree of sophistication, even an implicit theology. Yet Heidegger was only too well aware that we are all conditioned by the technology of which we are a part – it is impossible to stand 'outside' this technology. Are there any alternatives in the new biology that suggest a different approach to the mechanistic one dominant in biotechnology? I suggest that in ecology we find seeds of an alternative, but this is not one that simply draws on the idea of the earth as a giant ecosystem. Rather, the area of ecology that is most suggestive speaks about order, but also about chaos. Furthermore, the story of Barbara McClintock shows that a science resonant with wisdom is still possible, even within genetic science. Once again we find wisdom appearing, this time at the border of order and chaos.

I attempt to draw all these threads together in the concluding chapter of the book. Throughout I have tried to weave the image of wisdom with threads in science, to map out a new way of relating the two that does justice to the theological voice as well as the scientific one. Even though theology is progressively marginalised and excluded in academic communities, I suggest that many of its traditional ideas still carry something of the strength of a classic. The public sensitivity to theology, however implicit, is surely a warning to those in power that science left to its own devices will not finally win the day. Yet theology has important lessons to learn from contemporary culture as well. The temptation to turn inwards, to shelter in obscurantism must surely be resisted. This book on wisdom is a start in this direction. Yet I am conscious that there are areas of this book that are far from complete. It is my hope that it will be a stimulus to others in their search for wisdom.

The capitalisation of Wisdom appears in the text when Wisdom is personified or is referring to the divine Wisdom of the different persons of the Trinity. I use a lower case for wisdom when wisdom is impersonal, or associated with human, secular wisdom. In some cases wisdom hovers between divine and human activity and so cannot be categorised clearly as one or the other. In these cases I have generally preferred the use of lower case for wisdom.

Chester
Advent, 1999

Abbreviations

BSE	Bovine Spongiform Encephalopathy
CSEC	Centre for the Study of Environmental Change
ENDS	Environmental Data Services
HFEA	Human Fertilisation and Embryology Authority
HGAC	Human Genetics Advisory Commission
JB	Jerusalem Bible
MAFF	Ministry of Agriculture, Fisheries and Food
NJB	New Jerusalem Bible
NRSV	New Revised Standard Version
RSV	Revised Standard Version

The Search for Wisdom

The rise of the new biology

Few will doubt that one of the major challenges facing the human race is our new-found ability to change the natural world for our own ends through genetic engineering and biotechnology. James Watson's and Francis Crick's discovery of the structure of deoxyribonucleic acid (DNA) in 1954 opened up the molecular structure of life to human intervention in a way that was impossible prior to this event. Hence the new biology – a very new science – will undoubtedly be that which has the largest impact on our lives in the next millennium. Both the scientists and the public met the initial discovery with rapturous enthusiasm. Now it seemed that we held the key to life itself, and we could contribute to its improvement.

The multimillion-dollar-funded Human Genome Project, completed in draft form in June 2000, is a global response to the prospect of being able to map in detail the structure of human genetic information, the human genome. Such mapping, it is claimed, could contribute to the discovery of particular genes that lead to particular genetic diseases, or propensity to other diseases, such as cancer. It seems like a climax in biological research that now we have the skill to study and perhaps change the biological blueprint of living things. But there are some people who have qualms and these continue to grow. In the case of manipulation of the human genome, who

is to say that the knowledge will be used for good? The spectre
of eugenics and the Nazi dream still cast a shadow over all
claims for a biological utopia. The abuse of information by
insurance companies, the possible marginalisation of those who
are not genetically perfect, the exclusive nature of the access
to the technology and the possible strain on family and human
relationships are just some of the ethical issues that are currently
being aired.

Other anxieties are compounded by the infiltration of
genetically engineered food on to our supermarket shelves. It
seems that while we might have a choice over genetic testing,
few of us will have a choice about consuming unlabelled
genetically engineered food, such as soya beans. More and
more products are being tested through field trials. While
there are commercial benefits to the producers, the benefits to
the consumers have yet to reach the market place.[1] The unknown risks, distrust of government policy-makers in the wake
of the BSE food crisis and a sense that we are like human
guinea-pigs in a vast global experiment all serve to heighten
public anxiety. It is hardly surprising, then, that protestors
should target fields of genetically modified crops. While not
all will agree with their direct action, the perceived ecological
and health risks are sufficient to trigger a focused practical
response.

I will argue in this chapter that the ambiguous promise of
the new biology calls for a reassessment of scientific knowing.
I will suggest that there needs to be a reclamation of a more
integrated approach to our understanding that includes
goodness and knowledge in wisdom. Such a search for wisdom
in Christian theology has a basis in philosophy, but is also
rooted in a rich biblical tradition, beginning with that in the
Old Testament. This lays the foundations for further development of the wisdom motif as a basis for a theology of creation.
Such a theology is one that is grounded in the realities
confronting us in the new biology.

---

[1] For detailed examples of possible benefits see Nuffield Council on Bioethics,
Genetically Modified Crops: The Social and Ethical Issues, London: Nuffield
Council on Bioethics, 1999.

The assessment of risks

We might first of all want to ask ourselves how far public anxieties about genetic engineering are based on the real risks involved. The biotechnological companies are quick to point to the benefits in terms of medical and pharmacological uses or, in the case of food, improved efficiency and productivity. Environmental scientists are generally less convinced. The specificity of some of the genetic changes is in doubt. Scientists have, for example, been able to introduce a gene coding for an insecticide into maize plants, thereby removing any need for crop spraying with chemicals.[2] The genetic make-up of the maize is changed so that it can now synthesise its own insecticide internally. This seems to be environmentally beneficial, as heavy doses of chemical sprays are no longer required. However, recent experiments have shown that lapwings are also vulnerable to the insecticide, thereby upsetting the food chain due to the lapwing's premature death. Other possible dangers include the loss of biodiversity through use of herbicide-resistant plants. While the companies marketing the herbicides claim that this reduces the need for heavy herbicide spraying, environmentalists still worry that the wild species of plants around the crops will be killed, thus reducing biodiversity. Another possibility exists that there will be genetic 'leakage' through cross-pollination to wild species. Other possible ecological effects of genetically modified organisms include the threat of ecological invasion.

More direct effects on human health might include the possibility of allergic reactions to new proteins introduced into the food. While the risk is very small, even transfer of just a few genes from Brazil nuts into soya bean gives a positive reaction.[3] Hence, even though only a very small fraction of the total protein make-up of crops is changed, this still could lead to hitherto unknown allergic reactions. It is unlikely that such change could be monitored or detected adequately as it

---

[2] ENDS, 'The Spiralling Agenda of Agricultural Biotechnology', *ENDS Report* 283 (August 1998), 18–30.

[3] D. King, 'Genetically Engineered Food: How Safe is it?', *GenEthics News* 9 (November/December 1995), 8.

is likely to affect only a small number of individuals. The risk, however, remains. The possible threats to animal welfare relate to the way it is never possible to know in advance how far genes will change in expression once we move genetic material from one organism to another. In other words, the genetic environment in which the gene finds itself can lead to changes and unexpected effects. I have discussed this and other examples connected with animal welfare elsewhere.[4]

Counter-arguments in favour

When it comes to genetic engineering of the human genome, scientists are usually more cautious. Genetic engineering of the 'germ line' (egg and sperm cells) is currently banned in humans. As far as I am aware this prohibition is world-wide. There is always some risk in attempting to introduce genetic change in that while the techniques are relatively precise in terms of biological science, they are not one hundred per cent successful. Moreover, it is not normally known in advance where the new genetic material will be incorporated into the recipient's chromosomal DNA. The fact that there are billions of cells in any one person means that changing some cells in our body (somatic cells) will lead to localised effects. For example, those suffering from cystic fibrosis have a defective gene that codes for a particular protein. If the DNA of this gene is injected into lung cells, it is taken up by the cells in a fraction of cases and this is enough to promote some relief from suffering.[5] Some scholars have, nonetheless, argued that changes to the germ line should be permitted if it is for 'therapeutic' purposes, once the technical difficulties of success rates are overcome.[6]

An argument can also be made for the possible benefits of genetic engineering of non-humans. For example, genetically

---

[4] C. Deane-Drummond, *Theology and Biotechnology: Implications for a New Science*, London: Geoffrey Chapman, 1997, 83, 86.
[5] M. Reiss and R. Straughan, *Improving Nature? The Science and Ethics of Genetic Engineering*, Cambridge: Cambridge University Press, 1996, 202–6.
[6] A. Dyson and J. Harris (eds), *Ethics and Biotechnology*, London: Routledge, 1994.

modified bacteria or farm animals, such as sheep and goats, can produce the drugs needed for tackling human diseases.[7] The use of genetic engineering to produce crops containing vaccines offers considerable opportunities for disease prevention. For many the risks are worth accepting in those cases where medical benefits are obvious, though some are concerned about animal welfare issues. Crop plants, also, could be modified so that they grow in conditions that are normally unfavourable, such as areas of drought or high salinity. Moreover, it may be possible to engineer allergens out of particular crops, so that those who are allergic to nuts, for example, no longer have a reaction. Also a case has been made for introducing vitamins into crops of staples, such as rice or potatoes. Yet where these changes are intended to have an altruistic purpose, for example solving the crisis of Vitamin D deficiency in the poorer nations of the world, issues of social justice once again come to the surface. How do we know that those in the Third World necessarily want such genetically modified crops? Those most in touch with the grass-roots communities suggest that they do not, indeed this seems more like another example of imperialism with a different face.[8] Yet, closer to home, there are public fears about the possibility of a genetic underclass emerging in our society. How do we know, for example, that our new-found knowledge will be used for social good?

The crisis in knowledge

Once we scrape beneath the surface of biotechnology, it seems that the crisis is as much a crisis of knowledge as anything else. The promise of biotechnology is an ambiguous one. We are uncertain if our knowledge will be for good or ill. Gone is our implicit faith in science, that it will always solve our

---

[7] For further discussion of this see C. Deane-Drummond, *Genetic Engineering for a New Earth? Theology and Ethics of the New Biology*, Cambridge: Grove Books, 1999.

[8] See recent Christian Aid Reports related to this issue, *Selling Suicide: Farming, False Promises and Genetic Engineering in the Developing World*, London: Christian Aid, 1999; *Who Owns Who? Climate Change, Debt, Equity and Survival*, London: Christian Aid, 1999.

problems. Instead, it seems to be generating as many new difficulties as it solves. The presumed blessing of genetic technology seems a cruel parody of what it might become – namely a curse on the human race. The feeling of being out of control of our own destiny returns, even as we believe we have found the key to control our own futures.

Furthermore, we seem to have lost the wisdom to know the difference. The story of the Fall in the Garden of Eden takes on a different twist, with the tree of knowledge opening the way for unprecedented change in the way we construct the natural world. This impinges on the way we relate to one another socially and politically, hence the issue has implications far beyond the narrow confines of academic debate. Nonetheless, addressing the issue at an intellectual level may serve to generate a more socially responsible science, one that is in tune with cultural concern, rather than detached from it.

Modern distortions from ancient philosophy

In order to discern a little more clearly how we have arrived at the current position we need to consider how science has changed over the centuries. Ancient science was part of philosophy and included explorations into all areas of knowledge. The aim of ancient philosophy was the contemplation of life itself, the search for wisdom, rather than our modern preoccupation with fragments of knowledge. In other words knowledge was an aspect of the wider wisdom. Wisdom in the ancient philosophical sense is the active possession of knowledge, rather than just a 'string of information'.

The philosopher Mary Midgley believes that at the heart of all knowledge must be an understanding of goodness, as it shows the point of all other knowledge.[9] She suggests that modern science has lost this contemplative stance, so now it is just concerned with new discoveries. In other words it is always straining after the new, instead of taking stock of what is there already and reflecting on the implications. This is

---

[9] M. Midgley, *Wisdom, Information and Wonder: What is Knowledge For?* London: Routledge, 1989, 13–14.

particularly relevant to the contemporary meteoric rise of new biology that I mentioned above. Other philosophers make a similar comment, that our ingenuity has outstripped our wisdom.[10]

It is possible to trace historically the gradual shift in philosophical concern alongside the changes in patterns of science. While the early science was considered to be part of philosophy, with the rise in Enlightenment thinking scientific knowledge gradually became separated from wisdom. Kant attempted to overcome this crisis by separating moral knowledge and natural knowledge. Eventually philosophy became confined to the moral sphere, with natural philosophy translating into the domain of the natural sciences. The place of philosophy was eventually restricted just to thinking about why we know what we know.[11]

Much the same story could be told about theology, where considerations about God were part of ancient philosophy. Following Kant, theology became restricted to the moral sphere and eventually it was excluded from this as well, so that theology is just a way of thinking logically about 'religion', isolated from the rest of life. In other words the specialisation of science, which is so familiar to most of us, also applies to other areas of knowledge. Even those areas that might seem to be able to take a broader perspective, such as philosophy and theology, become part of the fragmentation process.

Nicholas Maxwell has called for a completely new understanding of the whole direction of philosophy, so that it is based on problems of life, rather than problems of knowledge. He calls this a *philosophy of wisdom*, tracing the idea back to the early philosophical stance of Socrates. He also goes a step further in arguing that the shrinking of our philosophy is a direct cause of the modern crises of our time, namely the nuclear threat, environmental challenge and global injustices of all kinds. He believes we need to learn to act in different

[10] N. Lash, *The Beginning and the End of Religion*, Cambridge: Cambridge University Press, 1996.
[11] Lash, *Beginning*, 116–17.

ways and such action is only possible once fundamental problems of living are given priority. He suggests:

> What I advocate is a radical change – a radical evolution – in the overall fundamental aims and methods of inquiry. At present we have a kind of academic inquiry that has, as its intellectual aim, to improve knowledge. This needs to be transformed, I shall argue, into a kind of rational inquiry that has, as its basic intellectual aim, to improve wisdom.[12]

He believes that this focus on wisdom is both more rational and more humane. More rational because it allows us to connect the personal with the public and concentrate on problems that are really important for life and living. More humane as it connects with the goals and aims of social life, instead of working in detached 'objective' isolation.[13] He believes that simply attaching social concern to existing science is not enough – rather it must be resourced from a different philosophical position rooted in wisdom. He argues that while science itself is not to blame, its lack of social co-operative rationality does make it responsible for the ills in society. For example, the justification of research is usually a far less 'rational' activity, simply because only the results of research are considered to be objects of inquiry.[14] This is based on a false philosophy of knowledge.

Maxwell mentions some heroes of a philosophy of wisdom, including some scientists such as Darwin, Popper, Einstein, who no doubt have behaved in responsible and socially aware ways.[15] However, it is not clear why he holds these up alongside Socrates, Jesus, Mill and Fromm. Mary Midgley has clarified this beautifully in her book *Wisdom, Information and Wonder*.[16] She compares two twentieth-century scientists, Sir Ernst Chain, who was the co-discoverer of penicillin, and Albert Einstein. For Chain, professional scientists cannot be expected to have the wisdom to deal with

---

[12] N. Maxwell, *From Knowledge to Wisdom: A Revolution in the Aims and Methods of Science*, Oxford: Blackwell, 1984, 3–4.
[13] Maxwell, *Knowledge*, 6–10.
[14] Maxwell, *Knowledge*, 55–6.
[15] Maxwell, *Knowledge*, 117.
[16] Midgley, *Wisdom*, 74–80.

personal relationships or give advice in wider public and political matters. He effectively seals off science from the rest of life, thus barring any potential confrontation and dialogue. His insistence that no quality of good or evil can be attached to scientific research removes all science from the realm of ethics. The responsibility of the latter is simply left to 'society'.

However, as Midgley points out, Chain is also a citizen as well as a scientist. It is simply not good enough to abdicate responsibility for science by claiming it is outside its jurisdiction to think about these things. Albert Einstein, by contrast, was able to think both as a scientist and as a citizen. He devoted himself to political campaigns for justice and peace once he saw the implications of the newly discovered nuclear capacity. For Einstein, science gave the intellectual equipment for clarity of thought on other issues. However, science needs a Puritan's restraint in being humble about its own capacity to provide the first principles for ethics.

This suggests that it is possible for scientists to become more socially responsible and aware. However, both Maxwell's and Midgley's typologies present certain difficulties. In the case of Maxwell's hypothesis, how realistic is his envisaged transformation of the aims and goals of all knowledge, including science? The most we can hope for is a shift in the direction of wisdom, rather than a radical replacement. Further, is his particular version of wisdom the only one worth considering? He seems to have put sociology at the top of a hierarchy, even while speaking in terms of dialogue and co-operation. Has this become a liberal democratic politic, dressed up in the language of wisdom? Furthermore, while Midgley gives us two clear examples from the stories of Sir Ernst Chain and Einstein, can we really expect scientists to become political agitators? We might also like to reflect on the good effects on society of the discovery of penicillin, in spite of the narrow social views of the individual concerned. Is a certain degree of narrowness necessary for scientific achievement?

Beyond science

I hope to show in what follows that to expect scientists on their own to come up with solutions to complex issues raised by science is unrealistic. The early scientists of the seventeenth century were more aware of a goal to work for the common good. Charles Raven, in particular, believed that this century was the only one in which theological ideas and science came together in a grand synthesis.[17] However, this synthesis was a fragile one and soon broke down once the argument for God from design had effectively been dismissed by Darwin's theory of evolution. Now it seemed that there was no need to implicate God as the designer of the intricacies of the natural world. Now, instead, we could explain the variety of species through a long process of natural selection. Science could be portrayed as the liberator from the magic and superstition of former times. In as much as it gave us more knowledge into the causes of events, this is a fair statement. However, science also attempted to split apart from value so that its method was seen as detached, objective and removed from subjective interference.

When seen in this light, science on its own is impotent to supply meaning. Instead, the trend in science seems to view the world as meaningless, freed from the tyranny of mythologies such as religion.[18] It seemed bent on destruction of religious foundations, but at the same time unable to fill the void created in the sphere of meaning. Some scientists, it is true, gloried in the ability of science to make discoveries. However, the presumption that science really was objective was to prove to be a shallow one. Science can never completely free itself from the particular subjectivity of the observer. To believe otherwise is itself a delusion. Nicholas Lash suggests that the delusion of total objectivity is now finally coming to an end. The tragedy of modern Western culture is the time it has taken to come to realise that there is no neutral starting point, no universal place from which to view reality.[19] In other words, whether we like it or not we are all conditioned by our particular culture and tradition that forms the context of our particular story.

[17] C. Raven, *Synthetic Philosophy in the Seventeenth Century: A Study of Early Science*, Herbert Spencer Lecture, 22 May 1945, Oxford: Blackwell, 1945.
[18] For a commentary see B. Appleyard, *Understanding the Present, Science and the Soul of Modern Man*, London: Picador, 1992, 83.
[19] Lash, *Beginning*, 18.

Science as commitment: Polanyi

How have contemporary scientists responded to these challenges? Michael Polanyi is one philosopher of science who was quite ready to admit that science is not the neutral, objective and sterile activity it is often portrayed to be. He suggested that all our knowledge comes though commitment that is highly personal.[20] He recognised the split between critical lucidity and 'intense moral consciousness'.[21] He believed that eternal purpose cannot be found in science and admired the pattern of thinking in Augustine, which put faith before reason. He argued that while this initially held up scientific progress, now the balance had to be addressed so that faith once more has room to breathe.

This seems to open up space for validity of truth explored in myth, poetry and ritual in a way that Lash does not really address. Nonetheless, Polanyi shied away from a specific religious content to his philosophy and while he found some parallels in the method of science and religion, he describes Christian worship as an 'eternal, never to be consummated hunch'.[22] These kinds of descriptions do not seem to bear much resemblance to the traditions found in theology or Christian religion. However, his ideas about indwelling a tradition and the intersection of tradition and novelty in science come some way towards healing the rift with religion. He was prepared to accept the idea that truth could be found in religion as well as science, indeed science could not survive in isolation from the rest of humanity's cultural heritage.

Most significant of all, perhaps, for our present discussion is Polanyi's idea of tacit knowledge. Tacit knowledge is the sense by which we become dimly aware of the direction in which we must seek for a solution, before its formulation.[23] Perception comes from sense organs and even worms have this ability to reach forward and try and make sense of the world around them. Such tacit knowledge has evolved from

[20] D. Scott, *Michael Polanyi*, London: SPCK, 1996.
[21] Scott, *Polanyi*, 180.
[22] Scott, *Polanyi*, 185.
[23] Scott, *Polanyi*, 46.

small beginnings. He also understood it to refer to the acquisition of basic skills, such as riding a bicycle, or cooking. Even though the detailed processes are not possible to specify exactly, it is still knowledge. Added to this is the idea of caring, of commitment, in other words that we have to believe that there is something to know. Tacit knowing is the everyday experience of ordinary people, but also the root of scientific knowing as well.

Polanyi's concept of tacit knowing goes some way towards recognising that the practice of science is a very human activity that has its roots in everyday experience. It therefore serves to remind science of its origin in human insight and perception, rather than giving it any more grandiose status. Nonetheless, there are some problems with his views. One in particular is his failure to address adequately the real possibility that scientific insights may be misguided or immoral. His views seem to suggest that as long as there is commitment, caring, then accurate perception of reality automatically follows. His vision of reality carried a religious gloss, but is this really adequate from a theological point of view? Rendering science into an activity that bears some resemblance to religious practice is not really dialogue at all.

Trends towards wisdom in the new physics

More recently physicists engaged in what has become known as the 'new physics' have thrown up fresh doubts about the nature of the reality that they seek. Instead of the fixity of the past, relativity theory, quantum theory and chaos theory all serve to challenge how far we really can have certainty about the world. In simple terms, relativity claims that there is no such thing as absolute time and space, quantum theory that we cannot have precisely controlled measurements and chaos theory claims that we cannot predict precisely the outcome of certain events.[24]

These results have led to a more cautious appreciation of knowledge that is discovered by science – it is a 'critical'

[24] For a lucid and popular introduction to this see Appleyard, *Understanding*, 156–63.

realism, which admits that the reality is subject to change as new discoveries are made. How far is the new physics different from the old, classical position that understood the world as a mechanism? Some would argue that the physics is genuinely new, that it represents a radical break with the mechanistic world that was assumed in classical physics.[25] Others prefer to see the change as more continuous, since we find elements of holism and mechanism throughout the history of science.[26]

Whatever the position we adopt, it is clear that the new physics lends itself to more possibilities of religious connotations. Fritjof Capra's classic book *The Tao of Physics* is a good example of this phenomenon.[27] Since then a variety of books have mushroomed on the relationship between the new physics and Eastern wisdom and philosophy.[28] However, one point is worth noting, that the Eastern wisdom seems to be accepted in an uncritical and descriptive way in contrast to the more thorough and critical treatment of the sciences. The language of dialogue, it seems, only goes as far as absorbing those elements of the religion that conform with scientific practice.

The search for a new consonance

Lash is particularly scathing about all the more recent attempts at dialogue between theology and the sciences. He suggests that the careful and critical use of theological language is abandoned, so putting it bluntly, scientists 'treat topics in philosophy and theology with a carelessness and unconcern for competence, which rightly irritates them when the boot is on the other foot'.[29] Lash also believes that all such dialogue goes very smoothly as long as 'both theologians and scientists

[25] Appleyard, *Understanding*, 183.
[26] J. Brooke and G. Cantor, *Reconstructing Nature: The Engagement of Science and Religion*, Edinburgh: T&T Clark, 1998, 96–101.
[27] F. Capra, *The Tao of Physics: An Exploration of the Parallels Between Modern Physics and Eastern Mysticism*, Berkeley: Shambhala, 1979.
[28] G. Zukav, *The Dancing Wu Li Masters: An Overview of the New Physics*, New York: Wilham Morrow, 1979; S. Grof (ed.), *Ancient Wisdom and Modern Science*, Albany: State University of New York Press, 1984.
[29] Lash, *Beginning*, 102.

operate as more or less sophisticated spectatorial empiricists'.[30]
In other words, theology is truncated in favour of the particular science. While his dismissal of scientists' understanding
of theology may be somewhat exaggerated, when science and
theology are engaged in dialogue it is normally theology which
turns out to be the weaker partner.

Those engaged in the contemporary debates between science
and religion have begun to speak of a 'new consonance'
between the two disciplines, in place of the enmity of past
generations. This consonance seems to mean finding 'corres-
pondence' or connections between the natural world as
portrayed by science and that portrayed in theology. However,
the relationship between them is not always clear. While for
some the ideal of consonance seems to mean harmony and
full accord, for others it is theology constrained by scientific
research. Both interpretations, however, seem to weaken the
role of theology in the dialogue process. Ted Peters, for
example, comments that there are a few writers prepared to
put theology in what he terms the 'leadership role' following a search for consonance, describing this as 'a courageous
move'.[31] Yet none seem to have given theology the opportunity
to speak first, to ask *science* to respond to its concerns and
epistemology.

Giving theology a voice
What kind of language does theology need to speak in order
to be heard by scientists? It seems to me that even though
theology and science operate through different frames of
reference, they are both, as Polanyi realised, profoundly human
enterprises. The new biology, which is of primary concern to
this book, differs from the new physics in that it is still largely
operating under the mechanistic world-picture that is characteristic of classical physics. It has therefore not had the same
degree of humbling that has led to much agonising in the
physics community. This, however, may be an advantage since
the more spurious connections with religion can be avoided.

---

[30] Lash, *Beginning*, 92.
[31] T. Peters, *Science and Theology: The New Consonance*, Oxford: Westview
Press, 1998, 10.

Furthermore, the classic understanding of the role of religion as the moral voice of science becomes relevant once again. The complex ethical issues surrounding the new biology bear an urgency that was not adequately recognised in the generation that heralded the rise of the new physics. Perhaps the breakdown of certainty that is part and parcel of the end of modernity and in tune with modern physics has allowed religious voices to be heard once again.

We need to search for a theology that will remind science of its human origins, that will speak from an ethical perspective and that will foster a broader approach which is in tune with global concerns. It is, on the one hand, a corrective to the narrow specialisation in science, while, on the other hand, offering a new vision of the way science may recover its original intention to work for the common good. While Lash has suggested that the wisdom of religion needs to be reinstated, the next stage is to spell out exactly what this wisdom might mean in theological terms. For Christian theology at least, wisdom has been a neglected area of study until comparatively recently. However, wisdom traditions, by their very richness as literature, lend themselves to addressing complex issues that we face in the new discoveries of science. Theology needs to recover its voice and speak again, to break out of the timidity in the face of science that has been characteristic of previous attempts at dialogue. The opposite extreme of condemnation of science is not fruitful either, as it refuses to recognise science's achievements and the positive benefit to humanity of many of its discoveries.

Wisdom in the Old Testament

Books about wisdom in theology abound, mostly connected with particular mystical writers of different periods. However, biblical wisdom is not just mysticism, though it may contain elements of this experience. In order to clarify the heart of the meaning of wisdom in the Christian tradition it is necessary to explore the biblical basis for this wisdom in the wisdom literature. In this chapter I will be focusing on wisdom in the Old Testament. I will explore wisdom in the New Testament in the following chapter. This biblical wisdom, as interpreted through different traditions, can then become the basis for a creation theology that is in tune with the latest developments in the new biology. A wisdom model is necessarily more complex compared with, for example, an incarnational model of the relationship between God, humanity and the world. By contrast, the reductionist philosophy of the new biology narrows our understanding so that wider complexities are avoided.

Wisdom as literature, as I mentioned above, is a relatively new area for intense biblical scholarship. The scope of the wisdom literature always includes the Psalms, Proverbs, Ecclesiastes and the Book of Job. Most scholars also include the Apocryphal books such as the Wisdom of Solomon and Ecclesiasticus or Ben Sira. Others extend the net to the Pseudepigraphal literature such as the Book of Enoch. The core stories of salvation history such as patriarchal promises or the story of the exodus and giving of the covenant are, by and large, missing from the wisdom literature. If we presume that salvation history is the core message of biblical theology, then wisdom will naturally retreat to the margins. The shift in emphasis has come from a realisation that any characterisation of wisdom as unhistorical is incorrect. History is not just a recollection of key events in the past, but it is also an analysis of daily experience in the lives of ordinary people. Furthermore, while the wisdom literature did not rehearse the events known as salvation history, such events were presupposed. There are also exceptions to this characterisation in that Wisdom of Solomon and Sirach include lengthy surveys of salvation history. However, any history is reinterpreted in the light of their prime concern, which is to transmit human and social traditions. For our purposes the absence of particular national frames of reference has certain advantages as it gives it a much wider validity and more universal significance that is also characteristic of science.

The human face of Old Testament wisdom
The renewed interest in wisdom literature also comes from a greater appreciation of its significance in informing the daily

lives of ordinary people. Murphy aptly describes wisdom as a
'Tree of Life'.[32] The basic assumption of wisdom writers was
that wisdom was a quality of life that could be learned. Hence
the primary wisdom writers were also teachers. While early
wisdom was likely to be a disciplined empiricism, engaged
with problems of government and administration, later wisdom
became more focused on ethical conduct.[33] The intention of
wisdom writers now was to instil an ethical consensus in
society, based on the accumulative experience of the past. The
advice given by the wisdom writers is based squarely on human
experience.

It is this pragmatic rooting of wisdom that gives the wisdom
literature some commonality with the practice of science.
Instead of the lofty words of the prophets, God's nature could
be discovered in ordinary human experiences of life and the
universe. However, wisdom writers were not secularists, even
if they shared some of their insights. For them any denial of
God is the attitude of a fool, rather than one who shows
wisdom. Instead of the law, which spelt out specific instructions
for living, wisdom was more open to different interpretations
becoming possible in different circumstances. For example,
Proverbs 26.4 and 26.5 give two opposite injunctions:

> Do not answer a fool in the terms of his folly
> for fear you grow like him yourself.
> Answer a fool in the terms of his folly
> for fear he imagine himself wise. (NJB)

Such contrasting injunctions invite a degree of freedom in
moral judgement, rather than strict legal adherence.[34] The
intention of the Proverbs is, then, to develop practical wisdom,
which will become more obvious with further experience.

Brown has suggested that the primary purpose of the
wisdom literature is to develop particular character traits that

---

[32] R. E. Murphy, *The Tree of Life: An Exploration of Biblical Wisdom Literature*,
2nd edn, Grand Rapids: W. B. Eerdmans, 1996.

[33] R. C. Hill, *Wisdom's Many Faces*, Collegeville: The Liturgical Press, 1989,
79.

[34] W. P. Brown, *Character in Crisis: A Fresh Approach to the Wisdom Literature*,
Grand Rapids: W. B. Eerdmans, 1996, 13.

lead to ethical conduct. He defines character as the self in relation, both to the perceived world and to God.[35] The development of character includes freedom of choice, but within a framework of ethical accountability of both the individual self and the community. Wisdom writings encourage, then, building up of moral virtues and moral integrity. Particular stories, or narratives, lead to the formation of character in the wisdom literature. They are not, however, uniform. Character as portrayed in Proverbs is very different from Job or Qoheleth. For Job, the conventional wisdom of suffering as the result of sin was no longer valid, he challenged such ideas by his own life story of events. For Qoheleth a lonely journey within led to a scepticism about the possibility of any real purpose of a life of virtue, which, like the wicked, inevitably ended in a sense of the 'absurd', of death and tragedy. Both stories remind the reader that lofty hopes of reward for righteous action are unrealistic and only lead to despair. Brown believes that Qoheleth is significant as he encourages a freedom from 'obsessive striving' that is a trap too easy to fall into within the traditional role of wisdom.[36]

It seems to me that all aspects of wisdom informing character – the freedom of choice for individual and community, the openness to new experiences, the strengthening of moral integrity and the lack of obsessive striving – have relevance for the practice of science. First of all, the literature recognises diversity of response and some flexibility in dealing with complex issues. Ethical conduct is not just about following a rulebook. Secondly, the experience of Job is a reminder that particular traditions may need to be revised in the light of new evidence, new experience. We have to be open to new possibilities, as well as call on the traditions of the past. Yet this very openness does not amount to a rejection of faith. Qoheleth continued to search for wisdom, but realised that too great an attachment can lead to despair. It amounts to 'chasing after wind'. Science, like theology, can easily become arrogant in its claims and presumption that it holds a key to

[35] Brown, *Character*, 8.
[36] Brown, *Character*, 145.

the future. The initial great relish with which the Human Genome Project has been greeted reflects just such arrogance and lack of humility.

It is also important that Qoheleth is allowed to speak in the wisdom corpus. Even though he is highly critical of his teachers, he still has a place in the canon. How far are scientists really open to criticism from within or outside? The temptation to dismiss the truths of those outside the subject becomes clear from reading books by Stephen Hawking or Richard Dawkins. The former rejects modern philosophy as simply the analysis of language.[37] The latter dismisses theology as having no more 'solid basis than fairies'.[38] In both cases the lack of supposed empirical knowledge seems to be the basis for the rejection. Lash believes that empiricism is now so much part of our culture, infused by the dominance of a scientific perspective, that grammatical procedure is considered obsolete and irrelevant.[39]

The variegated forms of wisdom

How might the wisdom literature serve as a corrective to this focus on cultural empiricism? While Brown is correct to highlight the role of wisdom in character formation, the picture he paints is not an accurate representation of the richness of the biblical sources. Wisdom is also a variegated discourse and includes various forms such as riddle, fable, parable, allegory, proverb, psalm, exhortation, dialogue, rhetorical question, didactic narrative and autobiographical narrative, to name just some examples.[40] Poetic and metaphorical language is included alongside empirical observations. Purdue suggests that the imagistic and aesthetic language of the wisdom literature is the most dominant.[41] He also goes further in suggesting that discursive language distorts the spirit

---

[37] S. Hawking, *A Brief History of Time*, London: Bantam Press, 1988, 175.
[38] R. Dawkins, 'A Reply to Poole', *Science and Christian Belief* 7(1) (April 1995), 46.
[39] Lash, *Beginning*, 18.
[40] Hill, *Faces*, 101.
[41] L. Purdue, *Wisdom and Creation, The Theology of the Wisdom Literature*, Nashville: Abingdon Press, 1994, 48.

and intention of the original authors. While I believe that it is important to keep the metaphorical aspects of the wisdom literature to the foreground, I also consider that its pragmatism does point to an empiricism that cannot be dismissed. Indeed its strength is to combine both types of knowing in one body of literature. One can inform and correct the other.

Wisdom as artificer in creation

Having dealt with the more anthropological emphasis in wisdom, it is time to consider another face of wisdom that deals with the *creation* and the *cosmos*. There are some scholars who believe that it is this face and not the anthropological one that comes through most clearly. Almost all scholars now recognise that wisdom literature includes creation theology, but differences exist as to how far creation can move to centre stage. Many scholars take this to be a distortion of wisdom's intention.[42] It seems to me that placing any theme at the centre of wisdom is too simplistic. The coherence of wisdom comes through its many faces, human, social and cosmic.[43] In the dialogue with science, the multifactoral nature of wisdom forces an exploration of wider issues of human ethical and social conduct. This contrasts with other theologies of creation, which just focus on the natural world. Having said this, we are now in a position to examine the relationship with the natural world that does form a significant strand of wisdom thought.

In Proverbs the metaphors used to describe the origin of the world are artistry, fertility, battle and struggle. For the sages, God uses wisdom to create and sustain the world. For example, Proverbs 3.13–20 speaks in the first strophe of the contentment of those who find wisdom. The second strophe uses language that elsewhere is applied to the deity, especially 3.17. The third strophe explores wisdom's role in the creation of the world. The pursuit of wisdom is not simply an intellectual exercise, but a commitment of the heart where Wisdom is the object of human love and affection, such as

---

[42] Brown rejects this idea, *Character*, as does Murphy, *Tree*.
[43] In this much I agree with Hill, *Faces*.

Proverbs 1.20–33. Human life and well-being are thus grounded in creation. Wisdom seems to function as the artificer of creation.

Wisdom's place in creation is elaborated further in Proverbs 8. The interpretation of this passage has been the subject of scholarly controversy. Proverbs 8.22ff. suggests that Wisdom is associated with the beginning of creation:

> Yahweh created me, first-fruits of his fashioning, before the oldest of his works. (NJB)

However, the meaning of *qānānî* in 8.22 may imply possession by God *or* creation by God, especially when linked with the idea of beginning. Whatever the interpretation this implies a close relationship between God and Wisdom. The actual role of Wisdom in creation described in Proverbs 8.30 has proved difficult to decipher because of the ambiguity associated with the word *'āmôn* in 8.30a:

> I was beside the master craftsman, delighting him day after day, ever at play in his presence. (NJB)

The possible alternatives include Wisdom as craftsman, or possibly less likely, foster child.[44] If the former sense is taken then Wisdom is intricately bound up with the creation of the universe, which reinforces 8.26b and 8.29, which imply that all of matter and all ordering comes about through Wisdom. The final outcome of 8.30b is the celebration of this fact, that wisdom is *also* a source of joy, wonder and praise.

Some of the most celebrated examples of meditations on creation are found in the wisdom literature. Psalms 8 and 19A and the creation passages in Job are just three examples. However, the literature is not just about the wonder of God as found in the natural cycles of sun, moon and stars, it is also expressive of the detailed observation of the natural world and how we can learn from such observations. This lends this literature some affinity with the practice of science. Consider the following passages, for example,

---

[44] For further discussion see C. Deane-Drummond, 'FutureNatural?: A Future of Science Through the Lens of Wisdom', *The Heythrop Journal* 40(1) (1999), 41–59.

The beginning, end and middle of the times,
the alternation of the solstices and the succession of the
    seasons,
the revolution of the year and the position of the stars,
the natures of animals and the instincts of wild beasts,
the powers of the spirits and the mental processes of
    men,
the varieties of plants and the medical properties of roots.
All that is hidden, all that is plain, I have come to know,
instructed by Wisdom who designed them all.

(Wisdom 7.18–21 JB)

Idler, go to the ant;
    Ponder her ways and grow wise:
no one gives her orders,
    no overseer, no master,
yet all through the summer she makes sure of her food,
    and gathers her supplies at harvest time.

(Proverbs 6.6–8 JB)

Creation is praised both in and of itself as a reflection of the glory of the Maker, as a source of human comfort through its medical properties and as an example for human conduct. While these observations showed that the writers were keenly aware of the natural world, 'there was only a rudimentary knowledge of what we could call natural sciences'.[45] There was also no sense that wisdom was a quest for order in the universe, in the sense of a Greek understanding of cosmos. Wisdom's cosmological dimensions are expressed through analogies between the human and the natural world as in Proverbs above, but this is not the same as finding a grand cosmic order. There is also little evidence that wisdom was used as part of a natural theology, rather the understanding of God as Creator was presupposed.

The seventeenth-century synthesis: wisdom as wonder
Seventeenth-century scientists did not hesitate, however, to construct a natural theology based on the themes of the wisdom

---

[45] Murphy, *Tree*, 114.

literature, especially the Psalms. The idea of the world as God's temple eroded the barriers between the disciplines in a way that would have been impossible in the medieval era, which accepted a more rigid scholastic system. The ideal of a system of knowledge founded on one method gave rise to a secular theology that was 'orientated towards the world'.[46] Natural theology, that is arguments for the existence of God from close observation of nature, formed part of this secular theology. Prior to this development only clergy taught theology, which was restricted to the arena of supernatural knowledge. Natural theology was developed within this secular theology, written by the laity for the laity.

John Ray's book *The Wisdom of God Manifested in the Works of Creation*, first published in 1692, was immensely popular and had numerous editions right up until the next century.[47] Charles Raven was to become recognised himself by his detailed biographical study of John Ray. For him the book:

> supplied the background for the thought of Gilbert White and indeed for the naturalists of three generations; it was imitated and extensively plagiarised; by Paley in his famous *Natural Theology*; and more than any other single book it initiated the true adventure of modern science, and is the ancestor of the *Origin of Species* or of *Évolution Créatrice*.[48]

Ray's book was significant as science, since it moved from just identification and classification schemes to interpretation of the significance of physical and physiological processes. It showed a wealth of observation on the behaviour of creatures. It brought order to a study that had been veiled in legendary and symbolic ideas alongside vague and confusing classification schemes. Furthermore, from his observations Ray went on to develop ideas about particular 'laws' illustrated by them, always searching for an integrated view of the universe. His

---

[46] A. Funkenstein, *Theology and the Scientific Imagination*, Princeton: Princeton University Press, 1986, 3–9.
[47] Now recognised as a classic text, it is still in print, J. Ray, *The Wisdom of God Manifested in the Works of Creation*, New York: Arno Press, 1977.
[48] C. Raven, *John Ray: Naturalist; His Life and Works*, Cambridge: Cambridge University Press, 1942, 452.

book was very wide ranging, taking in botany, zoology, and astronomy. He believed that the study of the natural world and uncovering its purpose and design amounted to 'thinking God's thoughts after him'.[49]

The wisdom of God was identified with the mind of God and the rationality and truth discoverable in the universe. Ray's search for wisdom in the works of creation led to a sense of wonder, of awe at the discoveries of the workings of the natural world. Another significant idea was Ray's belief that God was working continuously in creation, which contrasts with the more mechanical model of God as a divine watchmaker, which appeared later in Paley's works. One particular text of wisdom literature that Ray uses as a theological support for his ideas is Psalm 104.24:

> Yahweh, what variety you have created,
> arranging everything so wisely!
> Earth is completely full of things you have made.
>
> (JB)

Ray insisted that the reason things are the way they are is not by accident, but by divine design. His delight in the natural world brought a shift in attitude to nature as aesthetically satisfying. His work is novel in bringing together the natural and revealed, both springing from the one divine source in wisdom.

Another less well-known contemporary of John Ray, who came from a more explicitly theological perspective, is Thomas Traherne. His *Thanksgiving for the Wisdom of the Word*, published in 1699, showed his particular fascination for the Psalms. Meditating on these gave him the 'clue of Nature'.[50] Unlike his Puritan contemporaries, who held a very pessimistic view of human nature, Traherne perceived in the world 'the beautiful frontispiece of Eternity'.[51] For him, the wisdom of God was an active, energetic force, 'shaping painfully and at

[49] Raven, *John Ray*, 455.
[50] G. Dowell, *Enjoying the World: The Rediscovery of Thomas Traherne*, London: Mowbray, 1990, 35–42.
[51] Dowell, *Enjoying the World*, 44–45.

great cost, the symmetry, harmony and proportion that are the essence of all beauty'.[52] His search for wisdom as the unity behind the many identifies him with the Cambridge Platonists. For him only an 'innocent eye' can see clearly enough in order to perceive the true reflection of God in creation.

There were, nonetheless, difficulties with such views that translated the wisdom of God into a romantic vision of the natural world. Charles Darwin's *Origin of Species*, while coming from the same pedigree as Ray's *Wisdom of God*, was strikingly different. Darwin, who argued that the natural world arose through natural processes, effectively dismissed any necessity for the role of God in the world. While Traherne had claimed that we need an 'innocent eye' to perceive God's creation, this innocence now seemed to be shattered.

Lash argues that one of the most significant developments in the seventeenth century was the 'spectatorial' view of the natural world. He asks us to 'consider what happens when "observation" is made the paradigm of learning, and accuracy of representation (rather than, for example, soundness of judgement) becomes the standard of knowledge'.[53] He believes that the new way of acquiring knowledge came so to dominate the Western imagination that other ways of reading texts were excluded and marginalised. However, Traherne's work shows that the survival of the poetic imagination is still possible through observation. I also have my doubts whether observation *as such* was as destructive as Lash implies. It was rather a parallel step towards knowing as active, rather than passive, that seems to me to be the most significant development in the seventeenth century. Instead of allowing the natural world to trigger a sense of wonder and contemplation, the understanding that knowing could be achieved through *construction* came to dominate the thinking of the time.[54] It is true that many writers hesitated to argue that the natural world could be achieved by construction, since only God had knowledge of this realm. Yet once the natural world was no longer considered to be a divine creation, it was a short step to believe that

---

[52] *Christian Ethicks*, 69, cited in Dowell, *Enjoying the World*, 55.
[53] Lash, *Beginning*, 79.
[54] Funkenstein, *Theology*, 12, 297ff.

humans could come to know nature through this means as well.

A more serious criticism of the way wisdom is used in the seventeenth century relates to the lack of awareness of the nature and scope of wisdom literature. While the natural world was commonly celebrated as manifesting the wisdom of God, the idea of God as Creator was presupposed. The exclusive concentration on wisdom as found in creation ignores other faces of wisdom that are important correctives to this view. One in particular is the social face of wisdom that considers the way humans relate to one another. While wisdom literature is not explicitly political, it does deal with social relations across nations and thus has an international flavour. Wisdom highlights social injustice and calls for new social relationships. In most cases the assumption is that justice will be done through the power of God's righteousness.

The book of Job is a notable exception which challenges the idea that we can find justice in this life. The story of Job, which tells of a man broken by misfortune and loss, leads to his despair. He eventually falls silent in his attempt to understand God. Job's struggle to find meaning in an unjust world finally leads to his recognition of the action of God in the wildest and most remote places of the earth. He never finds a final answer to his question 'Where can justice be found?' Nonetheless, the very absence of any prospect of finding a solution lends to the wisdom literature a realism that prevents it becoming a shallow ideology. The search for human justice can continue, but it is set in the context of appreciation of the complexities of life that can frustrate its achievement.

The book of Ecclesiastes is similarly sceptical about the justice of God. Qoheleth challenges the equation of righteous living with well-being and life. The author also rejects the involvement of God in the natural rhythms of the universe. Whybray argues that it is incorrect to assume that the natural cycles are portrayed as futile – rather they simply show regularity.[55] Qoheleth's radical rejection of all natural theology,

---

[55] R. N. Whybray, 'Ecclesiastes 1:5–7 and the Wonders of Nature', *Journal for the Study of the Old Testament* 41 (1988), 105–12.

which is finding God in the natural world, empties it of divine purpose. It is important to include Qoheleth as it shows the sharp perception of the wisdom writers as a whole. If Ray had focused on Ecclesiastes for his wisdom instead of the Psalms he might have been more cautious about identifying the wisdom of God exclusively with the created order.

The plural faces of wisdom

Wisdom, then, shows a particular pluralistic view on life that includes social, human and cosmic aspects. The search for wisdom cannot, therefore, be restricted to one or other category. It seems to me to be particularly significant in developing an adequate theology of nature that is relevant to the discoveries of modern science. An adequate theology has to do more than merely look at either the God–world relation or the human–nature relation in isolation. If we limit ourselves in this way an aspect is missed which subsequently proves to be important. A better understanding of wisdom leads us to see the world in all its relational complexity.

Over time the wisdom literature developed a more specifically theological idea of divine Wisdom, as described in Proverbs 8. However, the theology of wisdom is more than this theological focus and to extract this concept in isolation from the rest of the literature also leads to distortions. I will be returning to a discussion of feminine wisdom and its significance for science later in this book. For the time being it is worth noting that while the word for wisdom is a feminine one, the reason why Wisdom is portrayed as a feminine figure remains something of an enigma for Old Testament scholars.[56]

Wisdom in science and theology

It is also worth reflecting on the relationship between wisdom as gift and wisdom as learned. While the earliest wisdom literature concentrated on wisdom as acquired through education and instruction, it also came to be thought of as a divine

[56] Murphy, *Tree*, 146.

gift. This relationship between education and gift also influences how we perceive wisdom in relationship with science. Both strands are also found in the writings of the early philosophers before the shattering of philosophy's association with science that I discussed earlier. According to the Aristotelian tradition wisdom is the crown of scientific knowledge and cannot exist apart from science. Yet even in this view knowledge *as such* was not identified with the highest achievement possible in the human mind. Plato's philosophy, on the other hand, pointed in a different direction: wisdom in the civic life was given by Zeus to all humanity, while wisdom for daily life was the responsibility of humans.[57] The notion of divine wisdom *as gift* developed into the Augustinian tradition, where wisdom becomes the foundation for science. Thomas Aquinas takes up the Aristotelian notion of wisdom as emergent from science, though he attempts to synthesise this with the Augustinian tradition.

The clash in the ways of relating wisdom and science becomes clear: is wisdom learned through science or given by God? Is it an achievement or gift? There are three possible positions that we can adopt. In the first, based on Aristotle, science is essential for wisdom and wisdom is its highest achievement. In the second and third, based on Plato, wisdom is essential for science. For the second case, science uses wisdom in order to attain its goals. But there is another possibility, or third case, namely that if wisdom is emphasised science may be *excluded* because of scepticism towards all human forms of knowledge. It is possible to find all three positions in ancient, medieval and sixteenth-century thought.[58] It is also worth emphasising that the meaning of science for Aristotle and Plato was not the experimental mode of science, as we know it today. Science then included all areas of knowledge. We

---

[57] Plato's, *Protagoras* 321c–d. See B. Hubbard and E. Karnofsky (eds), *Plato's Protagoras*, London: Duckworth, 1982, 17. Further discussion is in C. Deane-Drummond, 'Wisdom: A Voice for Theology at the Boundary with Science', *Ecotheology*, in press.

[58] R. G. Remsberg, *Wisdom and Science at the Port Royal and the Oratory: A Study of Contrasting Augustianisms,* Yellow Springs: The Antioch Press, 1940, 156.

will be returning to Aquinas's attempt at synthesis later in this book. The most significant shift towards modern experimental methods took place in the seventeenth century. The difference today is that modern experimental science still lays claim to be the exclusive basis for wisdom.[59]

Weaving an image of wisdom

The narrowing of wisdom to mean modern scientific knowledge is bound to lead to a distortion of wisdom. Daniel Hardy, similarly, recognises a trend in the history of science where wisdom becomes restricted from the transcendent ideal of Plato to human rationality alone.[60] Hardy has also suggested that wisdom is closely connected with our understanding of God and God's relationship with the world. Wisdom is the dynamic interwovenness of God, the whole cosmos and humanity. Wisdom is the means through which we discover how far our purposes are matched with those of God. It is the 'dynamic of human knowledge, understanding and practice on the one hand, and God and the fulfilment of God's purposes on the other'.[61]

His refusal to allow wisdom to be narrowed to knowledge or separated from the tradition of goodness is a welcome recovery of the idea of ancient wisdom. He includes human, cosmic and divine elements, which also fits in with the biblical tradition. However, it raises the question as to how such a vision can be applied to the practice of science. In particular how can we know what the wisdom of God means? His suggestion that wisdom is learned through worship is an interesting one, but is this enough? While he recognises that all human wisdom is insufficient, it seems to me that wisdom needs to face up to the question of theodicy as well as correcting our perceptions of the world. In particular, elements of social

---

[59] H. Brown, *The Wisdom of Science: Its Relevance to Culture and Religion*, Cambridge: Cambridge University Press, 1986.

[60] D. Hardy, 'Rationality, the Sciences and Theology', in G. Wainwright (ed.), *Keeping the Faith: Essays to Mark the Centenary of Lux Mundi*, London: SPCK, 1989, 284–8.

[61] D. Hardy, 'The God Who Is With the World', in F. Watts (ed.), *Science Meets Faith*, London: SPCK, 1998, 137.

justice and the recognition of the reality of suffering need to be included in any portrait of wisdom. I will be focusing on this particular aspect by looking at the particular insights from wisdom texts in the New Testament in the chapter that follows.

While I agree, then, with Hardy's use of ancient philosophical wisdom to challenge the modern presumption of knowledge as equivalent to wisdom, or a narrow view that fails to include a moral dimension, I believe that wisdom can also be used to develop an adequate theology of nature. Moreover, I am less sceptical than Hardy about drawing on other traditions of wisdom as found in classic Christian texts, such as Aquinas, while recognising that these traditions do have their limitations. Such texts, while they may not be complete, show insights from cultures that are less burdened by the fragmentation of society that we currently experience.

The appeal to wisdom allows theology to find a voice in the modern world in a way that still has relevance to our current situation. Pope John Paul II, in his encyclical letter *Fides et Ratio*, is anxious to point to the strength of the wisdom literature in healing the breach between faith and reason. Indeed for him wisdom's main function seems to be this, to put reason in its place so that 'reason is valued without being overvalued'.[62] It seems, then, that he puts faith in a primary position, so that, citing Proverbs 1.7, the fear of the Lord is the beginning of knowledge. He recognises the twin strands in Old Testament thought, that wisdom comes through observation, but also through divine revelation as gift. He also goes on to speak about the wisdom of the cross which I will return to in the next chapter. He affirms the search for truth as a valid human enterprise that drives many human activities, including the sciences.[63]

He insists that we need to explore the meaning of our existence within the complexities of suffering and death that confront us on a daily basis. In order to counter this he suggests that we need to

[62] Pope John Paul II, *Faith and Reason, Encyclical Letter Fides et Ratio*, London: Catholic Truth Society, 1998, 32.
[63] John Paul II, *Faith and Reason*, 41.

seek a final explanation, a supreme value, which refers to nothing beyond itself and which puts an end to all questioning. Hypotheses may fascinate, but they do not satisfy . . . personal existence must be anchored to a truth recognised as final, a truth which confers a certitude no longer open to doubt.[64]

This seems to suggest a refuge in unwarranted dogmatism, though he does allow for a searching truth and defines a human being as one who searches for truth. Yet his definition of truth as coming from two wings of faith and reason seems to me to be more akin to the notion of wisdom, which is altogether suggestive of a richer form of knowledge that he has already identified in both philosophy and Scripture.

He also believes that the truths found in science in no way contradict the truth of the revelation in Christ and that both have their origin in God.[65] Yet in the light of what has gone before, this seems to be too easy a reconciliation between the two forms of knowledge. While there may, in the end, be a fundamental unity underlying both, the truth perceived in one may not cohere easily with that in the other without hard and difficult discourse. He seems to be too ready to admit to a convergence in ignorance of the problems involved, though he raises these in a later context, as I will illustrate below. His attraction to Thomism also shows that he is open to giving reason more of a primary role, acknowledging that knowledge can mature into wisdom.[66] Rather than viewing Aquinas's separation of philosophical wisdom and theological wisdom as a problem, he believes that they needed autonomy 'if they were to perform well in their respective fields of research'.[67] Yet he does recognise that this split led to some 'fateful consequences' and led to the eventual sunder of faith and reason. He now takes on a more critical attitude to modern science:

In the field of scientific research, a positivistic mentality took hold which not only abandoned the Christian vision of the world, but more especially rejected every appeal to a metaphysical and moral

[64] John Paul II, *Faith and Reason*, 43–4.
[65] John Paul II, *Faith and Reason*, 52.
[66] John Paul II, *Faith and Reason*, 67.
[67] John Paul II, *Faith and Reason*, 69.

vision. It follows that certain scientists, lacking any ethical point of reference, are in danger of putting at the centre of their concerns something other than the human person and the entirety of a person's life. Further still, some of these, sensing the opportunities of technological progress, seem to succumb not only to a market place logic, but also to the temptation of a quasi-divine power over nature and even over the human being.[68]

These are strong words following the more conciliatory tone of his earlier reflections. Yet he holds on to a vision that only with faith can reason be prevented from taking side-tracks, and only with reason can faith be prevented from falling into superstition. Overall, he desires to reclaim the place of philosophical reasoning in theology, while still giving philosophy the autonomy to work from within its own rigorous rational criteria. Yet this is not the same as self-sufficiency. It is here that problems surface, since autonomy by definition seems to imply self-sufficiency. It is a delicate balance and one that is equally relevant to the relationship between theology and the sciences.

While recognising the truth of science, theology speaks of a wider truth that echoes a more ancient way of thinking about the world. It is for this reason that I argue for a theology of wisdom, rather than a theology of truth, for the latter can too easily slide into a narrow rationalism. Furthermore, while the truth seems to indicate a fixity of goal, a certainty, wisdom is more fluid and open to different possibilities. This gives wisdom another edge over truth as the means of linking faith and reason, since it allows different aspects to come into view depending on the context. John Paul II's final comments on the possibility of a new science accord very much with my own:

> In expressing my admiration and in offering encouragement to these brave pioneers of scientific research, to whom humanity owes so much of its current development, I would urge them to continue their efforts without ever abandoning the sapiential horizon within which scientific and technological achievements are wedded to the philosophical and ethical values which are the distinctive and indelible mark of the human person.[69]

[68] John Paul II, *Faith and Reason*, 70–1.
[69] John Paul II, *Faith and Reason*, 152.

But what might this sapiential dimension mean for the practice of science? Furthermore, how can we include not only the wisdom that comes from contemplation of the world, but also the wisdom of Christ? How might these insights serve to influence a particular theology of creation? It is to these questions that we turn in the chapter that follows.

2

The Wisdom of the Cross

The idea that science will lead to progress for humanity is a relatively recent cultural construct, tracing back a few hundred years.[1] More recent critics of science have laid on its doorstep blame for pollution, overpopulation, power of armaments and so on. Some point to science as responsible for the narrowing of the imagination and even claim that it is destructive of culture, a spiritual cul-de-sac. Such parodies of science fail to do justice to the way it is conducted in practice through an effort of the imagination. Further, they ignore the real benefits of science that we tend to take for granted. Nonetheless, I have tried to show in the previous chapter that any arrogance in science, or for that matter theology, needs to be challenged through opening up dialogue with other ways of thinking and knowing. Hanbury Brown believes that science itself is not at fault, rather it is the way we use the knowledge we have. Hence 'If the first major lesson of the Scientific Revolution was that knowledge is power, the second is that our ability to produce new knowledge greatly exceeds our ability to use that power wisely.'[2] He suggests, then, that it is the *uses* of science which are at fault, rather than science as such. Furthermore, while he recognises the importance of wisdom, for him it seems to amount to religion catching up with the knowledge that

---

[1] H. Brown, *The Wisdom of Science: Its Relevance to Culture and Religion*, Cambridge: Cambridge University Press, 1986, 101.
[2] Brown, *Wisdom of Science*, 107.

science provides.[3] He believes that the churches must respond to the challenge, otherwise they will 'slowly pass into oblivion and their place will be taken by other, perhaps more adaptable faiths'.[4] Is it really possible to have it both ways? Brown seems to be asking religion to contribute wisdom, but also adapt to the findings of science. He assumes that science itself remains untouchable, merely strengthened by absorption of wisdom.

What might be the alternatives to a mechanistic science available to us today? The Gaia hypothesis of James Lovelock may be one answer, aligned as it is with creation-centred spirituality. However, I will argue in this chapter that both Gaia and creation spirituality lack credibility as a basis for a theology of creation. Instead, an exploration of how Christ is viewed in terms of wisdom in the New Testament serves to integrate the theme of redemption into an understanding of creation. I will argue that this strand of wisdom is essential, as it is able to take into account the ambiguities in human existence and in the existence of all life forms. Furthermore, it challenges concepts of Christ that are narrowly conceived in terms of anthropology, broadening their scope in order to develop a cosmic Christology.

Alternative visions

God and Gaia

James Lovelock is one maverick scientist who has consistently argued that we need to challenge not only the way we apply science, but also the way we do science. Traditional experimental science works through a process of 'reduction', where the whole is understood as the product of the parts. Lovelock has challenged this method by suggesting that we need to look at the whole earth system, rather than its parts. He called his idea the *Gaia* hypothesis, and by so doing imparted to his idea a religious metaphor. His hypothesis could have been called the 'geo-physiology' hypothesis, since it proposed that life as a whole regulates the gaseous composition of the earth,

---

[3] Brown, *Wisdom of Science*, 143.
[4] Brown, *Wisdom of Science*, 182.

keeping it within certain limits so as to sustain life. He used his observations to predict that other planets, such as Mars, could never have sustained life.[5]

While no one disputes that the earth is unique in its ability to keep its gaseous composition and temperature constant, in spite of the increasing solar intensity, there are many debates as to how this might happen. At one end of the spectrum traditional scientists argue that living things influence the environment. At the other end of the spectrum Gaia becomes the framework for an ideological quest. Those who draw on Gaia in this way believe that humankind is forced to think of itself in more modest terms. There is a shift from seeing ourselves as 'toolmakers', using the earth's resources for our own good, to a more harmonious and balanced relationship with the earth.[6] I have discussed the various scientific interpretations of Gaia and their ethical ambiguity elsewhere.[7] For the present discussion it is important to note that Lovelock envisages a different way of doing science so that now it is conducted from a holistic perspective. While to some extent the science of ecology performs the same function, Gaia theory embraces the ecology of the whole earth system and thereby becomes a much bolder challenge to traditional science. The gradual accumulation of scientific evidence seems to favour at least partial systems of Gaia.[8] It is the way particular questions are asked that seem to lead to new patterns emerging that would have previously passed unnoticed.

One reason why more traditional scientists are wary of Gaia is the extent to which religious concepts become fused with Gaia theory. Furthermore, the particular way the fusion has happened portrays Gaia as a challenge not just to reductionism as such, but also to the scientific belief in the absence of purpose, or teleology, in the universe. Lovelock has always

[5] J. Lovelock, *Gaia*, Oxford: Oxford University Press, 1988.
[6] K. Pedler, *The Quest for Gaia*, London: HarperCollins, 1991, 13–21.
[7] C. Deane-Drummond, 'Gaia as Science Made Myth; Implications for Environmental Ethics', *Studies in Christian Ethics* 9(2) (1996), 1–15.
[8] P. Bunyard (ed.), *Gaia in Action: Science of the Living Earth*, Edinburgh: Floris Books, 1996. I will come back to a discussion of the relationship between Gaia and ecology in Chapter 6.

claimed that his own particular interpretation of Gaia is consistent with the scientific rejection of teleology. Yet his own
writings seem to posit a kind of consciousness to Gaia that
implies she has a purpose. Taken to its scientific limit it seems
that the purpose of Gaia is the survival of life, particularly the
micro-organisms, rather than higher life-forms, including
humans.[9]

Gaia was the name for the ancient goddess of the earth and
the image of God as Gaia has been taken up by a number of
feminist writers, including Rosemary Radford Ruether.[10] I
intend to return to a discussion of the way eco-feminists
have used Gaia by way of comparison with their use of Sophia
in a more detailed exploration of Sophia as feminine divine
in Chapter 4. For the moment it is worth noting that most
feminist writers seem either to ignore Lovelock's Gaia almost
entirely, or adopt Gaia as part of a basis for a new philosophy.[11]
Just as there is a variety of different interpretations of Gaia as
science, so too there is a variety of interpretations of Gaia as
theology. Hugh Montefiore has managed to incorporate Gaia
into a more traditional theological framework, apparently
equating the work of Gaia with the Holy Spirit. For him 'Gaia
is a kind of sacrament through which the power and wisdom
of God shines . . . the outward and visible earth shows us
something of the inner workings of the Holy Spirit within
it'.[12] It is, nonetheless, more usual for Gaia to be taken up by
those who advocate a more monistic understanding of the
relationship between God and the world. In this Gaia seems
to cohere with the New Age spirituality.[13]

[9] See Deane-Drummond, 'Gaia as Science Made Myth', 8.
[10] R. Radford Ruether, *Gaia and God: An Ecofeminist Theology of Earth
Healing*, London: SCM Press, 1992.
[11] Anne Primavesi, for example, makes only cursory and positive reference to
Lovelock's Gaia. A. Primavesi, *From Apocalypse to Genesis*, London: Burns
& Oates, 1991, 14 and 34. Elizabeth Sahouris finds in Gaia clues to human
behaviour, E. Sahouris, *Gaia: The Human Journey From Chaos to Cosmos*,
New York: Pocket Books, 1989.
[12] H. Montefiore, *Credible Christianity: The Gospel in Contemporary Culture*,
London: Mowbray, 1993, 31.
[13] L. Osborn, 'The Machine and the Mother Machine Goddess: The Gaia
Hypothesis in Contemporary Scientific and Religious Thought', *Science and
Christian Belief* 4(1), 1992, 27–42.

Historians John Brooke and Geoffrey Cantor suggest that Lovelock's Gaia and New Age writing in general bears some resemblance to the romantic works of Goethe or Oken.[14] Such romantic views of science are certainly not new, they have recurred throughout the history of the relationship between science and religion. There remains the question as to why the earlier more romantic portrayals of science failed to overturn more mechanistic ones. Brooke and Cantor suggest that one reason may be that the romantics failed to influence leading scientific institutions.[15] Lovelock is only too well aware that the idea of the earth acting as a living organism has a long history, promoted by scientists such as James Hutton (1788) and at the turn of the twentieth century the Russian, Vladimir Vernadsky.[16] The mechanistic scientists eventually won the day, so those such as Hutton or Vernadsky, who held on to more organic or vitalistic perspectives, were seen as anachronistic. It remains to be seen how far Lovelock's Gaia will continue to be viewed as marginal to mainstream science. Its adoption by New Age writers, however spurious from Lovelock's point of view, would tend to engender a hostile reaction within the confines of institutional science. It therefore seems unlikely to influence science on a wider scale. Nonetheless, like creation-centred spirituality which I will discuss next, it still has significance as a contribution to a movement for social change. Public perception of science will continue to be influenced by Gaia, regardless of its adoption by the scientific, or for that matter theological, hierarchy.

Creation-centred spirituality

Creation-centred spirituality is closely allied to more idealistic views of Gaia. Thomas Berry is a pioneer for this kind of spirituality in its most recent form. Like Lovelock, he searches for a holistic perspective. However, his is less a model of science than as a deliberate creation of what he terms a functional

[14] J. Brooke and G. Cantor, *Reconstructing Nature: The Engagement of Science and Religion*, Edinburgh: T&T Clark, 1998, 95.

[15] Brooke and Cantor, *Reconstructing Nature*, 96.

[16] J. Lovelock, 'The Gaia hypothesis', in Bunyard *Gaia in Action*, 15–16.

cosmology.[17] He suggests that our scientific culture has split us apart from the natural world and humanity has lost its sense of connectedness and sense of belonging. It is only when we tune into the world process that we see our own insignificance. Such a call to identification with the earth has striking parallels with romantic portrayals of Gaia. In both cases the earth is the primary source for human reflection. The difference is that Berry has attempted to draw in traditional Christian concepts and reinterpret these in the light of creation spirituality. He views the universe as a story, a narrative that we must once again adopt in order to awaken a sense of reverence for the earth.

Matthew Fox has taken up the call of Thomas Berry and developed a more systematic reinterpretation of Christian history, focusing on creation themes. His fourfold path of creation spirituality, set out in his book *Original Blessing*, locates humanity firmly in the context of the earth.[18] To summarise these ways:

1. The *via positiva*, or Befriending Creation.
2. The *via negativa*, or Befriending Darkness, including a letting go and letting be.
3. The *via creativa*, or Befriending Creativity and befriending our divinity.
4. The *via transformativa*, or Befriending New Creation, including compassion, celebration and erotic justice.

Fox believes that our understanding of Christianity has been hampered by a failure to appreciate the work of the mystics, many of whom had a much deeper sense of the divine in creation. He argues that it is essential that we see creation in terms of blessing, rather than the traditional understanding of Fall and redemption. Yet even at the start of his book he identifies his search as a search for wisdom. It is wisdom 'that the people may live'.[19] By this he means a cosmic creation

[17] T. Berry, *The Dream of the Earth*, San Francisco: Sierra Club Books, 1988.
[18] M. Fox, *Original Blessing: A Primer in Creation Spirituality*, Mexico: Bear & Co, 1983.
[19] Fox, *Original Blessing*, 9.

story that resonates strongly with that of Thomas Berry. Instead of the split between science and religion we must now seek the 'wisdom that nature can teach us and the wisdom that religious traditions can teach us'.[20] For him the religious tradition that we need to recover is restricted to an affirmation of creation.

Fox does seem to allow for human weakness through his concept of *via negativa*. However, this is a weak strand in his work and he has laid himself open to a barrage of criticism, especially with regard to his rejection of original sin.[21] Other scholars have suggested that his lack of political acumen is one of the main reasons why Fox fails to respond adequately to environmental questions.[22] Nonetheless, the continued growth of creation spirituality and its networks, especially in the USA, point to its sociological and political significance in terms of a new social movement.[23] Fox seeks to re-image Christ as the cosmic Christ, rather than the historical Christ. He does acknowledge briefly the influence of Hebrew wisdom in the Church's understanding of the cosmic Christ. However, his prime emphasis is to find scriptural and other evidence for cosmic Christology, rather than specifically Wisdom Christology.[24] It seems to me that the main difficulty with Fox's re-interpretation is not so much the cosmic scope of Christ's activity, but his much weaker acknowledgement of the historical Jesus. Added to this are his more spurious mystical treatments of the cosmic Christ in which he speaks of Christ in erotic dimensions. Furthermore, in his anxiety to escape from the notion of sin and redemption it is unclear as to what

[20] Fox, *Original Blessing*, 10.
[21] See, for example, a vehement attack by Lesslie Newbigin in a Letter to *Reform* (United Reformed Church), December, 1993.
[22] M. Goodall and J. Reader, 'Why Matthew Fox Fails to Change the World', in I. Ball, M. Goodhall, C. Palmer and J. Reader (eds), *The Earth Beneath: A Critical Guide to Green Theology*, London: SPCK, 1992, 104–19.
[23] For a discussion of new social movement theory see A. Melucci, *Nomads of the Present*, London: Hutchinson Radius, 1989. I am indebted to Peter Cox, my PhD student, for his interpretation of creation-centred spirituality as a new social movement.
[24] M. Fox, *The Coming of the Cosmic Christ: The Healing of Mother Earth and the Birth of a Global Renaissance*, San Francisco: Harper & Row, 1988, 21, 83–109.

Christ's healing signifies, other than a return to an idealised past, an original blessing.

The appeal of Fox's creation spirituality is that it seems to portray God as immanent, earthed and earthy, in tune with creation. His views fill the void created by the lack of adequate reflection on the immanence of God in creation and what it means in today's world of science and technology. As Linda Woodhead has pointed out, creation spirituality is still reliant on the philosophy of modern thought, even though it is postmodern in its appeal to consumer culture.[25] She suggests that experience in Fox's interpretation is both authoritative and ahistorical. While it seems to me that a description of Fox as fundamentalist is overdrawn, there are clear connections between Fox's work and that of other New Age and some feminist writers who demand a radical egalitarianism. The problem with an overemphasis on immanence is that God becomes indistinguishable from creation.[26] However, Woodhead's suggestion that the detachment from tradition opens the way to tyranny of powerful personalities seems an idealisation of tradition. Powerful personalities can just as easily strongly influence the way tradition is interpreted. Fox has always claimed to draw on traditional Christianity, though many regard him as a heretic. Woodhead also suggests that the new spirituality, which includes Fox, fails as it directs the gaze within, rather than without. I have already pointed out his seeming lack of awareness of political issues in the green movement. However, in his more recent work he has highlighted the division between rich and poor as a major cultural crisis.[27] Woodhead also notes that the new spirituality, unlike earlier mysticism, fails to find strength in weakness. While, as I noted above, this is not strictly true since Fox includes a *via negativa*, this theme is never properly incorporated into his creation spirituality as a whole.

[25] L. Woodhead, 'Post-Modern Spiritualities', *Religion* 23 (1993), 167–81.
[26] L. Woodhead, 'Sophia or Gnosis?', in S. Barton (ed.), *Where Shall Wisdom be Found? Wisdom in the Bible, the Church and the Contemporary World*, Edinburgh: T&T Clark, 1999, 275.
[27] M. Fox, *A Spirituality Named Compassion: The Healing of the Global Village*, San Francisco: HarperCollins, 1990.

A further consequence of Fox's view is that creation becomes a vehicle of direct knowledge of the Creator. While I believe that the emphasis on realised eschatology is characteristic of creation spirituality, the suggestion that it 'wants direct knowledge, not future hope' seems to me to be exaggerated.[28] It is fair to say that there is a tendency to search for gratification now, but Fox suggests a *via transformativa*, where the present is gradually transformed and healed. However, it is a present transformed in the light of an older past, 'when the just harmony and order ruled the cosmos'.[29] Fox's image of the kingdom is one that can be realised in the present, but it is in the light of a mythical golden age. It is as if the past is recast in the image of a future that knows no bounds of blessing. As such his eschatology is not as 'realised' as it appears at first glance. Hope is kept alive by what Eliade once described as the 'myth of the eternal return'.[30] I suggest that this return to a cosmic blessing at the beginning is a completely inadequate basis for hope as it fails to take into account either human history or God's action in the future. As Moltmann has pointed out, this is a false idea of God's presence, where 'the horror of chaos is ordered and sanctified by means of sacred festivals which celebrate the epiphany'.[31] I will come back to a discussion of the future of creation in Chapter 5.

Overall, we can view creation-centred spiritualities as a reaction to the institutional Church's lack of emphasis on the immanence of God in creation and its preoccupation with history. It also seems to meet the need for what appears to be more egalitarian ways of thinking and knowing. However unsophisticated Fox's theology appears, it has an appeal to the heart and his writing strikes chords that seem to fill a gap left in traditional hierarchical frameworks. Yet while bearing some of the marks of Christian theology, it is clearly inadequate

---

[28] Woodhead, 'Sophia or Gnosis?', 275.
[29] Fox, *Original Blessing*, 260.
[30] M. Eliade, *The Myth of the Eternal Return*, New York/London: Routledge & Kegan Paul, 1954.
[31] J. Moltmann, *Theology of Hope*, trans. J. W. Leitch, London: SCM Press, 1967, 98. See also J. Moltmann, *God in Creation*, trans. M. Kohl, London: SCM Press, 1988, 104–9.

as a basis for a theology of creation. While Fox identifies a form of spirituality, it lacks any self-critical reference. In general theologians have dismissed his work, even though academic theology which loses all touch with grass roots 'popular' theology fails for other reasons.[32] What is needed is an adequate academic theology of creation that lends itself to more popular reinterpretations. I intend to argue in this book that a theology of creation based on wisdom does just that. It can retain some of the strengths of Fox's approach in its appeal to immanence, imagery, symbolism, yet avoid the weakness of a creation spirituality cut off from the rest of salvation history.

Christ and Wisdom

Jesus, teacher of wisdom

The Gospels portray the relationship between Jesus and the wisdom tradition broadly in two distinct ways. In the first, characteristic of the Synoptics, Jesus is the teacher of wisdom. In the second, characteristic of the Johannine texts, Jesus himself becomes identified with God's Wisdom, leading to an emergent Wisdom Christology. I will discuss the latter in the next section. However, the Synoptic tradition is important as it reminds us of the historical reality of Jesus and his teaching ministry. Furthermore, it connects the historical Jesus with the wisdom tradition of the Old Testament, which I discussed in the last chapter.

The way Jesus as portrayed in the Synoptic Gospels drew on the proverbial and parabolic traditions of the sages of Israel is very familiar. In the Synoptic tradition there are over a hundred wisdom sayings of Jesus.[33] Many of them require no privileged revelation, but are simply maxims for living based on human experience. Like the sages, Jesus is described as one who drew on everyday events from the natural world in

---

[32] Margaret Goodall and John Reader believe that he may not be worth taking seriously, 'the man is an entertainer, not a serious theologian', M. Goodall and J. Reader, 'Matthew Fox', 105.

[33] C. E. Carlston, 'Proverbs, Maxims and the Historical Jesus', *Journal of Biblical Literature* 99 (1980), 91.

order to point to deeper truths. The appeal to the order of creation often comes first, as in the Sermon on the Mount, where the affirmation of the meek inheriting the earth comes before appeals to keep the law. Parables such as the lost sheep, the sower, the woman with the lost coin all point to the radical generosity of the love of God. Like Qoheleth who questioned traditional wisdom, Jesus' teaching is radical in that he challenged the traditional wisdom of the Pharisees, who kept themselves separate from those who failed to keep the law. However, unlike Qoheleth, there is a positive outcome for those who have ears to hear and eyes to see. Jesus is shown as one who deliberately chooses to eat with publicans and sinners, extending the compassion of God to include those normally on the margins of society. His parables unsettled and reversed expectations.

It seems likely that the earliest disciples of Jesus viewed him as another teacher and prophet of wisdom.[34] The earliest tradition in Q ascribes to the ministry and teaching of Jesus a greater significance compared with the great wisdom teacher Solomon:

> The queen of the South will arise at the judgement with the men of this generation and condemn them; for she came from the ends of the earth to hear the wisdom of Solomon, and behold, something greater than Solomon is here. (Luke 11.31 RSV)

While Elisabeth Schüssler Fiorenza interprets Jesus as a prophet of Sophia in a long succession that continues in the Q community, Richard Horsley interprets Jesus as the climactic figure in a long line of Israelite prophets.[35] The difference seems to be related to the fact that Fiorenza intends to place more emphasis on Wisdom as the key figure in the story, rather than Jesus. I will leave a full discussion of the way Christ might be considered as Wisdom incarnate until the next section. For the moment I am anxious to point to the identification of Jesus with the wisdom traditions in the earliest

---

[34] E. Schüssler Fiorenza, *Jesus: Miriam's Child, Sophia's Prophet*, London: SCM Press, 1994, 139–43. I will return to a fuller discussion of the significance of wisdom for a feminist theology in Chapter 4.

[35] R. A. Horsley, 'Q and Jesus: Assumptions, Approaches and Analyses', *Semeia* 55 (1991), 206.

Christian communities. This can subsequently become the basis for linking Christ and creation.

The way the figure of Jesus serves to combine elements of the prophetic and wisdom traditions allows him to portray a powerful mixture of images that in ancient Israelite texts were more commonly kept separate. Hence to speak of Jesus as a prophet of wisdom poses something of a challenge to traditional, more static, images engendered by the wisdom theology of the Old Testament. Nonetheless, the activity of a scribe as described in Sirach includes law and wisdom as well as prophecy and wisdom, so the connection does have some precedents in the earlier literature.[36] The possible link between prophecy and wisdom is significant in that it hints at the way wisdom in the New Testament can be related to an eschatological hope that was more difficult in much of the Old Testament literature. How far the apocalyptic tradition meets and interacts with the wisdom tradition in the New Testament is a matter for scholarly debate.[37]

We find in the wisdom teaching of Q not just sayings related to human experience, but also a personification of Wisdom. In the story of the children in the market place, for example, described in Luke 7.31–35, Wisdom is personified and both John and Jesus are her children.[38] Furthermore, the crowds are rebuked for not recognising the messenger of God foretold by the prophets.[39] Here we have an example once more of the link between prophecy and wisdom.

In other sayings, such as Luke 11.49–51/Matthew 23.34–36 Jesus is portrayed as one who draws directly on wisdom

---

[36] J. Marböck, 'Sir. 38.24–39, 11: *Der schriftgelehrte Weise*', in M. Gilbert (ed.), *La Sagesse de L'Ancient Testament*, 293–316, cited in C. E. Carlston, 'Wisdom and Eschatology in Q', in J. De Lobel (ed.), *Logia – Les Paroles de Jesus – The Sayings of Jesus*, Leuven: Leuven University Press, 1982, footnote 15, 103.

[37] See, for example, R. Horsley, 'Wisdom and Apocalypticism in Mark', in L. G. Purdue, B. B. Scott and W. J. Wiseman (eds), *In Search of Wisdom; Essays in Memory of John Gammie*, Westminster: John Knox Press, 1993, 223–44; also B. B. Scott, 'The Gospel of Matthew; The Sapiential Performance of an Apocalyptic Discourse', in Purdue *et al.*, *In Search of Wisdom*, 245–62.

[38] Carlston, 'Eschatology', 102–3.

[39] This may be a reference to the messenger sent by God foretold in Exodus 23.20 and Malachi 3.1.

teaching, quoting a saying about wisdom sending the prophets in order to reinforce his own words of judgement.[40] In Jesus' lament over Jerusalem in Luke 13.34–36/Matthew 23.37–39, it is Wisdom who weeps and declares judgement, but now the identification between Wisdom and Jesus is much closer. There are, in addition, other passages in Q that are less obviously connected with wisdom, but seem to use a wisdom framework for the story. For example, the temptation of Jesus shows some parallels with the book of Job: like Job there is a dispute with the devil, a dialogue about right conduct and the worship of God, and the vindication of the righteous one by God. Carlston notes the numerous other maxims and sayings that suggest Q found the wisdom categories proper vehicles for understanding both the person of Jesus and his message. He concludes that 'the sheer bulk and variety of wisdom materials in Q shows that wisdom is a basic, not an adventitious element in the theological outlook of the Q community'.[41]

Once we move beyond Q to examine the interpretation in Matthew's Gospel we begin to find hints of an even closer identification of Jesus and Wisdom. While this becomes much clearer in the Gospel of John, James Dunn has argued that certain passages in Matthew point to Christ as not just teacher of wisdom, but Wisdom incarnate.[42] For example, whereas in Luke Jesus says 'Wisdom is vindicated by all her *children*' (Luke 7.35), in Matthew 'Wisdom is vindicated by her *deeds*' (Matt 11.19), which turn out to be the deeds of Christ (Matt 11.2). This is reinforced by the saying 'Take my yoke upon you and learn of me' (Matt 11.29) echoing 'Put your neck under her [wisdom's] yoke, and let your soul receive instruction' (Sirach 51.26).

Another possible feature of Jesus as teacher of wisdom found in the Gospels is how far this portrayal of Jesus draws on the Greek Cynic philosophy as well as the Jewish wisdom tradition. The Cynics, like Jesus, were sharply critical of society and

---

[40] Most scholars seem to attribute the wisdom citation used by Jesus to a document that has since been lost, see Carlston, 'Eschatology', 105.
[41] Carlston, 'Eschatology', 112.
[42] J. Dunn, 'Jesus, Teacher of Wisdom or Wisdom Incarnate?', in Barton, *Where Shall Wisdom*, 78.

social conventions. However, as Dunn points out, parallel themes do not necessarily imply dependence and the comparison with Cynic teaching seems to be very selective.[43] We can reach the conclusion that Jesus was viewed in his own life and in the earliest Christian community as a teacher of wisdom and that this is reflected in the New Testament.

Wisdom Christology

As I have hinted above, the image of Jesus as wisdom teacher is complemented by another strand, most noticeable in the Gospel of John, that Jesus can be understood as identified with Wisdom. In the previous chapter I pointed to the complex and plural images that are bound up with wisdom in the Old Testament. Nonetheless, the figure of Wisdom, as described in Proverbs 8, is more likely a personification of divine Wisdom, rather than a separate ontological agent, or hypostasis, distinct from God. Wisdom reflects, then, the immanence of God in creation. In Ben Sira we find Wisdom's status elevated by identification with the Torah. James Dunn has argued that 'the doctrine of the incarnation began to emerge when the exalted Christ was spoken of in terms drawn from the Wisdom imagery of pre-Christian Judaism'.[44] This process began in the wisdom passages of Paul's letters, but only in the Gospel of John in the post-Pauline period does the concept of Christ as the incarnation of Wisdom emerge fully. I intend in this section to discuss the overall shape of Wisdom Christology. At its heart is the Pauline idea of the wisdom of the cross, which I will discuss in some detail in the following section. For the moment it is worth noting how the New Testament accounts came to identify Jesus with Wisdom.

In Matthew we find Jesus portrayed as teacher of the way of wisdom, but in John he himself becomes the way. In Mark we find a more oblique reference to wisdom in pointing out obstacles to the hidden wisdom of God. John develops this portrayal still further, so that obstacles to wisdom are set in

---

[43] Dunn, 'Jesus', 85.
[44] J. Dunn, *Christology in the Making*, London: SCM Press, 2nd edn, 1989, 259.

the context of a cosmological framework of conflict between light and dark, good and evil, God and the devil.[45] The wisdom motifs in John's Gospel are numerous and the parallels with Logos are striking.[46] I intend to give a few examples here by way of illustration. John 1.1a echoes Genesis 1.1, so that Logos is identified as pre-existent and active with God in creation. Similarly in Proverbs 8.22–23 Wisdom is presented as the first of God's creatures, in co-operating with God in the creative process. As Martin Scott remarks concerning Wisdom: 'She existed in the heavens before the world was formed, and shares responsibility for the orderly nature of creation. This is precisely the role given by the opening words of John's Prologue to the Logos.'[47] In Proverbs we find Wisdom as agent of creation, but in John, Logos fulfils this role (John 1.3). The search for light and life given by Logos in John 1.4 echoes the thought of Proverbs 8.35, where the search for life is the search for Wisdom.

Nonetheless, the portrayal of Christ as the embodiment of Wisdom is not confined to the Prologue in John, but extends to the main body of the text as well. Jesus is described as pre-existent in terms that echo the characterisation of Wisdom. The descent–ascent trajectory that characterises the whole Gospel of John begins with the coming of the divine Logos in the Prologue and ends with the ascent of Christ following his crucifixion.[48] Similarly, Wisdom is pre-existent with God, descends and is manifested through the prophets and the law, returning eventually to heaven following rejection by some and acceptance by others (Prov 8; Sirach 24; 1 *Enoch* 42). In other words, the structure of Johannine Christology looks to the question of where the Logos/Son is going to as well as where he is from. Furthermore, Wisdom is sent from above,

[45] S. Barton, 'Gospel Wisdom', in Barton, *Where Shall Wisdom*, 104–10.
[46] Noted by Rudolf Bultmann in 1923, 'The History of Religions Background of the Prologue of the Gospel of John' reprinted in J. Ashton (ed.), *The Interpretation of John*, London: SPCK, 1986, 18–35. See also Dunn, *Christology*, 213–50.
[47] M. Scott, *Sophia and the Johannine Jesus*, Sheffield: JSOT Press, Sheffield: Academic Press, 1992, 96.
[48] Barton, 'Gospel Wisdom', 104–5.

as a gift of God, as in Wisdom 8.21; just as Jesus is sent by the Father in passages such as John 3.16–17, 3.34.[49] The purpose in both cases is that humanity might find communion with God, as in Wisdom 9.10 and John 3.17.

The relationship between Jesus and the Father is one of mutual love (e.g. John 3.35; 5.20; 10.17; 15.9). Although there is scant reference to a relationship of love between God and Wisdom, in Wisdom 8.3–4 this does seem to be the case, 'She glorifies her noble birth by living with God and the Lord of all loves her'. Love and knowledge are meshed together in Wisdom 8.4 and in John 10.14–15, 10.17. Michael Willett notes that 'it is not immediately clear what it means to speak of God's love for a personification of divine action in the world'.[50] Scott believes that we need to move to a richer understanding of Wisdom, not just as personification of a divine attribute. In certain passages found in the Wisdom of Solomon 'Sophia is effectively God in feminine form, equivalent to the more common Jewish expression of God in masculine form, Yahweh'.[51] Such a view necessarily leads to a tension between Jesus as Logos incarnate and Jesus as Wisdom incarnate. I will discuss in Chapter 4 how far Wisdom might be described as a separate feminine divine. For the time being it is worth noting that the shape of Wisdom Christology is influenced by whether we view Wisdom as a personification of an attribute of God or having a separate ontology. Most scholars would support the former, though the latter presents an interesting challenge to the traditional portrayal of Jesus as the incarnation of the divine Logos, understood as a 'masculine' category.

Another parallel between Wisdom and Jesus that is relevant in this context is revelation. Just as Jesus reveals the Father's name in John 17.6 and all that he has heard and seen comes from the Father (e.g. John 3.11–12, 8.26, 38; 15.15), so too Wisdom reveals God (Wisd 7.25–26). The vocabulary now is rather different: Wisdom is described as the revealer of secrets and those who love Wisdom gain intimacy with God.

[49] M. E. Willett, *Wisdom Christology in the Fourth Gospel*, San Francisco: Mellen Research University Press, 1995, 60–2.
[50] Willett, *Wisdom Christology*, 79.
[51] Scott, *Sophia*, 77.

Images of Jesus such as light, bread, water which echo those of Wisdom are all bearers of revelation. More generally the Father–Son language, although unusual in the Old Testament, is more prevalent in the late sapiential literature, especially the Wisdom of Solomon, chapters 1–11. The idea of familiar relationships is extended to the disciples, who in John become Jesus' children, in parallel with the notion that Wisdom also has her children (e.g. Sirach 4.11; 6.18).

The most striking parallel between Wisdom and Jesus is perhaps the idea of Jesus as the bread of life in John 6.27, echoed in Proverbs 9.1–26. Wisdom prepares a banquet and she invites those at the table to come and drink her wine and eat her bread (Prov 9.5). Furthermore, the image of Jesus as the vine reflects Wisdom in Sirach 24.17, where 'like the vine I bud forth delights'. The image of Jesus as the water of life connects with the river of Wisdom found in Sirach 24.30–34. Images of Jesus such as bread, wine and water undoubtedly have a sacramental inference.[52] However, this need not detract from the parallels found with the wisdom tradition.

The sign-miracles in John seem to echo the way the exodus miracle stories are retold and interpreted as symbols of salvation in the first eleven chapters of the Wisdom of Solomon. John uses his stories to reinforce a more general theme that human destiny depends on the acceptance or rejection of Jesus. A parallel sense of the critical importance of the acceptance or rejection of Wisdom is illustrated in the Wisdom of Solomon.

The above examples show, in an unambiguous way, the indebtedness of John to the wisdom tradition. In a recent commentary on John, Ben Witherington III believes that recognising Jesus as God's Wisdom, Wisdom incarnate, 'is the key to understanding the presentation of this character of the story'.[53] John's indebtedness to the wisdom tradition seems to be related to the school in which he wrote, where wisdom literature and

---

[52] P. Borgen, *Bread From Heaven; An Exegetical Study of the Concept of Manna in the Gospel of John and the Writings of Philo*, Leiden: E. J. Brill, 1965, 154–8.
[53] B. Witherington III, *John's Wisdom: A Commentary on the Fourth Gospel*, Louisville: Westminster/John Knox Press, 1995, 20.

thinking influenced his writing. In all likelihood wisdom was very popular in early Judaism. Wisdom's universal appeal would have suited the mixture of Jews and Greeks characteristic of the earliest Christian community around John.[54] The Wisdom that Christ portrays in John's Gospel is one fully incarnate in human form, unlike the divine agent of Wisdom who is accepted by some and rejected by others. The search for wisdom as expressed in Pilate's question, 'What is Truth?' comes in the person of Jesus, manifested in his life and death. Above all the most significant transformation of wisdom in John is the idea of Christ's death as the portrayal of wisdom. I will discuss the way this unfolds, beginning with the Pauline texts in the section that follows.

The wisdom of the cross

The very idea of linking wisdom with crucifixion can come as something of a shock, especially when we think of wisdom as the positive alluring quality that we learn or are given as God's gift. However, Paul's first letter to the Corinthians does make such a bold claim. Overall his chief intention seems to be to challenge the pride that comes with too much faith in human wisdom alone. 1 Corinthians 1.8 – 2.5 deliberately seems to pitch human wisdom (*sophia*) against the 'word of the cross' (1.18). The background to this passage is the apparently boastful arrogance of this community, engaged in bitter rivalry against one another and convinced of either their own or their leader's superiority and rhetorical eloquence.[55] Hays would refute any suggestion that Paul in 1 Corinthians intended Christ to be understood as the incarnation of Wisdom. However, it seems to me that the seeds of Wisdom Christology emerge and its foundation is the identification of God's wisdom with the wisdom of the cross. For Paul the wisdom of God *is* the wisdom of the cross, which overturns the wisdom of the world. In the Corinthian setting the human wisdom that Paul refers to is really esoteric or superior knowledge expressed through

---

[54] Witherington, *John's Wisdom*, 19.
[55] R. B. Hays, 'Wisdom According to Paul', in Barton, *Where Shall Wisdom*, 113ff.

powerful Hellenistic rhetoric. It has, in other words, a tendency towards Gnosticism. This is very different from much of the Jewish wisdom tradition that is grounded in reflection on daily life and experience that I discussed in the last chapter. Hence Paul is pointing to the behaviour of the Corinthians and their misguided attachment to certain forms of knowledge that they believed made them superior to others. Paul quotes Isaiah 29.14 in 1 Corinthians 1.19 when he suggests that God 'will destroy the wisdom of the wise and the discernment of the discerning I will thwart'. Isaiah is writing to the leaders of Judah, who were mistaken in trusting their own wisdom and plans to form an alliance with Egypt, instead of trusting in God.[56] In other words, Paul is not so much dismissing the Jewish wisdom tradition as a whole, rather he is pointing to the pitfalls of an over-reliance on human wisdom. According to human wisdom the idea of God manifested in a cross seems like sheer foolishness.

At the time crucifixion was the most humiliating and demeaning form of torture and to declare this as the action of God seemed to most to be unthinkable. The low social status of many of those in the Corinthian church reinforces this apparent sense of God's foolishness by the world's standards, indeed 'God chose what is foolish in this world to shame the wise' (1 Cor 1.27). The ability of God to start again with what seems unlikely material is part of the sense that this is a new creation, a new action of God. This new action where we find 'Christ the power of God and the wisdom of God' (1 Cor 1.24) culminates in the suggestion that Christ 'became for us wisdom from God, and righteousness and sanctification and redemption' (1 Cor 1.30). This idea revolutionises the idea of wisdom – Christ crucified is the wisdom of God. There are various possibilities as to what Paul means by the wisdom of God here. He may have been identifying Jesus as the new Torah, wisdom and Torah having previously been identified in earlier literature, such as Ben Sira.[57] Alternatively he may

---

[56] Hays, 'Paul', 114.
[57] J. A. Davis, *Wisdom and Spirit: An Investigation of 1 Corinthians 1.18 – 3.20 Against the Background of Jewish Sapiential Traditions in the Greco-Roman Period*, Lanham: University Press of America, 1984.

simply be taking over the language of his opponents in an ironical way.[58] Nonetheless, it seems unlikely that Paul had a highly developed Wisdom Christology in mind when he made this claim. His prime concern is to challenge all those who wish to be wise to reflect on the scandal of the cross.

The idea that Christ crucified expresses the wisdom of God still comes as something of a shock even to modern ears and could lead to a kind of morbid introspection unless we search for the reason for God's action. We find this in the way Paul links wisdom with righteousness, sanctification and redemption. Righteousness implies covenant, which leads to sanctification and redemption. In other words God's wisdom seems to be pointing to the wisdom of the cross as the plan of salvation.[59] Furthermore, if we explore the idea of covenant we find at its heart the love of God. For Paul, those who are spiritually mature act in love towards one another (1 Cor 3.1–4). Such wisdom is only possible through the action of the Holy Spirit (1 Cor 12.13). The foolishness of God is wiser than human wisdom (1 Cor 1.25) because it is the foolishness of divine vulnerability and love. The cross, then, expresses the passion of God for creation, and his compassion.[60] As Denis Edwards has suggested, 'It is an extreme expression of identification between the Lover and the beloved – between God and suffering creation'. [61] He suggests, further, that the reference to Christ's role in creation in 1 Corinthians 8.6 implies that Jesus is understood as divine Wisdom.[62] I am less convinced that Paul's letter to the Corinthians links Jesus explicitly with divine Wisdom in the sense that Christ then takes on characteristics of Wisdom, such as pre-existence. Some

[58] For a discussion of different alternatives see E. A. Johnson, 'Jesus: The Wisdom of God; A Biblical Basis for Non Androcentric Christology', in *Ephemerides Theologicae Lovanienses* 61 (1985), 261–94.

[59] Dunn, *Christology*, 211–12. Dunn seems to trace the earliest *origin* of the idea that Jesus is the embodiment of divine Wisdom to the first letter to the Corinthians. The idea then spread to all the Hellenistic churches, as indicated by, for example, Colossians 1, Hebrews 1.2ff., Matthew and John.

[60] J. Moltmann, *The Passion for Life*, trans. M. D. Meeks, Philadelphia: Fortress Press, 1978.

[61] D. Edwards, *Jesus the Wisdom of God: An Ecological Theology*, Homebush: St Pauls, 1995, 75.

[62] Edwards, 'Jesus', 38.

scholars have laid claim to an alternative eschatological and even apocalyptic tradition that dominates Paul's thinking in 1 Corinthians.[63] What seems more likely is that both sapiential and apocalyptic elements are present in Paul's theology.[64] The apocalyptic elements are suggestive of a future that is not readily conceived by the wisdom traditions alone. I will be returning to a discussion of the relevance of the relationship between apocalyptic and wisdom to the future of creation in Chapter 5.

John's Gospel is much more explicit in developing a Wisdom Christology that culminates in reflection on the cross. The purpose of Paul writing to the Corinthians and that of John's Gospel are very different. As I pointed out earlier, John was writing in the context of a community well versed in wisdom literature. For John the scandal of the cross could not be ignored, even though he explicitly identified Christ with Wisdom and the divine Logos. Furthermore, the way he incorporated the cross into his Christology takes us to another level of meaning concerning the wisdom of the cross.

Wisdom writers frequently referred to how we can profit from suffering. Such exhortations are taken up in 1 Peter, James, Hebrews and Luke-Acts.[65] In Sirach 2.1–2a, 4–6, for example, we find

> My child, when you come to serve the Lord
>   prepare yourself for testing . . .
> Accept whatever befalls you,
>   and in times of humiliation be patient.
> For gold is tested in the fire,
>   and those found acceptable in the furnace of
>   humiliation.
> Trust in him, and he will help you;
>   make your ways straight, and hope in him. (NRSV)

---

[63] For a discussion see E. E. Johnson, 'Wisdom and Apocalyptic in Paul', in Purdue *et al. In Search of Wisdom*, 263–83.

[64] Johnson, 'Wisdom and Apocalyptic'. Johnson also points out that the letter to the Corinthians cannot be reduced just to a discussion of Paul's Christology, rather he is concerned with the action of God in human history.

[65] C. H. Talbert, *Learning Through Suffering: The Educational Value of Suffering in the New Testament and its Milieu*, Collegeville: The Liturgical Press, 1991.

Similarly in Wisdom 3.4–6a:

> For though in the sight of others they [the righteous]
>   were punished,
> their hope is full of immortality.
> Having been disciplined a little,
>   they will receive great good,
> because God tested them and
>   found them worthy of himself;
> like gold in a furnace he tried them. (NRSV)

In Paul's letter to the Romans we find a similar connection, where our boast of the hope of God's glory (5.2) is found paradoxically in the suffering and tribulations of Christian experience (5.3). There are, however, differences compared with the wisdom tradition. In these cases the sufferer will endure, as God is faithful and will rescue the righteous. For Paul suffering can only be endured as it points to a future hope that rests on the love of God 'poured out into our hearts through the Holy Spirit' (5.5). Hope is not so much an optimistic attitude about a positive future, as a trusting that God will complete what was begun at the cross.[66] The ultimate triumph of God is expressed in the resurrection of Christ. Without the cross suffering can just as easily lead to despair and resignation, as the book of Job testifies.

John's Gospel takes us even further into an exploration of the relationship between the cross and glory. Willett suggests:

> The Gospel transforms the cross from humiliation (as in the synoptics, Acts and Paul) to glorification. Here pre-existence assists in that process of transformation. The glory which shines in the hour is the luminous glory of pre-existence. The cross is glory because it is the pre-existent Word who is on the cross.[67]

He seems to be suggesting that the glory comes from an understanding of Christ's origin, as well as a knowledge of where he is going to. John points back to the pre-existent Logos, as identified with pre-existent Wisdom, in order to reveal the

---

[66] Johnson, 'Wisdom and Apocalyptic', 279.
[67] Willett, *Wisdom Christology*, 52.

cross as a manifestation of the glory of God. Jesus' death is not just a sign, but displays the glory of God and acts like a 'final sign'. A parallel can be drawn with the Wisdom of Solomon, where Wisdom's final sign is the drowning of the Egyptians (19.1–9).

However, John does not just look back to Christ's origin in order to claim that the cross is one of glory. Now the light of the resurrection seems to shine back to the crucifixion event, revealing it as one that displays the glory of God. His 'lifting up' on the cross leads to an ascent into heaven. He also looks to the final vindication of Christ in the resurrection. It is possible that the theme of kingship, characteristic of the wisdom literature, is influential here. If Christ is understood as king, then the passion narrative can be reinterpreted as victory and glorification.[68]

The concept of the cross as one of glory permeates the Gospel in less obvious ways. Jesus is portrayed as one who identifies his own flesh and blood given up at death as an offering of life to those who believe. Jewish tradition looked to Wisdom or Torah as the bread from heaven. In John 12.24 we find a saying of Jesus, that 'unless a grain of wheat falls into the ground and dies, it remains a single grain; but if it dies, it bears much fruit'. This seems to be a commentary on his death, as in the previous verse we find 'The hour has come for the Son of Man to be glorified'. Again the link between his glory and his death comes as something of a surprise, explained by the parable of the grain of wheat. Here the fruit of eternal life for all manifests the wisdom of God, expressed paradoxically in the cross.

Hence in John we find that creation, incarnation and salvation history are kept together through reflection on the cross as the cross of God's glory. I suggest that it is the wisdom traditions that permit John to embrace such a broad compass. However, wisdom left on its own without the critical lens of the cross opens up a multiplicity of different possible interpretations of wisdom that may be more or less identified with the Christian tradition. Wisdom theology that remains

[68] Willett, *Wisdom Christology*, 121–2.

Christian theology cannot afford to ignore or marginalise the wisdom of the cross.

Denis Edwards has pointed to Jesus as the Wisdom of God in order to develop a basis for an ecological theology. His refusal to split creation and incarnation puts a welcome emphasis on the love of God for the world, as expressed in both movements of creation and incarnation. Jesus as Wisdom of God is both a teacher of wisdom and Wisdom incarnate. However, it is only in his section on Jesus and ecology that he begins to incorporate the wisdom of the cross. I have already pointed out the important insight that the wisdom of the cross displays the love of God for all creation. Nonetheless, I believe that the cross offers a critical challenge to human wisdom that we ignore at our peril. The cross is certainly the vulnerable love of God, but it is more than this as well. As Paul's letter to the Corinthians shows, the cross challenges all human wisdom and forces us to reconsider our own futures in its light. One of the reasons why Edwards seems to resist this aspect of Wisdom Christology is related to his desire to see the incarnation as an act of love, following the position of Duns Scotus. He views this as an alternative to the Thomist position where the incarnation functions to restore and redeem what is broken by human sin.[69] He does allow for the redeeming influence of Christ in creation, but it is redemption for future glory, rather than salvation from sin.[70] However, it seems to me that both interpretations of Christology are appropriate and serve to complement one another. Christ's death on the cross is a sign of vulnerable love, but only when it is added to the saving, redeeming quality does it become the cross of glory. I believe that if we weaken this aspect of Wisdom Christology we open the door to it becoming yet another romantic spirituality, with all the problems that this anticipates. Furthermore, I do not think we can stop at the reflection on Christ as the Wisdom of God. The Holy Spirit, too, manifests God's Wisdom, as I will explore in Chapter 4. This lends itself to a powerful Trinitarian image of Wisdom. Yet the cross remains the lens through which

[69] Edwards, *Jesus*, 70–1.
[70] Edwards, *Jesus*, 86.

this Wisdom can be understood. Richard Hays suggests that the meaning of wisdom needs to be controlled by 'Christ crucified'. He comments:

> This word of warning applies both to scholars who may be tempted to idolise learning for its own sake and to those whose celebration of Sophia tacitly becomes a form of human self-affirmation. Wisdom is a dangerous category and it can be employed rightly within the grammar of Christian theology only when it is grounded firmly within the canonical narrative whose climax is the death of Jesus.[71]

Yet the death of Jesus is surely not so much the *climax* in the way he suggests, as part of the double movement of cross and resurrection. The cross makes sense in the light of the resurrection and the resurrection is marked with the signs of the cross. As Moltmann comments: 'In the light of the cosmic dimensions of his resurrection, his death on the cross takes on universal significance.'[72]

Richard Hays is also particularly wary of those writers who celebrate Christ primarily as the teacher of wisdom. However, such a view can, it seems to me, become part of our understanding of the relationship between Christ and wisdom. It also serves an important function in grounding wisdom ideas in the historical Jesus. However, the event of the cross cannot be ignored either. The way Christ and creation can be understood in terms of Wisdom Christology depends on an adequate appreciation of the cross, in the light of the resurrection, as I will discuss next.

Christ and creation

The first chapter of the letter to Colossians has a much fuller account of the relationship between Christ and creation. The hymn of Colossians (1.15–20) is thought to have its origin in the wisdom tradition. While the background context for this hymn is a matter for some debate, for example it could have derived from a pre-Christian Gnostic setting, or have its roots

---

[71] Hays, 'Paul', 123.
[72] J. Moltmann, *The Way of Jesus Christ*, trans. M. Kohl, London: SCM Press, 1990, 282.

in rabbinical Judaism or Hellenistic Judaism, most scholars agree that the language used indicates that of Jewish wisdom literature.[73] However, Christ is presented as one who is greater than wisdom, as wisdom is never portrayed as the goal of creation.[74] The first stanza seems to speak of Christ as active in the creation of the world. He is the image of the invisible God, the first born of creation (Col 1.15), so that 'all things were created by him and for him. He is before all things, and in him all things hold together' (Col 1.16–17). This echoes the idea of Wisdom as the image of the invisible God (Wisd 7.26), acquired at the beginning of God's way (Prov 8.12). The idea that Christ holds all things together in unity (Col 1.17) bears some resemblance to Wisdom as the mediator of creation (Wisd 7.21; 8.1, 6).

Dunn suggests that in this passage Christ is simply defining what Wisdom is, the power revealed in Christ is the same power that God used in creating the world through Wisdom.[75] He resists any suggestion that originally this hymn implied that Christ was pre-existent and active in creation. Rather, it is the continuity of God's action that is being celebrated. He suggests that the more obvious interpretation that Christ is involved in creation does not necessarily follow. Rather, creation is pointing to Christ through the activity of Wisdom. In other words, the movement here is from creation to Christ, rather than the other way round, from Christ to creation. However, as I argued above, the idea of Christ's pre-existence becomes much more obvious in the Gospel of John. Subsequent Christian interpretations of Colossians would naturally read into this passage the concept of Christ as *Pantocrator*. Nonetheless, if Dunn's exegesis is correct, then it forms an important corrective to over-enthusiastic interpretations of

---

[73] Käseman, for example, traces the text to pre-Christian Gnosticism, E. Käseman, 'A Primitive Christian Baptismal Liturgy', in *Essays on New Testament Themes*, trans. W. Montague, *Studies in Biblical Theology* 41, London: SCM Press 1964, 149–68. For a survey of different positions see R. P. Martin, *Colossians: The Church's Lord and the Christian's Liberty*, Exeter: Paternoster Press, 1972, 40ff.

[74] Martin, *Colossians*, 58.

[75] Dunn, *Christology*, 190.

the relationship between Christ and creation. It certainly cannot be used to imply that Christ has exclusive involvement in the initial creation of the world, over against the Spirit.

The second stanza speaks of Christ as mediator of redemption, so that 'through him to reconcile to himself all things, whether things on earth or things in heaven, by making peace through his blood, shed on the cross' (Col 1.20). The pre-existence hymn appears to have been modified by adding a reference to the Church in verse 16 and the blood of the cross in verse 20.

Some commentators have suggested that the additional reference to the Church implies that *all things* in verses 17 and 20 refer just to the Christian community and not to creation. Eduard Schweizer, for example, believes that the redaction process has effectively denied Christ's cosmic role in redemption.[76] However, it is hard to see why the authors would have bothered to place Christ so firmly in the wisdom tradition if this was not the case. The overall tenor of this hymn seems to be to celebrate the glory of Christ, rather than to diminish his role in creation. Dunn sees the significance of this passage, not so much in terms of final redemption of creation, but more generally as underlining the significance of the Christ event. Furthermore, it is Christ as risen and exalted that Paul seems to have in mind. Following the resurrection, 'the power and purpose in creation cannot be fully understood except in terms of Christ, and so too Christ cannot be fully understood except in terms of that wise activity of God'.[77] At the time this passage was written the involvement of Wisdom in the creating and saving action of God was part of common culture, now Christ is identified with this Wisdom. Even if we accept this more limited interpretation, it is clear that Christ and creation have to be considered together, rather than separately.

Edwards is more confident that this passage supports the notion that 'Human beings form one universe with other creatures, and human bodiliness cannot be separated from

[76] E. Schweizer, *The Letter to the Colossians; A Commentary*, Minneapolis: Augsburg Publishing House, 1982, 273–7 and 290–302.

[77] Dunn, *Christology*, 194.

the sphere of bodiliness – the physical universe. The whole universe will share in the consummation of all things in Christ.'[78] But the question still remains, how far will the consummation of all things in Christ mean a completely new creation and how far can we think of the process as already begun on this earth? The very idea of the relationship between God and creation being one of intervention is resisted by most of those working at the interface of theology and science.[79] This seems to be related to the fact that God is understood as one who works within the processes of the natural world, rather than through some sort of supernatural process. In consideration of the relationship between Christ and creation, as shown in Colossians, we need to ask how the redemptive process might be operative in creation.

It is possible to retain the idea of a non-interventionist God by suggesting with Edwards that 'the risen Christ is already the secret heart and center of the created universe, then, through God's gracious act, the transformation of matter has begun from within the processes of the universe'.[80] This is indeed an attractive proposal that keeps creation and redemption closely meshed together. Joseph Sittler has argued that the hymn in Colossians can serve to challenge the dualism in the Western Church between nature and grace.[81] I intend to come back to a fuller discussion of the difference between the Eastern and Western approaches to nature in the next chapter. However, the suggestion that Christ is already at work secretly in the universe raises some interesting questions. If Christ is really at work in the way Edwards suggests, then what is the purpose of the Christian community? How do we distinguish between creation and new creation in Christ? If the influence of Christ is automatic, as he seems to suggest, then would this imply that the world will inevitably become more and more Christocentric, rather in the manner of the writing of Teilhard de Chardin? A purely evolutionary interpretation of cosmic

---

[78] Edwards, *Jesus*, 86.
[79] See, for example, T. Peters (ed.), *Science and Theology: The New Consonance*, Boulder: Westview Press, 1998.
[80] Edwards, *Jesus*, 87.
[81] J. Sittler, *Essays on Nature and Grace*, Philadelphia: Fortress Press, 1972.

Christology that sees evolution as a given, rather than in need of redemption, fails as it seems to ignore the cost of the creative process. Jürgen Moltmann also affirms a cosmic Christology, but clarifies the way the cosmic Christ can act as agent of salvation in the natural world:

> Cosmic Christology cannot identify the lordship of Christ with the one supposedly existing 'harmony of the world', for its starting point is the reconciliation of all things through Christ; and the premise of this reconciliation is a state of disrupted harmony in the world, world powers which are at enmity with one another and threatening chaos. Cosmic Christology talks about a reconciled, Christ pervaded cosmos and in this way differs from every other cosmic mysticism, old and new, whether Indian or 'postmodern'.[82]

The idea of the eschatological transformation of nature expressed through a cosmic Christology brings us to a discussion of the future of creation. While I agree that there has to be some continuity between creation and new creation, we need to distinguish carefully the two movements in salvation history. Moltmann is again helpful here, distinguishing as he does between *adventus*, that is the future promise of God breaking into the present, and *futurans*, the future unfolding that is in continuity with the present.[83] I will be returning to this issue again in Chapter 5.

Romans 8.21 speaks of a groaning of all creation, waiting for redemption. While there is some controversy about whether the creation refers specifically to the whole natural order, it is unlikely to be a specific reference to cosmic Christology. I have argued elsewhere that if we channel all the sufferings of

[82] Moltmann, *Way*, 278. It is worth noting that while Moltmann acknowledges the link between Christ and Wisdom, especially in Paul's letter to the Corinthians, he does not develop this further much beyond noting that the connection is there and that in the earliest Christian communities there was a Wisdom Christology, 'and as such cosmic Christology', see *Way*, 282. Hence he is able to say 'In the final "greening of the earth" the cosmic Wisdom-Christ will come forth from the heart of creation, setting that creation in the light of God's glory', 280.

[83] J. Moltmann, *The Experiment Hope*, trans. M. D. Meeks, London: SCM Press, 1975, 52; see also J. Moltmann, *The Future of Creation*, trans. M. Kohl, London: SCM Press, 1979, 29–31.

the cosmos into Christ's suffering we lose a sense of the suffering of God with creation through the Holy Spirit.[84] Although
I have highlighted the wisdom of the cross from a Christological perspective in this chapter, it needs to be complemented
by an adequate pneumatology, as I will discuss in Chapter 4.

Given this view of the groaning of all creation, waiting for
redemption, we could ask where we might find signs in the
present of future hope. If we return to the Wisdom Christology
in John, then Christ promises life to all those who partake
in his body and blood. This signifies the eucharistic meal that,
as I have shown earlier, echoes the feast of Wisdom portrayed
in Proverbs 9. Furthermore, the spiritual blessings that come
to those who are united in Christ's death, include the gift of
wisdom and understanding. 'In him we have redemption
through his blood, the forgiveness of sins, in accordance
with the riches of his grace that he lavished on us with all
wisdom and understanding' (Eph 1.7–8). Marcus Barth has
pointed to the rich meaning of wisdom and prudence in this
text.[85] In the next few verses we find once again a summary of
the relationship between Christ and creation expressed in
wisdom language. In Ephesians 1.9 the purpose of the mystery
of God's will comes to the fullest expression in verse 10, 'to
bring all things in heaven and earth together under one head,
even Christ' (1.10). This verse bears some resemblance to
Colossians 1.20, where the blood of the cross is mentioned. If
this interpretation is correct, then it may hint at the reconciliation of broken relationships between God and all creatures.
It is, however, unlikely to refer to recapitulation of all things.
More likely explanations either stress the leadership of Christ,

---

[84] C. Deane-Drummond, *Ecology in Jürgen Moltmann's Theology*, Lampeter:
Edwin Mellen Press, 1997, 253–6.
[85] M. Barth, *Ephesians 1–3*, Garden City, NY: Doubleday & Co., 1974, 84–5.
Possible interpretations include first, that God does not squander grace at
random; second that both wisdom and prudence point to the addition of the
gift of revelation to salvation and third that wisdom and prudence are given
to humanity in order to aid right conduct. All wisdom includes God's wisdom
as well as that of humanity. Furthermore, prudence is added to wisdom to
clarify that it is wisdom operating in prudence that is important in this context,
the terms 'wisdom' and 'prudence' are not distinct as in the theoretical and
practical wisdom of the Greek philosophers.

or simply that all things are summed up in Christ.[86] We arrive at a paradox very similar to the one we reached in Colossians. Is this passage really indicating reconciliation of all things in Christ, or pointing to Christ as the sum of all things?

It is of note that both Colossians and Ephesians include reference to the death of Christ alongside reference to the relationship between Christ and creation. Ephesians, however, points to the specific effects of Christ's saving work through forgiveness of sins. While reference to sin is specific to the human community, Christ's power extends to the disarming of negative cosmic forces (Eph 1.21). Such a power is expressed now through the Church, so that 'His intent was that now, through the church, the manifold wisdom of God should be made known to the rulers and authorities in the heavenly realms, according to his eternal purpose, which he accomplished in Christ Jesus our Lord' (Eph 3.11). The passage does not suggest that any cosmic function of Christ is now given, instead, to the Church. The Church does not so much replace Christ in his cosmic function as proclaim by its existence the Wisdom manifested in Christ.[87] However, the Church's remit is to witness to the entire world, so that 'political and social, cultural and religious forces, also all other institutions, traditions, majorities and minorities are exposed to her testimony'.[88]

Other references to Christ disarming cosmic forces include 1 Corinthians 15.24; Philippians 3.21; Colossians 2.15; 1 Peter 3.22. Colossians connects the power that Christ has over cosmic forces with the cross, 'And having disarmed the powers and authorities, he made a public spectacle of them, triumphing over them by the cross' (Col 2.15). The author of 1 Peter focuses more on the power of the ascended Christ, 'It saves you by the resurrection of Jesus Christ, who has gone into heaven and is at God's right hand – with angels, authorities and powers in submission to him' (3.22). However, this is set in the context of the saving effects of Christ's death (3.18). All these verses suggest that we need to consider Christ's

---

[86] Barth, *Ephesians*, 89–91.
[87] Barth, *Ephesians*, 345, 363–5.
[88] Barth, *Ephesians*, 365.

death and resurrection together in reflecting on the relationship between Christ and creation. Jürgen Moltmann suggests that while the epistemological foundation for cosmic Christology is in Christ's resurrection, the ontological foundation lies in his death on the cross.[89] An adequate cosmic Christology includes the wisdom of the cross, seen, as in John, in the light of the resurrection.

The challenge for biotechnology

How do these theological insights impinge on the way we perceive ourselves and the natural world, in particular the way we have developed the power to create new life-forms through genetic engineering? Lovelock's Gaia hypothesis, while it challenges the reductionism that is at the heart of genetic engineering, fails in a number of respects to provide an adequate basis for a theology of nature. In the first place the number of different possible scientific, theological and ethical interpretations of Gaia produces a diffuse perception of the relationships between God, humanity and the natural world. In its limited scientific form it is only likely to consider genetic engineering in terms of its possible effects on the global ecology of the earth. As long as the whole geo-physiological process was not disturbed, such actions could be considered as having relatively little significance. In its more ideological form, while it is removed from some of the dangers of extreme forms of anthropocentrism, it seems to portray humanity in highly nega-tive terms as a 'parasite' on the earth. More important, perhaps, it is suggestive of a particular form of ethical naturalism. In this view there are no means for dealing with ambiguity, suffering and nature's 'crying need for grace', as Rahner has put it.[90]

From a theological perspective, creation-centred spirituality has shifted the theological agenda from an exclusive focus on human sin and redemption to creation. It has helped to foster

[89] Moltmann, *Way*, 281–6.
[90] G. A. McCool (ed.), *A Rahner Reader*, London: Darton, Longman & Todd, 1975, 194. See also Chapter 4 for further commentary.

a recovery of the immanence of God in all things, though verging at times to embrace a form of pantheism. However, along the way it has presented a naïve view of nature that does not seem to take adequate account of the sheer waste, suffering and pain that is part of the evolutionary process. While arguing for a cosmological theology, it tends towards an ideology that is out of touch with political and social issues. In addition it attaches itself to a particular form of science, especially that of the new physics, that seems to welcome in an uncritical way organicism in science in opposition to scientific reductionism. This theology would seem, then, to have very little to say to genetic engineering other than rejecting its mechanistic approach to the natural world.

The biblical wisdom tradition seems to be a more fruitful avenue for exploring an adequate understanding of ourselves in the age of the new genetics. Jesus, as teacher of wisdom, identified with the wisdom writers of the Old Testament in their affirmation of creation as a gift from God. He saw in creation, through story and parable, means through which his teaching could carry a sense of disclosure. While acknowledging the wisdom in the natural world, he challenges his listeners to go beyond this to consider moral and spiritual implications. While of no direct relevance to genetic engineering as such, it is clear that Jesus as teacher of wisdom affirms the natural world and the order of creation as it is. This affirmation comes from the Jewish faith that God is ultimately the Creator of the world. Would this suggest that humanity is forbidden to interfere with the natural order of creation? The parables and other passages that identify Jesus as teacher of wisdom do not allow us to come to this conclusion. However, they do suggest that his ongoing purpose is to overturn our presuppositions about what wisdom really is. He identifies with the poor, the sinners and the outcast to an extent that challenged the received wisdom of the day. Christ's concern extended from the poor to the natural world. Hence the relevance today is to look at genetic engineering from the side of the poor and disadvantaged as well as the natural world. How far are we contributing to the impoverishment of the so-called 'underdeveloped' nations by

genetic engineering? Can we really justify the particular interference we seek if it leads to suffering and death of sentient
animals?[91]

Wisdom Christology remains narrow in its scope as long as
it is defined in terms of Jesus as teacher of wisdom. We can
trace the emergence of this Christology to the earliest Christian
communities who struggled to make sense of who Christ is.
Wisdom was the most all-embracing category within the Jewish
tradition that could be used to describe Christ. Yet it is striking
that within a few years of Christ's death we find a hymn
celebrating and elevating Christ as the Wisdom of God in the
letter to the Colossians. The parallels between Logos, Wisdom
and Christ in the Gospel of John leave little doubt as to the
existence of a Wisdom Christology. Such a discovery is relevant
today as it provides a means of linking creation, incarnation
and redemption. The separation of either creation and incarnation, or creation and redemption in much of the history of
Christian theology needs to be challenged.

The above is fleshed out further through reflection on the
wisdom of the cross. Just as Jesus in his role as teacher of
wisdom challenged previously held views, so Paul made his
stinging critique of the so-called wisdom of those in the
Corinthian community. He asks them to consider how far their
pride and arrogance were justified on the basis that the wisdom
of God is expressed in the cross. These insights are relevant to
all those who are captivated by the wisdom of science and
seem to suggest that it will always forge the right path in its
search for truth. Today the temptation to be swept along by
technique and method can blind us to the reality of what we
are doing, as well as the future consequences. Consider the
cloning of Dolly the sheep in our most recent history. It was
done to solve a particular problem in the medical/agricultural
world, but it has opened up a floodgate of debate about the
possibility of human cloning, with all the associated ethical
issues.[92] I am not suggesting that new advances in science

---

[91] For a discussion of these questions see C. Deane-Drummond, *Theology and
Biotechnology: Implications for a New Science*, London: Geoffrey Chapman,
1997.

should all be prevented, rather that we need to be more critical of whether a particular 'advance' is creating the kind of world we really want. Perhaps theologians have become too complacent, too bemused by a sense of marginalisation to have the courage critically to appraise the new developments. In addition, we need to ask: How far are these developments going beyond the acceptable ethical and moral limits of human intervention in the natural world? In the case of human cloning and most animal cloning, for example, it seems to me that we have overstepped these limits.

The wisdom of the cross as expressed in the Gospel of John reminds us that the ultimate outcome of suffering was the glory of the resurrection. The cross is lit up from ahead by the light of the resurrection and from behind by the glory of his pre-existence. I have argued that it is possible to develop a cosmic Christology, both on the basis of the biblical analogies drawn between Christ and Wisdom, as well as through more explicit references such as are found in the letter to the Colossians. This leads to the idea that the natural world is caught up in the double movement of creation and redemption. What does this signify for genetic engineering? First it means that where we are contributing to the suffering of creation, we are indirectly contributing to the suffering of Christ. His death is for the victims of nature in the evolutionary process, including the victims that humans create through their own specific manipulations. Yet this by no means justifies such actions, rather we need to be critical of all the processes we undertake and ask whether this measures up to the gaze of Christ on the cross. Are we helping to create an entrapped or liberated nature? While Christ can forgive every sin, including sins against nature, is it time we moved towards a more humble attitude of repentance? The manipulation of even plant species so that they become more and more genetically uniform in order to boost yields, at least in the short term, seems to me

---

[92] For a commentary on cloning see C. Deane-Drummond, 'Biotechnology: A New Challenge to Theology and Ethics', in C. Southgate, C. Deane-Drummond, P. D. Murray, M. R. Negus, L. Osborn, M. Poole, J. Stewart, F. Watts, *God, Humanity and the Cosmos: A Textbook in Science and Religion*, Edinburgh: T&T Clark, 1999, 355–87.

to destroy the very variety and diversity that is at the heart of the creative process of evolution. However we envisage God in Christ involved in the evolutionary process, few would wish for dead-ends to be created by human manipulation.

Finally the wisdom of the cross reminds us that the prime movement of God towards the creation is the movement of love. It is love that is powerful enough to face humiliation, death and crucifixion. How far do we reflect the image of God if we fail to show love for creation? Christ's love was expressed through identification with us. While it is impossible for us to identify with the natural order, we need to find ways of seeing the world through the perspective of other creatures – a tuning into the natural world that makes us more sensitive to its particular gift as creation. One way we might begin to do this is through the celebration of the Eucharist, bringing evocative memories of Wisdom's banquet. Creation, Christ and redemption come together in one eucharistic celebration. This is a reminder, too, that wisdom cannot be divorced from worship, that it is through worship that we can begin to have an inkling of what divine wisdom means.[93]

Conclusions

I have argued in this chapter that we need to find more adequate ways of relating science and theology in order to face the pressing issues that arise through new biotechnology. While Gaia and creation-centred spirituality are at least a start in putting creation back on the theological map, they lack an adequate critique of science other than a simplistic rejection of mechanistic philosophy. A theology of creation through Wisdom, grounded in the wisdom of the cross, can help us to move to an appraisal of both theology and science. Wisdom Christology is one of the earliest Christologies that emerged in the fledgling Christian community. However, I believe that it still has relevance today. Pauline wisdom reminds us that the wisdom of the cross challenges all our presuppositions

---

[93] See D. Hardy, 'The God Who Is With the World', in F. Watts (ed.), *Science Meets Faith*, London: SPCK, 1998, 144–9.

about progress and sophistication in method that has dominated much recent biotechnology. The Wisdom Christology of John takes us to a deeper reflection on the mystery of the cross as glory, reflected in the light of the resurrection. The resurrection gives us reason to hope for reconciliation, not just for ourselves, but for the created order as well. As we move to a deeper reflection on the meaning of cosmic Christology for today we are reminded of the eucharistic banquet, that celebrates the love of God for creation and its redemption. The Orthodox Divine Liturgy evokes a cosmic Christology, with Christ as Pantocrator. We are now in a position to explore further insights from Eastern Orthodoxy and ask in the chapter that follows what this might offer us in the struggle to develop a more enlightened science.

3

East Meets West

The rise of modern experimental science is a curiously Western phenomenon. Nonetheless, few would doubt that in pre-modern times the Eastern nations were responsible for considerable advances in science. Needham's extensive historical research on the relationship between science and society in the East and West suggests that it was the prevailing social, intellectual and economic conditions of Renaissance Europe that were primarily responsible for the breakthroughs in science occurring in the West. He rejects possible alternatives, such as different 'physical-anthropological' or 'racial-spiritual' factors compared with the East.[1] However, on close examination of his argument it is clear that philosophical/religious factors did influence the prevailing social conditions that he suggests are primarily responsible for the difference. The principle of letting Nature take her course (*wu wei*) is part of Taoist philosophy and led to particular non-interventionist practices among magistrates, along with the Chinese being the 'greatest observers among all ancient peoples'.[2] The experimental science that flowered in Europe seemed too interventionist to be philosophically respectable. Needham rejects the idea that Chinese science was stagnant after the seventeenth century, rather it did not expand at the

[1] J. Needham, *The Grand Titration: Science and Society in East and West*, London: Allen & Unwin, 1969, 190.
[2] Needham, *Grand Titration*, 211.

same rate. Another relevant difference between East and West was in the idea of order in creation. For the Chinese, order in the world was present but it was not determined by a rational and personal being. This led to a lack of confidence that any laws of nature could be discovered through reason. He suggests that if the social conditions in China had been different and had not been inhibited by bureaucratism, then a different, more organic form of science might have emerged.

More recently Western science has come under a stinging critique from Seyyed Nasr. He argues that the detachment of Western science from its religious moorings has led to a lack of any sense of the sacred in nature. He criticises the West for its almost exclusive focus on environmental ethics, rather than a reassertion of the religious understanding of the order of nature.[3] His impressive synthesis of aspects of different religious traditions serves a common purpose, namely to re-instate a sense of the sacred in nature, to recognise its purpose and spiritual meaning for humanity both now and in the future, and to explore the interrelationships between social and natural law.[4] He argues that religious factors were among those responsible for the flowering of modern experimental science in Europe. However, the emergence of modern science was accompanied by both an eclipse of the sapiential religious symbolic cosmology and the rise in rationalism and Renaissance humanism.[5] He suggests that Aquinas's idea of natural law, once secularised, allowed an even greater detachment of human reason from the divine will. His suggestion that we need an adequate understanding of both the order of nature and ethics, rather than one or other in isolation is, it seems to me, a valid one. It is the task of this chapter to explore the wisdom cosmology of Eastern traditions of Christianity and combine this with Aquinas's understanding of wisdom as discernment. I will argue that it is only by combining both traditions that Christianity can develop the resources necessary for an adequate contemporary theology of creation.

[3] S. H. Nasr, *Religion and the Order of Nature*, Oxford: Oxford University Press, 1996, 1–8.
[4] Nasr, *Religion*, 64.
[5] Nasr, *Religion*, 130–3.

Sophia of the East

Sophiology anticipated in early Eastern Christian traditions

Gregory of Nyssa (AD 335) had the most extensive knowledge of the sciences among the Cappadocian Fathers.[6] Of particular interest is his way of viewing salvation history and nature. He stressed the idea of the 'eternal now', where the cosmos is created with humanity at the centre. This sense of the eternal present leads to a unity of thought in both the beginning and the end of the cosmos in such a way that humanity is never outside the divine supernatural life. There is no separation of nature and grace, moreover the idea of nature itself is different. For Western thinkers nature is commonly thought of as the intellectual and physical/animal life of humanity. Supernatural grace is then added on to this nature. In Gregory nature means the intellectual life and the supernatural life – the animal life is then added. This explains an understanding of human nature as good in the Greek tradition. The image of God is found in the whole person, rather than just the intellect. He was also keen to insist on the work of all three persons of the Trinity in both creation and redemption.[7] Gregory gives to the Holy Spirit the same characteristics as God, namely one who is life-giving, everlasting, changeless, just, wise and good.[8] Gregory is also known for his mystical theology, in particular his recognition of the apophatic tradition, leading to his sharp distinction between Creator and creation.[9] His appreciation of the value of culture, especially his attempts to incorporate Platonic modes of thought, alongside a healthy scepticism that the mind is simply an instrument that must surrender to the mystery in our understanding of God, marks him out as a theologian worth remembering today. Anthony Meredith comments that it 'is precisely in the fruitful alliance between

---

[6] G. A. Maloney, *The Cosmic Christ: From Paul to Teilhard*, New York: Sheed & Ward, 1968, 148–58.
[7] A. Meredith, *Gregory of Nyssa*, London and New York: Routledge, 1999, 38.
[8] Meredith, *Gregory*, 42.
[9] Meredith, *Gregory*, 100–1.

this search for exactness and the perils of such a search that we meet in Gregory of Nyssa'.[10]

While Gregory of Nyssa sought to mediate between science/ Platonic philosophy and religious faith, Maximus the Confessor develops a fully cosmological Christology. For him all things are created in Christ and all things will be reunited through Christ. As I discussed in the previous chapter, an understanding of Christology in terms of wisdom linked into a view of Christ as Logos. A Logos Christology gradually replaced the earlier Wisdom Christology. In Maximus, however, we find a strong sense of the importance of the wisdom of God, though this wisdom is bound up with reason. Furthermore, the attributes of God, such as wisdom, justice and omnipotence, are distinct from the being or ontology of God.[11] Nonetheless, such attributes are 'fully divine and in no way compromise His divine simplicity'.[12]

He marks out the stages in the spiritual life in the following way.[13] In the first stage the task is to remove vices caused by self-love which act as impediments to the grace of God. In the second stage humanity encounters the mind of God through divine gift. Once that inner nature, or logos, is perceived in each creature, then humanity can use that creature according to divine intention. The *logoi* in all creatures reflect a principle of harmony, corresponding to the wisdom of God in all things. Furthermore, it is only through the action of the Spirit that humanity can come to an accurate perception of the mind of God. The Holy Spirit not only produces virtues, but also, following the Book of Daniel, 'bestows wisdom and knowledge'.[14]

The third stage of the spiritual life is in mystical contemplation of the Trinity. For him it is only insofar as humanity has become like God that the true knowledge of God can be

[10] Meredith, *Gregory*, 131.
[11] K. Ware, *Free Choice in St Maximus the Confessor*, Canan: St Tikhons Seminary Press (USA), 1989, 181.
[12] Ware, *Free Choice*, 219.
[13] Maloney, *Cosmic Christ*, 171–3.
[14] Maximus the Confessor, 'Chapters on Knowledge' in *Maximus the Confessor: Selected Writings*, trans. G. C. Berthold, introduction by J. Pelikan, Mahwah: Paulist Press, 1985, 161.

revealed. Such a gift comes through an active infusion of the love of God in the human soul. In the Church we find that the Holy Spirit and the active co-operation of humanity work to bring together the following principles:

> reason with mind, prudence with wisdom, action with contemplation, virtue with knowledge, faith with enduring knowledge; without any of these things being inferior or superior to the other in such a way that all excess or defect be eliminated from each of them ... For thought is the act and manifestation of the mind related as effect to cause; and prudence is the act and manifestation of wisdom, and action of contemplation, and virtue of knowledge, and faith of enduring knowledge. From these is produced the inward relationship to the truth and good, that is to God, which he used to call divine science, secure knowledge, love and peace in which and by means of which there is deification.[15]

Furthermore, he goes on to suggest that this deification of humanity is linked with the transfiguration of the material cosmos. Humanity achieves an inner unity that leads to a corresponding cosmic unity in the material world. Like Gregory of Nyssa, his antithesis was between natural and unnatural, rather than natural and supernatural. Hence 'the only true evil was the unnatural. It consisted in thwarting, through self-love, man's nature in its destiny to be united with God and with all things in and through God'.[16] A life lived according to nature was a life lived according to God's intention. The difference between Augustine's understanding of free choice and that of Maximus the Confessor, is that for Augustine humanity has just one choice, between good and evil. For Maximus the choice is between several good alternatives.[17] Such free choice is a natural good, though any rejection of those choices in favour of evil comes from personal employment of the will. Furthermore, the starting point for his anthropology is not fallen humanity, as in Augustine, but the deified humanity of Christ and the saints in the eschaton.

---

[15] Maximus, 'Chapters on Knowledge', 193.
[16] Maloney, *Cosmic Christ*, 179.
[17] Ware, *Free Choice*, 221.

Maximus is significant in that he anticipates the development of the idea of the virtue of wisdom, taken up in the thought of Thomas Aquinas. However, at the same time he outlines a cosmic Christology that retains the wisdom motif. In this he anticipates the cosmic theology of the Russian Orthodox writers that we will turn to next. However, any specific use of the wisdom tradition remains undeveloped in his thinking.

The emergence of Russian Sophiology

It is in the Russian Orthodox tradition of the nineteenth century that we find a full flowering of a form of theology that elaborates the notion of wisdom. Prior to this various different forms of wisdom are represented in popular iconography. In the fourth century Constantine dedicated a cathedral church in Constantinople to Sophia, rebuilt again by the Emperor Justinian after its destruction in 532. In the cathedral itself, we find the image of Christ, and it is Wisdom portrayed as Logos that is common in Byzantium, where the dedication of Hagia Sophia is the feast of Christmas. Yet after the council of Ephesus in 431, where Mary was proclaimed Mother of God, a common tradition of associating Sophia with Mary developed. The Cathedral of St Sophia of Novgorod (1045) celebrated its feast day on the feast of Mary's Assumption. In the Russian Orthodox tradition, by the late seventeenth century, we find other representations of Sophia in addition to that associated with Sophianic representations of Christ and the Mother of God.[18] First, there is the Novgorod type in which Sophia is portrayed as a fiery-faced angel. Second, there is the Kievan type in which a Woman of the Apocalypse stands for Sophia. Third, we find a representation of Wisdom as surrounded by pillars or as host at a banquet based on an allegory of Proverbs 9:

> Wisdom has built herself a house, she has erected her seven pillars, she has slaughtered her beasts, prepared her wine, she has laid her table. (9.1–2 JB)

[18] E. K. Zelensky, 'Sophia the Wisdom of God: The Function of Religious Imagery During the Regency of Sofia Alekseevna of Muscovy', in L. Fradenburg (ed.), *Women and Sovereignty*, Edinburgh: Edinburgh University Press, 1992, 198.

To the fool she says, 'Come and eat my bread, drink the wine I have prepared! Leave your folly and you will live, walk in the ways of perception.' (9.5–6 JB)

Finally, there is the Iaroslavl type where a crucifix, surrounded by seven gifts of the Holy Spirit, stands for Sophia. Other iconographic representations depict Wisdom through rhombic symbolism.[19] All these illustrations show that Wisdom keeps surfacing in popular piety, but she cannot be contained by any one image.

There seems to be no traceable theological reflection on the theme of wisdom in Russian religious thought prior to the nineteenth century.[20] Vladimir Solovyov (b. 1853), Sergii Bulgakov (b. 1871) and Pavel Florensky (b. 1882) are key figures in the development of Sophiology. I intend to concentrate most on the work of Bulgakov, as his work is a conscious attempt to develop a fully orthodox theology.

Vladmir Solovyov's work was both poetical and philosophical. His early encounter with Wisdom is in the form of a beautiful female figure. A few years before his death he wrote an autobiographical poem, describing the three mystical experiences of Sophia he had during his lifetime. His first experience is revealing:

> Suddenly my eyes could not focus,
> Without a trace the earth disappeared.
> Passion's storm faded away,
> I was surrounded with heavenly blue.

> You too are radiant blue! A blossom
> Of supernatural beauty in your hand.
> With gracious goodness you smiled at me,
> Nodding – then the heavenly image was gone.[21]

His subsequent experiences speak of visions surrounded by 'golden light and radiant blue', the radiance shining especially

---

[19] D. M. Fiere, 'What is the Appearance of Divine Sophia?', *Slavic Review* 48(3) (1988), 449–76.

[20] R. Williams, *Sergii Bulgakov: Towards a Russian Political Theology*, Edinburgh: T&T Clark, 1999, 113.

[21] Extract from *A Poem* (1898) cited in T. Schipflinger, *Sophia-Maria: A Holistic Vision of Creation*, trans. J. Morgante, York Beech: Samuel Weiser, 1998, 257.

from her eyes, 'like a day's light at dawn's creation'.[22] Given
these images, it makes sense to describe these visions, as does
Urs von Balthasar, as visions of Our Lady.[23] Other poems speak
of his sense of the presence of Sophia in all creation:

> O earth, my mistress, since the days of youth
> I have felt your sweet breath,
> Heard the beat of your heart in the veil of your
>   blossoms
> And touched the pulse of all life . . .
>
> On that day, the light from the vaults of heaven,
> Flowed down differently, clear and unclouded;
> Between the old familiar trees of earth
> Appeared mysteriously pale eyes, so blue.[24]
>
> The ice is melting, clouds yield to light,
> Flowers blooming all around me,
> Silent tones in ether of transparent sounds,
> I sense you everywhere. [25]

He had a considerable influence on other Russian symbolists
of the time who looked to the Divine Feminine, rather than to
Christ, for inspiration. It is possible that Jacob Boehme (1575–
1624) had a major influence on Solovyov. Boehme's concept
of Sophia seems to have been suggested to him by the Jewish
cabalistic lore based on the Book of Zohar. David suggests
that 'Sophia supplied above all the final principle of integration of the correlative physical and moral elements in God's
essence, the tie linking man to God and his nature, and the
latent basis for the perfection of man and through him of the
world'.[26]

---

[22] Solovyov, *Poem*, 258–9.
[23] H. Urs von Balthasar, *The Glory of the Lord: A Theological Aesthetics*. Volume
3, trans. A. Louth, J. Saward, M. Simon and R. Williams, Edinburgh:
Edinburgh University Press, 1986, 292.
[24] Extract from *O Earth, My Mistress* (1886), cited in Schipflinger, *Sophia-
Maria*, 253–4.
[25] Extract from *I Am Always There, Both Day and Night* (1898), cited in
Schipflinger, *Sophia-Maria*, 255.
[26] Z. David, 'The influence of Jacob Boehme on Russian Religious Thought',
Slavic Review 21 (1962), 45.

Solovyov took up the mantle of a chivalrous knight, liberating the world through a holy war.[27] He wrote in a context where positivism, materialism and atheism seemed to him to be the dominant strands among the nineteenth-century Russian thinkers of the time.[28] By combining Neoplatonic ideas of the Eternal Feminine with an Orthodox concept of Sophia, he hoped to reclaim both philosophy and religion for the purposes of combating what he saw as a dangerous and empty materialism and nihilism. Sophia is the Eternal Feminine, incarnate in the Virgin Mary. He arrives at an image of Sophia as a grand synthesis between humanity, the Virgin Mary and the Church, combining to produce an organic link between heaven and earth. For Solovyov, Christology alone could not produce a satisfying theology of creation, even in its cosmic forms. Neoplatonic influences come out clearly in that the world is formed after the pattern of divine Wisdom, so that 'In Sophia the fullness of the ideal forms contained in the Word is reflected in creation'.[29] Sophia becomes an ideal form of humanity, envisaged as both the crown of creation and the microcosm of the world.

He tries to explain evil in the universe by speaking of a cosmic fall, in which the world-soul exerted her powers apart from God and through alienation from the Logos. Here we have a coincidence of creation and fall that bears some resemblance to Maximus the Confessor. Von Balthasar points out that in Solovyov the world-soul and Sophia are not identical, but insofar as the world-soul is structured by Sophia and enters into the same goal, then the two become one.[30] This allows Solovyov to speak of the fall of the world-soul, without implicating Sophia as such. This is not so much a second Fall as coincidental with the Fall of humanity. For Solovyov, evil is not just ignorance, it is a deliberate rejection of love. It seems

---

[27] S. D. Cioran, *Vladimir Solovyov and the Knighthood of the Divine Sophia*, Waterloo: Wilfred Laurier University Press, 1977.

[28] G. L. Kline, 'Russian Religious Thought', in N. Smart, J. Claydon, S. Katz and P. Sherry (eds), *Nineteenth Century Religious Thought in the West*, Vol. 2, Cambridge: Cambridge University Press, 1985, 208–17.

[29] Cioran, *Solovyov*, 107.

[30] von Balthasar, *Glory*, 314–16.

likely that his confrontation with the apocalypse at the end of
his career shifted his position so that he took more account of
evil.[31] Solovyov believed that it is only once Christ is incarnate
that the unity between Logos and Sophia is restored and Sophia
becomes once again the determining principle of the cosmos.
Yet the Logos is still the active principle, the world-soul in the
guise of Sophia becoming 'fertilised' by the Logos. The world-
soul carries forward the cosmic process begun with the initial
act of creation. The potency of creation is established in the
beginning, but it is given form by the Logos. It is then that
knowledge becomes possible for humanity, understood as
participation in Sophia, the ground of all harmony in the
cosmic order. He believed that the evil in this world is transitory, rather than eternal. There are additional theological
difficulties with his theodicy. The restoration of order,
following a cosmic fall of the world-soul away from Logos,
shows considerable indebtedness to Gnostic thought. How
far is his utopian metaphysical vision in touch with the world
as we know it? Is evil really a transitory force in the way he
suggests?

   One particular difficulty with his synthesis, especially in
the light of contemporary feminist theology, is his archetypal
representation of male and female which assumes an unequal
dualism. Such a dualism offers a complementary image of
masculine and feminine, but the feminine still suffers from
being placed in a subordinate position. Man is envisaged as
the active subject and woman the passive object; man is the
seat of reason and woman that of emotion and instinct and so
on.[32] Moreover, for him it is still Logos or Word that remains
the active unifying principle and Sophia emerges as that which
is produced by the activity of the Word.[33] For all her majesty,
Sophia seems to take on the role of a passive receptacle of the

---

[31] von Balthasar, *Glory*, 290–7. In this respect Solovyov moves beyond a
Teilhardian synthesis, though the two writers show remarkable parallels in
other respects, as I will discuss below.

[32] B. Meehan, 'Wisdom/Sophia, Russian Identity, and Western Feminist
Theology', *Cross Currents* 46 (1996), 149–68, especially 155.

[33] V. Solovyov, *Lectures on Divine Humanity*, revised by B. Jakim (ed.), Hudson:
Lindisfarne Press, 1995, 107–8.

active principle of the Logos. She is like a world-soul, holding together in unity that which was broken apart and disordered. Nonetheless, he distinguished between the imperfect world-soul and the Wisdom of God in suggesting that the Sophia is fixed and eternal, while the world-soul is subject to time and space, created in the image of Sophia.[34]

Pavel Florensky took up Solovyov's work, but developed it in an even more mystical way and one that was more indebted to the ecclesiastical and liturgical traditions. Like Solovyov, he had a formative influence on Bulgakov, not least because he moved in the same social circles. He believed that all created realities are expressions of the Wisdom of God. In other words, once we understand the meaning of creatures and creation we are given an insight into the Wisdom of God. Hence wisdom is the 'fruit of a living religious consciousness', rather than the invention of philosophical speculation.[35] Cosmology, anthropology and theology come together in a grand organic synthesis of Sophiology. The relation between God and creation is one of love and entreaty, rather than compulsion or coercion. The being of creation is the realised love of the Creator, and this beauty in the union of love between Creator and creation is Sophia. Hence Sophia is the living link between God and creation. Sophia becomes, for Florensky, the transcendental unity of all created beings and the mystical basis of the cosmos. She is 'the great Root of the creature . . . by means of which the creature penetrates into the intimacy of the divine life and through which it obtains eternal life from the Source of Life'.[36] Yet the Logos is still the ground of the created order and Sophia the counterpart to the Logos or his bride. As bride she becomes associated with the Church, who is also the bride of Christ. Sophia as the outgoing divine love uncovers the true vocation of the Church, to show that the world is grounded in divine love. In her transformation of creation, Sophia becomes the ideal personality, encompassing the 'psychic content' of the

---

[34] Cioran, *Solovyov*, 24.
[35] R. Slesinski, *Pavel Florensky: A Metaphysics of Love*, Crestwood: St Valdimir's Seminary Press, 1984, 70.
[36] Slesinski, *Florensky*, 177.

God-Mind, forever linked as the 'eternal Spouse of God's Word'.

For Florensky, compared with Solovyov, Sophia is more intimately linked with the effect of divine love and action.[37] For him, Sophia is experienced as relationships, especially friendships, an idea that attracted considerable criticism. Even more controversial was his notion that Sophia is a distinctive hypostasis, alongside the Holy Trinity of Father, Son and Spirit. This distinction may be related to his determination to keep the essence of Sophia separate from the other persons of the Trinity. His approach led to charges of heresy and Gnosticism. Bulgakov developed his theology to counter such a trend and also to attempt to show how Sophiology can be true to the Orthodox faith, against the charge of heresy. His earliest work on Sophiology, the *Philosophy of Economic Activity* (1912) shows the influence of Schelling, Kant and Hegel, reflecting his determination to engage with European intellectual traditions.[38] Sophia is depicted as the world-soul, the subject of human productivity and an idealised form of humanity.

Sergii Bulgakov, like Solovyov and Florensky, had mystical experiences that fed into his theology. However, he was able to use these as an inspiration for deeper theological reflection that remained underdeveloped in both Solovyov's and Florensky's work. Bulgakov's description of his experience of Sophia in the cathedral church of Hagia Sophia highlights the mystical elements in his theology:

> It creates a sense of inner transparency, the weightiness and limitations of the small and suffering self disappear; the self is gone, the soul is healed of it, losing itself in these arches and merging into them. It becomes the world. I am in the world and the world is in me . . . It is the bliss of some final knowledge of the all in all in oneself, of infinite fullness in multiplicity, of the world in unity. This indeed is Sophia, the real unity of the world in the Logos, the co-inherence of all with all, the world of divine ideas . . . It is neither heaven or earth, but the vault of heaven above the earth.[39]

---

[37] Williams, *Bulgakov*, 119–20.
[38] Williams, *Bulgakov*, 120–1.
[39] J. Pain and N. Zernov (eds), *A Bulgakov Anthology*, London: SPCK, 1976, 13–14.

Another significant aspect of his experience of Sophia is his encounters of her through the beauties of the world. His first experience of Sophia was through standing on a snow-capped mountain in the Causacus:

> I saw your ice sparkling from sea to sea, your snows, reddening under the morning dawn, these peaks piercing the sky, and my soul melted away with delight . . . In front of me shone the first day of the World's creation. Everything was clear, everything became reconciled, and filled with ringing joy . . . But there was no word, no NAME, there was no 'Christ is risen' to be sung to the mountain summit. A limitless and powerful IT reigned, and this IT, by the fact of its being, extinguished in that moment . . . all the cards of my 'learning'. And that moment of meeting did not die away in my soul, that apocalypse, that wedding banquet, the first meeting with Sophia.[40]

Other similar experiences of Sophia came to him while on an ocean-going vessel in late November. In seemed to him that like the red of God's dawn, Sophia interpenetrates the whole of creation from the beginning, before the first days of creation. Such experiences of Sophia led to charges of pantheism, though, as I will show later, he was also accused of Platonism and Gnosticism. He rejected any charges of pantheism, insisting that his was a pan-en-theism, the world contained in God. As such, his theology coheres with more recent panentheistic theologies of creation, though he was writing in a period before they became fashionable.

Bulgakov, like Solovyov, argued that it was through Wisdom that God created the world, incorporating the idea of divine prototypes. He believed that his theology was more theologically orthodox, developing the idea that cosmic Sophia is the intelligible basis of the cosmos in his book *The Unfading Light*, published in 1917. While he intended this to be a sequel to *Philosophy of Economic Activity*, it is far more theological, drawing on the work of both Maximus the Confessor and Gregory Palamas for both an apophatic theology and a cosmic transfiguration of the cosmos. Following Nikolai Fyodorov

[40] S. Bulgakov, *Avtobiograficheskie zametki (Posmertnoe izdanie)*, 1946, 62–3, cited in Meehan, 'Wisdom/Sophia', 161.

(1828–1903), he distinguishes between the work of humanity as aligned with God's action, or 'theurgy', and the exalted achievement of humanity in economics and technology.[41] He rejects any sense that there can be an abstract philosophical system in isolation from concrete experience. Florensky's influence is clear at this stage in his description of Sophia as the fourth hypostasis, though he insists that Sophia is also revelatory of the divine life of the Trinity. Sophia acts on the border between God and the world. For Bulgakov,

> this frontier, which by definition stands between God and the world, creator and creature, is neither the one nor the other, but something quite distinct, simultaneously itself united with and divided from both God and creation ... This angel of creation, the beginning of the ways of God, is 'holy wisdom', Sophia. It is the loving of love.[42]

Sophia is a living being with a personal hypostatic life. She becomes the 'eternal object of the divine love, bliss, joy and gratuitous delight or play'. Yet she is also the subject of love as well, and in this sense is a personal hypostasis. Bulgakov rejects the idea of a quaternity of persons, since Sophia does not share in the intra-divine life of the Trinity. Sophia remains a receptacle of divine love, an Eternal Feminine understood in the passive mode of receiving. The whole Trinity acts in Wisdom in order that the world comes into being, so that

> It takes into itself the single and complete Godhead in its tri-personality, as Father, Son and Spirit. In so far as it receives its substance from the Father it is the creation and daughter of God. As that which is known by the divine Logos, it is the bride of the Son (as in the Song of Songs), the Spouse of the Lamb (as in the New Testament, especially the Apocalypse). As receiver of the outpouring of the Spirit's gifts, it is the Church, and so too the mother of the Son who was incarnate from the flesh of Mary, the heart of the Church; and as such Sophia is also the ideal soul of creation, Sophia is beauty.[43]

[41] Williams, *Bulgakov*, 126–7.
[42] S. Bulgakov, *The Unfading Light*, trans. R. Williams, cited in *Bulgakov*, 134.
[43] Bulgakov, *Unfading Light*, in Williams, *Bulgakov*, 136.

In receiving the Logos, Sophia becomes Sophia-Christ and the object of the Father's love. Yet Bulgakov pulls back from the idea of Sophia as created, for in Sophia there is 'only a yes to everything'. Yet neither is she the Absolute, but is rather the 'image of God', lacking the nothingness that is in the world. His image of Sophia at this stage seems to portray her as the intermediary between God and creation. Confusingly, perhaps, she cannot be fully identified with either, she is not the Absolute, yet is full of divine love. She is not created, but is still the feminine principle of the world.

An active role for Sophia in creation becomes more obvious in his suggestion that she is the yearning love of God, the eros in creation, the love of earth for heaven. Such yearning eventually culminates in beauty, echoing Dostoevsky's aesthetics. Sophia in this sense becomes the eschatological goal for creation. Reflecting on the Pauline image of all creation groaning in Romans 8, he suggests that 'all living things instinctively strive towards grace and beauty, harmony of movement, an inner rhythm of their life'.[44] The speech of creation remains 'tongue-tied' and only in humanity is there 'secure knowledge'. Yet such knowledge as we have now is still subject to a sense of a lack of true reconciliation, as we yearn for a 'higher self'. The discovery of our higher self can only come through 'our real and substantial participation in Sophia'. The task of human creative power is to discover its eternal image in Sophia. Such a transformation to ultimate Beauty can only come about through the gift of God.

Bulgkov sketches out the basis for human behaviour, an ethic, as active co-operation with the transformation of the world according to Sophia. He is strongly critical of any basis for human behaviour in economics alone, for it has a 'pseudo-eschatology'. He asks, in particular, if we can ever overcome the problem of poverty, both at the natural and communal level. In particular, he sees the task of humanity as crucial. He asks if economic labour can ever deliver the earth from its curse. His reply is that economic activity is only to be tolerated, reconciled like any worldly activity. Curiously, he suggests that

[44] Bulgakov, *Unfading Light*, in Williams, *Bulgakov*, 138.

Christian freedom is to be found in rejection of 'the wisdom of this world with its economic magic', including Marxism and other radical movements, and acceptance instead of 'divine folly'.[45]

In 1927 the Holy Synod of the Russian Émigré Church accused the St Sergius Theological Institute in Paris, where Bulgakov was dean, of heresy. It seemed to them that he put forward a new doctrine of God as Sophia, replacing the idea of Christ as the Wisdom of God. The idea of Sophia being superior to the Mother of God seemed offensive, as was the concept of a fourth hypostasis.[46] By 1935 the Moscow Patriarchy accused him of intellectualism, Gnosticism, and infusing masculine and feminine elements into the Trinity. They recommended that he be banned from serving as a priest or teacher. The Metropolitan of Paris nonetheless defended him.

His book, *Sophia: The Wisdom of God*, was published in 1937 in an attempt to defend himself against charges of heresy. Here, compared with *The Unfading Light*, Sophia was more specifically theological. He spelt out in a clearer way his vision for Sophia as encompassing the whole of theology. He argued that the legacy of the Reformation and the Counter Reformation was a refusal to consider anthropology and cosmology together. He suggested that Sophiology is a particular dogmatic interpretation of the world that has a rightful place alongside Thomism or Barthianism. For him Sophiology is crucial for all theology, not just a theology of creation:

> The future of living Christianity rests with the Sophianic inter-
> pretation of the world and of its destiny. All the dogmatic and
> practical problems of modern Christian dogmatics and ascetics
> seem to form a kind of knot, the unravelling of which inevitably
> leads to Sophiology. For this reason in the true sense of the word,
> Sophiology is a theology of crisis, not of distinction, but of
> salvation.[47]

---

[45] Bulgakov, *Unfading Light*, in Williams, *Bulgakov*, 149–52.
[46] C. Bamford, foreword to S. Bulgakov, *Sophia: The Wisdom of God: An Outline of Sophiology*, Hudson, NY: Lindisfarne Press, 1993, xix–xx.
[47] Bulgakov, *Sophia*, 21.

His insistence on the salvific role of Sophia was more likely to fuel the fire of his critics, who believed that the role of salvation could be attributed to Christ alone.

In a manner not apparent in his earlier work, he seems to be more ready to link Sophia with the being (*ousia*) of God. He suggests that God's *ousia* should not be separated from wisdom-glory, where wisdom signifies *content* and glory *manifestation* of all persons of the Trinity. As in his earlier work, he rejects any notion that wisdom is confined to the Logos, since this would suggest that the Father and the Spirit are without wisdom. Wisdom is characteristic of all three hypostases, just as the divine *ousia* is shared by them all. Once we accept the idea that Sophia is part of the being or *ousia* of God, then it seems to me inevitable that Sophiology and salvation are connected in an intimate way. Sophia is the means through which divine ideas become reality, so that the life of truth, identified with the Logos, when it becomes fully transparent is beauty, identified with the Spirit, and hence reflecting the divine glory. He picks up his earlier aesthetic theme, but spells out more fully the theological implications. In this way 'The life of Truth in its full transparency is beauty, which is the self-revelation of the Deity, the garment of God, as it were, it is the divine glory that the heavens declare'.[48] It is this beauty that seems to be the mark of salvation, and as such shows the involvement of all persons of the Trinity.

For Bulgakov Sophia is the 'Eternal Feminine' of the God-head, becoming *both* the internal love of God *and* the connection between the created world and the eternal world of the triune God. Whereas in *The Unfading Light* he developed the idea of Sophia as 'frontier', sitting uneasily between the divine persons of the Trinity and creation, now he clarifies this dis-junction by considering Sophia as both divine and creaturely. Divine Sophia becomes creaturely Sophia in the creation, expressed because of the love of God. Sophia in her creaturely and divine modes is expressed through the joint action of Word and Spirit, both pointing to the love of the Father, rather than themselves. In this he has retained the

[48] Bulgakov, *Sophia*, 49.

primacy of the role of the Father in creation, but it is through the participation of the Word and Spirit. The eternal Son becomes the Logos of the world and the Spirit becomes the beauty and glory of the world, created through Sophia as an expression of God's love.

The Spirit is present as creaturely Sophia at the beginning of creation before the first 'Let there be' of God's creative act. She is like the first mother who brings forth life to all that exists in the created world. I find the link that he develops between Sophia, the Logos and the Spirit fascinating. The bringing forth of life in creation becomes a Trinitarian act, not just 'Mother' in place of 'Father', but a movement of Trinitarian love through Sophia. While he never uses the term the 'Eternal Feminine', his somewhat stereotypical representation of the feminine needs some modification. His theology does, however, lend itself to reappraisal of our image of God in a way that is inclusive of both masculine and feminine metaphors. As Brenda Meehan has pointed out, his insistence on Sophia as *ousia* of God is of particular significance, since, from the point of view of feminist theology, Sophia is not simply a feminine principle bolted on, as it were, to an otherwise masculine image of God.[49]

Although Bulgakov was anxious to avoid charges of heresy, his ideas were severely criticised. His notion of divine and creaturely Sophia led to the charge of Platonism. Yet some form of dualism seems inevitable if the distinction between Creator and creation is going to be preserved. The opposite equation of divine Sophia with the world leads to an even more problematic pantheistic notion of God. Vladimir Lossky believes that Bulgakov has put the personhood of God before God's nature, since Wisdom is the common revelation of the persons.[50] He believes that this is an exaggerated reaction to the theology of the Western Church, which sees the Holy Spirit as no more than the bond of love between Father and Son. For Lossky, the Wisdom of God is just one of God's

---

[49] Meehan, 'Wisdom/Sophia', 159–60.
[50] V. L. Lossky, *The Mystical Theology of the Eastern Church*, trans. the Fellowship of St Alban and St Sergius, London: J. Clark, 1957, 79–80.

energies, like Life, Power and Justice. Any attempt to identify Wisdom with God's being or *ousia* seems offensive to Orthodoxy, since God's ontology can never be so described. Furthermore, there is a problem with identifying Christ as Logos incarnate and as Wisdom incarnate if Wisdom is no longer identical with the divine Logos. The preferred Orthodox position seems to be to restrict Sophia to the second person of the Trinity, understood as Logos/Sophia incarnate. While recognising that Bulgakov draws on the Orthodox tradition, those who adopt Lossky's stance prefer to think of him as a religious philosopher, rather than an orthodox theologian. While Bulgakov's Sophiological scheme is perhaps too elaborate, to reduce Wisdom to just another energy like Justice or Life seems to me to fly in the face of the biblical traditions of Wisdom as person. Furthermore, to restrict Wisdom to Christology does not do justice to the variety of the wisdom texts, as I will elaborate further in the following chapter. It is fair to say that Bulgakov has incorporated the personal nature of God into God's being, but a separation of person and nature in the way Lossky seems to suggest is unnecessary and artificial. John Zizioulas is one contemporary Orthodox theologian who has suggested that God's being and that of the Church are best understood in terms of communion, which speaks of personal interrelationships.[51] Furthermore, once the *ousia* of God is described in personal terms it is no longer possible to understand the being of God simply in the abstract. Bulgakov's identification of Wisdom with the *ousia* of God clearly marks out both the novelty and controversy in his theology.[52]

A more serious criticism of all Sophiological schemes is whether sufficient consideration is given to evil present in the universe. However, Bulgakov, at least, does devote some space to this issue. Compared with Solovyov's Gnostic notion of a cosmic fall of the world-soul, Bulgakov's scheme is more theologically coherent. He suggests that the counterpart to

[51] J. Zizioulas, *Being as Communion*, Crestwood: St Vladimir's Seminary Press, 1993.

[52] B. Newman, 'Sergius Bulgakov and the Theology of Divine Wisdom', *St Vladimir's Theological Quarterly* 22 (1978) 39–73.

creaturely Sophia is 'creaturely nothingness', an idea that he hints at in his earlier work, *The Unfading Light*. However, while in this work Sophia has nothing to do with such nothingness, now this is developed into an idea of Sophia's shadow, or 'dark face'.[53]

Sophia of the West

Intimations of Sophia in Pierre Teilhard de Chardin: the Eternal Feminine

Before moving to consider the work of Aquinas relevant to wisdom, it is appropriate to reflect briefly on the possible contribution of the thought of Teilhard de Chardin (1881–1955). Significantly, perhaps, his life spanned a similar period to that of Bulgakov. While Bulgakov originated in Russia and was an Orthodox priest who spent many years in the Western world in Paris, Teilhard was a French scientist and Jesuit priest, who spent many years in China. His fascination with Eastern religions, especially their mysticism, is well documented.[54] He recognised the differences between pantheistic and monistic/theistic mysticism, but sought to see how they are related to each other in an organic way. He was probably mistaken in thinking that the Eastern religions were more unified than they were in reality. Having said this, Teilhard sought to find a new road for Christian mysticism, that took into account his perception of the mysticism of the East. Ursula King suggests that one of his main achievements was to search for this new way between East and West:

> Perhaps it is Teilhard's main achievement to have sought a new formulation for a mysticism of the West, that is to say, a mysticism rooted in the Christian doctrines of creation and incarnation, but expressed in a new manner. However, the use of the term *via tertia*, the references to a new 'road', to a not yet existing mysticism, all point towards a synthesis going beyond past distinctions of West and East.[55]

[53] C. Graves, *The Holy Spirit in the Theology of Sergius Bulgakov*, Geneva: World Council of Churches, 1972, 26.
[54] See, U. King, *Towards a New Mysticism: Teilhard de Chardin and Eastern Religions*, London: Collins, 1980.
[55] King, *New Mysticism*, 203.

He distinguished between theistic and monistic forms of mysticism by suggesting that it is a sense of personal, mutual love between God and humanity that is a distinctive aspect of theistic forms of faith. In other words, while monism leads to a mysticism of unification, theism leads to a mysticism of identification. Yet he wanted to modify the Western idea of personal love and include the more Eastern concept of love as energy, animating the life of the world. For Teilhard, Eastern religion did not fully understand love in its highest and most personal form. It is significant that the Sophiologists of the Russian Church also sought to redefine mysticism in terms of both personal encounter with Sophia, but retained the idea of love as energy, invigorating and sustaining the world. There is a similar tension between the unification idea implicit in the concept of the world-soul, and the identification with Sophia in her various guises as Christ, Mary or simply Lady Wisdom. Like Bulgakov, Teilhard sought to unite anthropology with cosmology. However, for Teilhard the overriding concern was to bring theology into line with evolutionary categories and biological and scientific forms of thought. Bulgakov was more interested in engagement with political forms of thinking, though he ultimately seems to have rejected Marxism as bearing any ultimate hope for humanity.

Given these similarities, is there anything in Teilhard's theology that points to a concept of Sophia? The closest he seems to have come to this idea is through his notion of the Eternal Feminine, which perhaps resonates more with Solovyov's poetic Sophiology. Teilhard commonly speaks about the 'Soul of the World', which he believed was the primordial guiding principle of the cosmos, intimately connected with his notion of the Omega. In a poem entitled *The Eternal Feminine* (1918), he related his concept of the guiding principle of the cosmos to the figure of Wisdom in the Old Testament and then to the Virgin Mary in the New Testament.[56]

The introductory line to the first part of this poem cites Ecclesiastes 24.14a, which speaks of Wisdom: 'From eternity

56 P. Teilhard de Chardin, 'The Eternal Feminine' in *Writings in Time of War*, trans. R. Hague, New York: Harper & Row, 1968, 191–202.

in the beginning he created me.' Like the figure of Wisdom, Teilhard's poem is written as a monograph, under the figure of Beatrix. The first part of the poem draws on Proverbs 8.22–31 and Genesis 1.1. The following extract makes this clear:

> When the world was born, I came into being. Before the centuries were made, I issued from the hand of God – half-formed, yet destined to grow in beauty from age to age, the handmaid of his work. . . .
>
> Through me, all things have their movement and are made to work as one.
>
> I am the beauty running through the world, to make it associate in ordered groups: the ideal held up before the world to make it ascend.
>
> I am the essential Feminine.
>
> In the beginning I was no more than a mist, rising and falling: I lay hidden beneath affinities that were hardly yet conscious, beneath a lose and tenuous polarity.[57]

He also speaks of her as 'the bond that held together the foundations of the universe'. When life came, she was embodied in those beings that were chosen to be in her image, becoming the 'archetypal bride and mother'. She is the passion, the fire that burns in human hearts and allows them to be creative in the magnetism of the Feminine. He seems to be uncritical of the human explorations of science, viewing them as expressions of the passion of the Feminine:

> He builds up power, he seeks for glory, he creates beauty, he weds himself to science. And often he does not realise that, under so many different forms, it is still the same passion that inspires him – purified, transformed, but living – the magnetism of the Feminine.[58]

While he suggests that human love echoes her creative work in the universe, once humanity tries to grasp her for itself, seeking her through pleasure, then she becomes the Temptress. This echoes the theme of Woman Folly in the Proverbs, the

57 Teilhard, 'Feminine', 192.
58 Teilhard, 'Feminine', 194.

dark side of Lady Wisdom. He suggests that had Christ not come, humanity would have in all probability kept her 'in the camp of evil', that is, in the folly of his ways.

The introductory line of the second half of this poem draws on Ecclesiasticus 24.14b which speaks of Wisdom: 'and for eternity I shall remain'. Here Teilhard reflects on the Feminine after the coming of Christ, rather than in primordial creation. Yet he insists that the two are interconnected in an intimate way, 'In the regenerated world I am still, as I was at my birth, the summons to unity with the universe – the world's attractive power imprinted on human features'.[59] She seems to be an intermediary between Christians and God, so 'my reality has risen aloft, drawing men to the heights: it floats between the Christian and his God'.[60] But now love is transformed so that she becomes the ideal Virgin. Chastity is the alternative and ideal way of expressing the summons of Christ's love. She becomes Beatrix, the dream of all arts and sciences in each culture, so that 'I am the unfading beauty of the times to come – the ideal Feminine'.[61] It seems that she fosters an eschatological goal of beauty in a way that parallels that of the Russian Sophiologists. Furthermore, the idea that she is the love-energy of love that we find in Bulgakov goes further in suggesting that she lured God into the incarnation.

> Without the lure of my purity, think you, would God ever have come down, as flesh, to dwell in his creation?
>
> Only love has the power to move being.
>
> If God, then, was able to emerge from himself, he had first to lay a pathway of desire before his feet, he had to spread before him a sweet savour of beauty.[62]

This seems to be a reference to the Virgin Mary. He suggests that the role of Mary is to draw down the saviour of the world, a theme that appears later in his *Le Milieu Divin*, for

---

[59] Teilhard, 'Feminine', 197.
[60] Teilhard, 'Feminine', 197.
[61] Teilhard, 'Feminine', 199.
[62] Teilhard, 'Feminine', 200.

He had first of all to raise up in the world a virtue capable of drawing him as far as ourselves. He needed a mother who would engender him to the human sphere. What did he do? He created the Virgin Mary, that is to say He called forth on earth a purity so great that, within this transparency, He would concentrate Himself to the point of appearing a little child.[63]

Teilhard, like Bulgakov, sees her as the link between God and the earth: 'Lying between God and the earth, as a zone of mutual attraction, I draw them both together in a passionate union.'[64] Yet this is 'until the meeting takes place in me, in which the generation and plenitude of Christ are consummated throughout the centuries. I am the Church, the Bride of Christ. I am Mary, the Virgin, mother of all human kind.'[65] The idea of generation refers to Christ's corporeal body born of the Virgin Mary and animated by the Word. The idea of plenitude hints at the mystical Body of Christ that is the Church. In this way we find the maternal nature of the Virgin Mary and the Church becoming mystically identified with each other. Yet this has cosmic significance, since she becomes the basis for the divinisation of the cosmos, the unfolding of alluring forces containing the elements of the work of the Spirit.

Henri de Lubac's commentary on this poem makes it clear that while Teilhard does draw on the figure of Wisdom as an inspiration for his poem, a compelling influence seems to be his search to explain the significance of the Virgin Mary for the practice of chastity. She becomes an exemplar for chastity, the practice of which he believed preserved the dynamism of the Feminine. This influence is combined with his intention to explain the puzzle of life itself and human development of character.[66] These twin influences lead him to explore the role of Our Lady in the cosmos, so that for him the attractive cosmic elements of the Feminine working in the cosmos become incarnate in the Virgin Mary. The poem is

[63] P. Teilhard de Chardin, *Le Milieu Divin*, cited in H. de Lubac, *The Eternal Feminine: A Study on the Poem by Teilhard de Chardin*, trans. R. Hague, London: Collins, 1971, 28.

[64] Teilhard, 'Feminine', 200.

[65] Teilhard, 'Feminine', 200–1.

[66] de Lubac, *Feminine*, 17.

dedicated to Beatrix, as the veiled Virgin. Teilhard wrote this poem just before he made his religious profession of final vows. His struggle to come to terms with the vow of perpetual chastity, alongside other vows of renunciation of the world comes through clearly in the poem.

Like Bulgakov's theology, Teilhard's poem shows the influence of Platonism in his portrayal of love as a cosmic force. His description of different levels of love-energy seems to echo that found in Plato's *Symposium*. Yet he tries to avoid any charge of dualism by seeking to discover the evolution of the spiritual and the relationship between spirit and matter.[67] He is also likely to have been influenced by the German romantic poet Goethe, for whom the Eternal Feminine becomes incarnate in the Virgin Mary. Another influence is Dante, who speaks of the love of a young girl, Beatrice, in *The Divine Comedy*. As in *The Divine Comedy*, love becomes universalised into an incarnation of the loving Church. Dante, too, links this love with eternal Wisdom and the Virgin Mary. Yet his interpretation is noticeably different. Teilhard deliberately dedicates his prologue to Beatrix, who, as veiled virgin, is distinguished from the young woman Beatrice. Moreover, a universal cosmic role for the Eternal Feminine is missing from Goethe's account.[68]

Of particular relevance to the present discussion, however, is the close parallel between Teilhard's poem and Solovyov's *The Meaning of Love*. Henri de Lubac suggests that this cannot have been a direct influence on Teilhard, since although it was published in 1894 it was not translated into French until 1946.[69] I have already noted similarities between Teilhard's work and Solovyov's poetic mysticism. Nonetheless, the evolutionary aspects of creation, alongside his determination to stress the life of chastity as an ideal, mark out differences between Teilhard and Solovyov. Both tended to focus on the Virgin Mary and the Church as the expression of the universal Feminine. Both suffered from the stereotypical representation

---

[67] de Lubac, *Feminine*, 32–3.
[68] de Lubac, *Feminine*, 20; 37–8.
[69] de Lubac, *Feminine*, 39.

of the idea of Feminine. Both were mystical, poetical and philosophical rather than theological formulations. Furthermore, it seems to me that while Solovyov made a conscious effort to seek Sophia and saw in the Virgin Mary an expression of that Wisdom, Pierre Teilhard de Chardin sought the Virgin and discovered in her the Eternal Feminine, as foreshadowed in the writings on Wisdom. In other words, while Teilhard's poem was primarily a mystical reflection on Mary, Solovyov's poem was primarily a dedication to Sophia. Henri de Lubac's comments are relevant here, in that for Teilhard

> it is not an abstract principle which is personified in the Virgin – it is the Virgin, existing in her own individuality, who is universalised in the principle . . . If, then we speak of symbol, we shall not be saying that in this context the Virgin Mary is the fully realised symbol of the universal Feminine, but rather that this universal Feminine must be understood, in its pure essence, as the Virgin Mary.[70]

This ascription of the universal to Our Lady parallels that of the role of Christ, and it is Teilhard's intention to find an equivalence between the perfect man in Christ and the pure, ideal woman he saw in Our Lady. While he believed that the dedication to Our Lady was a correction to the 'masculinization' of the Church, he also viewed God as having a maternal nature. Yet he resisted any notion of femininity being attributed to the inner Godhead. Mary represents, rather, the 'outer atmosphere or envelope', the perfect model of what a creature should be before God.[71] As inseparable from Christ, Mary performs a crucial role in Christogenesis, the means through which Christ activates and vivifies the evolution of the world.

It seems to me that Teilhard's close association of the Eternal Feminine and Wisdom with the Virgin Mary leads to some theological restraints. On the one hand, he is prevented from using female language to describe God, as he is keen to insist that Mary is still creature. On the other hand, the language of cosmic divinity used to describe Wisdom exists in tension with his attempt to universalise the function of the pure

---

[70] de Lubac, *Feminine*, 119.
[71] de Lubac, *Feminine*, 126–8.

creature, the Virgin Mary. The relationship between the cosmic Christ and the cosmic functions of Mary remain obscure, except insofar as both are expressed through the birthing of the Church. Furthermore, once we restrict Sophia to Mariology she can no longer take on the full theological significance she deserves. By separating creaturely Sophia and divine Sophia, Bulgakov was able to demonstrate the link between Wisdom and Mary, who as perfect incarnation of creaturely Sophia, could remain distinct from Christ as incarnation of divine Sophia through the Logos. Nonetheless, Teilhard's achievement, perhaps, is in envisaging a cosmic role for the Eternal Feminine. Like Bulgakov and the Russian Sophiologists, the development of the more practical elements of the wisdom tradition that we find in the biblical witness is missing.

Wisdom as a practical basis for ethics in Thomas Aquinas

The strand of biblical tradition that associates wisdom with right action is developed in the theology of Thomas Aquinas. For Aquinas wisdom is one of the intellectual virtues. Reason is both speculative and practical. The three virtues of speculative reason are wisdom, *scientia* and understanding. The two virtues of practical reason are prudence and art. *Scientia* is the comprehension of the causes of things and the relationship between them, while understanding means grasping first principles. Wisdom is the understanding of the fundamental causes of everything and their relationship to everything else. It informs both speculative and practical reason. For Aquinas the fundamental cause is God, so wisdom is ultimately knowledge of God's nature and actions.

Aquinas believed that the true end of all the virtues is goodness and loosely speaking we can think of prudence as the means of attaining this end. Aquinas states that 'In the order of all human life, the prudent man is called wise, in as much as he directs his acts to a fitting end: thus it is said wisdom is prudence to a man (Prov 10.23)'.[72] Prudence is a clear perception of reality and is required for the practice of

[72] *Basic Writings of Saint Thomas Aquinas. Summa Theologiae*, Part 1–1, A. C. Pegis (ed.), New York: Random House, 1944, 1.6.

all the other moral virtues, namely courage, justice and temperance. However, Jean Porter has shown in a convincing way that we cannot analyse prudence simply through a standard means/ends type of analysis.[73] This might apply where the specific purpose in mind is justice, where it is more obvious what the goal might be. However, in many cases we cannot separate the goal from the action. The task of prudence becomes what Aquinas describes as discerning, through the use of reason, the right course of action in order to express a particular virtue; both for the good of the individual and the good of the community.

Prudence finds what Aquinas terms 'the mean' in moral virtues, since the virtue itself cannot determine what that mean might be. The mean of a virtue is based on reason. For an individual a 'rational mean' is reached when an individual's motivation is in accordance with the ultimate good for that individual. On the other hand a 'real mean' is reached when an individual decides to act so as to preserve relationships of mutual equality in a community. In both cases the use of reason is involved and it is the task of prudence to decide what the mean might be in each concrete situation. In other words, prudence is the right choice of actions working for the good of the individual and community which together lead to a life of virtue. It is part of the human condition to possess wisdom in various degrees and thereby its counterpart, foolishness. While Aquinas frequently states that it is self-evident that good is to be pursued and evil avoided, it is only in the notion of prudence that he elaborates how this might come about.

Another aspect of prudence in Aquinas is the ability to have a clear perception of reality in a specific situation. This requires virtues that Aquinas names as allied to that of prudence, namely memory of the past, insight into the present and shrewdness about the future, along with reason, understanding, openness to being taught, circumspection and caution.[74] The need for memory of the past is both individual and collective,

---

[73] J. Porter, *The Recovery of Virtue*, London: SPCK, 1994, 155–60.
[74] Aquinas, *Summa Theologiae*, Vol. 35, London: Blackfriars, 1972, 2–2, 48.1.

so that if memory is either suppressed or obscured, then insight into the present is impaired along with a distorted assessment of goals for the future. Prudence gives us the habit that allows us to compare any new situation with the old and by noticing differences between them it allows us to act appropriately for the good. Prudence helps us notice very subtle differences in situations, rather than simple application of certain rules and generalisations from past experiences.[75] It encourages, then, flexibility in thought that is very different from the conditioned responses pre-programmed by past experience.

Aquinas's idea of prudence as I have discussed it so far seems to be following Aristotle's treatment of prudence or *phronesis*, sometimes translated as 'practical wisdom'. Aristotle suggests that prudence has the following three components, namely to take counsel, to judge what has been discovered and to act in a certain way.[76] Where actions are those of prudence, the desire is to attain a true good. For Aristotle, to take counsel means the will chooses by use of reason a certain course of action in order to reach a particular end. If this is an act of prudence then that end will be chosen in order to attain a true good. Prudence includes the specific action and only those actions that arise out of prudence are correctly named virtuous actions.[77]

However, Aquinas goes further than Aristotle does in that he translates his philosophical notion of prudence into a much more theological concept of wisdom. Indeed wisdom and theology are intricately related, so that

> he who considers absolutely the highest cause of the whole universe, namely God, is most of all called wise. Hence wisdom is said to be the knowledge of divine things, as Augustine says . . . The knowledge of this science comes through revelation, not natural reason.[78]

---

[75] J. W. Kay, 'Getting Egypt out of the People: Aquinas's Contribution to Liberation' in G. S. Harak (ed.), *Aquinas and Empowerment*, Washington: Georgetown University Press, 1996, 10.

[76] Porter, *Recovery*, 162–3.

[77] Aquinas, *Summa Theologiae*, Vol. 23, London: Blackfriars, 1963, 1–2, 63.1.

[78] Aquinas, *Basic Writings, Summa Theologiae*, 1–1, 1.6.

First of all the life of a truly virtuous person comes from a settled commitment to lead a good life. Other virtuous actions may be praiseworthy even if they do not come from this commitment, but they are still prone to deviation.[79] For Aquinas the virtue of prudence will never reach its desired aim of goodness through human effort alone because of the distortions of human sin. How may prudence be fully achieved and become that which is aligned to God's wisdom? For Aquinas this is only possible through the gift of the Holy Spirit, engendering the theological virtues of faith, hope and charity in addition to wisdom. While wisdom may be acquired by use of reason and study, it may also come through the gift of the Holy Spirit inclining the individual towards a life of virtue. The seven gifts of the Holy Spirit are courage, piety, fear, counsel, understanding, *scientia* and wisdom. Counsel is part of prudence, hence four of the intellectual virtues are analogous to the gifts of the Spirit. When virtues are acquired through the use of reason, they are intellectual virtues; when they come as gifts from God, then they are gifts of the Holy Spirit. The precise way God infuses such gifts into the mind is left obscure. It is love that is the supreme means through which humanity can know intuitively the mind of God. However, this is not simply an unthinking response to the Spirit. As John Mahoney points out:

> From a consideration of the many texts in which Aquinas writes of this internal teaching of the Holy Spirit we can see how important for him was not only the activity of the Spirit but also the activity of man's own intelligence under the influence of the Spirit. For the Spirit does not work by blind impulses (an activity more characteristic of the 'spirit of the devil'), nor indeed is he a substitute for reason.[80]

Above all Christian wisdom rooted in the love of God allows the individual to discern God's wisdom in practical contexts. Such wisdom leads to an alignment of both heart and mind to the will of God through the Holy Spirit.

---

[79] Aquinas, *Summa Theologiae*, Vol. 23, 1–2, 57.5; 1–11, 58.4.
[80] J. Mahoney, *Seeking the Spirit: Essays in Moral and Pastoral Theology*, London: Sheed & Ward, 1981, 71.

Aquinas also develops the notion of community discernment. He recognises that those responsible for the distribution of shared goods in a community must possess political prudence. For him 'political prudence and distributive justice are in effect two components of one virtue by which rulers govern wisely and well'.[81] If that ruler is a monarch, then they must exercise regnative prudence. Yet even though he seemed to favour the idea of monarchy, he still insists that all persons in a community in some sense need to share in political prudence. The exercise of wisdom in a community allows it to conform to the ordering in the universe that for Aquinas is an expression of the divine wisdom. While he saw this ordering through the lens of medieval cosmology, it was no static fixed realm, but still open to the creative work of God.

The natural good is never realised in a human community because of sin, so that conflicts are always bound to arise. Given this limitation, Aquinas ascribes to love a unifying function, to which all the virtues are ultimately directed. For Aquinas, then, wisdom in a community, like that in an individual, finds its fulfilment through love, understood as charity. For him 'wisdom is the gift of the Holy Spirit that corresponds to charity'.[82] Through the gifts of God's grace in faith, hope and charity, humanity becomes deified. Aquinas links the three gifts associated with the speculative intellect with two of the three theological virtues, faith and love. While understanding and *scientia* are linked with faith, it is wisdom that is supremely linked with charity. Significantly the beatitude associated with wisdom is that of the peacemakers. He suggests that the friendship of charity is crucial, as it removes the clash of wills that leads to discord and instead promotes peace.

The task of humanity is not just to accept the order given by God, but to bring order into it through active co-operation with God. For Aquinas, it is in the Church, through the Holy Spirit, that wisdom comes to find its fullest expression in both individuals and community. While not all individuals are given the same degree of wisdom, they are part of a community of

---

[81] Porter, *Recovery*, 164.
[82] Porter, *Recovery*, 169, see *Summa Theologiae*, Vol. 35, 2–2, 45.1, 45.2.

the Church, and it is in this community that some are given a gift of wisdom for the benefit of all the others.

The opposite of wisdom is folly, interpreted as rooted in the sin of *luxuria*, or lust, that is the absence of self-discipline in desires of this world.[83] Moral evil undermines wisdom by corruption of the intellect as well as the will. The one who has no wisdom at all is a fool, characterised by a dull conscience, wrong standards and self-deception. But the shift towards folly is a gradual process, 'as a result of a series of wrongdoings in which his will and intellect progressively misprogram each other, as Aquinas' account of intellect and will explains'.[84] Hence, for Aquinas the will is involved in the pursuit of wisdom or folly.

Aquinas's understanding of wisdom as an *intellectual* virtue that is acquired by the will seems to many contemporary philosophers to be counter-intuitive, since they are more accustomed to thinking of the excellence of the mind in terms of intelligence.[85] For Aquinas wisdom is acquired through active participation of the will, and is not innate as is intelligence. For Aquinas the will desires the good by nature, but it is the task of the intellect to judge something as good. The task of judging is influenced by the passions, so that the passions, will and intellect act together to lead to certain actions. For example, under the influence of anger something may seem good that shows itself in a different light once the anger has subsided. Moreover, Aquinas suggests that the will influences the intellect, commanding it to adopt a particular belief. The idea that the will can in some sense control the intellect and in particular our belief systems is resisted by many contemporary philosophers. Nonetheless, any outright rejection of the notion that the will can in some cases modify our beliefs seems too crude to sustain.[86] While Aquinas is certainly unaware of the social dimensions of existence that condition all our choices, the tendency today is to look for biological or

---

[83] Aquinas, *Summa Theologiae*, 2–2, 46.3.
[84] E. Stump, 'Wisdom: Will, Belief and Moral Conduct', in *Aquinas' Moral Theory: Essays in Honour of Kretzman*, S. MacDonald and E. Stump (eds), Ithaca and London: Cornell University Press, 1999, 61–2.
[85] Stump, 'Wisdom', 28.
[86] Stump, 'Wisdom', 34–46.

social determinants of human action, instead of facing the real possibility of human freedom.

While it is important to be realistic about social conditioning and fully aware of the factors which influence human choices at an individual and community level, Aquinas holds forth a vision of practical wisdom that is particularly relevant today. Furthermore, contemporary secular philosophers, such as Alasdair MacIntyre have taken up and developed the idea of a virtue ethic.[87] In his early work Stanley Hauerwas develops an ethic of character.[88] He considered this approach a way out of the sterility of utilitarianism, which focuses simply on the problem in hand. He draws on Aquinas's idea that humans are masters of their actions through their ability to chose.[89] An act becomes moral in the light of particular intentions, though the goodness or evil of moral acts is prior to intention of the will. Significantly, Hauerwas seems to link his idea of character formation with the notion of prudence in Aquinas: 'It does not seem to be an unwarranted conclusion that the unity given to the virtues by prudence at least seems to have some similarities to what we mean by character, for the good of prudence is the good of the agent himself.'[90]

In his later work Hauerwas shifts to consider the community dimension of moral discernment and speaks more in terms of narrative. As I discussed earlier, Aquinas's understanding of prudence includes this community aspect, especially that in the Church, in a way that is more difficult for Hauerwas's character ethic. Hauerwas's idea of narrative bears some resemblance to MacIntyre's belief that human action, to be intelligible, needs a particular historical setting, a particular place in a particular story. The idea of narrative is also significant in that it suggests ways in which an individual may change and develop. While Aquinas certainly does not posit a narrative approach to ethics in any formal sense, he does recognise the need for discernment in a community and

---

[87] A. MacIntyre, *After Virtue: A Study in Moral Theory*, London: Duckworth, 2nd edn, 1985.

[88] S. Hauerwas, *Character and the Christian Life: A Study in Theological Ethics*, San Antonio: Trinity University Press, 1975.

[89] Hauerwas, *Character*, 61–7.

[90] Hauerwas, *Character*, 79.

faithfulness to the traditions of that community. Furthermore, the idea of wisdom in Aquinas is linked with the concept of natural law. This gives his ethics a cosmological dimension that is missing from Hauerwas's ethics based around character and narrative.

Aquinas's eternal law of God or wisdom of God is imperfectly expressed in *both* moral laws and natural laws. In as far as the natural laws in creation participate in the wisdom of God, they are expressions of God's wisdom. Hence while Bulgakov uses the language of creaturely Sophia, Aquinas speaks in terms of natural law. I have focused in this chapter on Aquinas's understanding of wisdom as discernment, that is in the application of wisdom, rather than wisdom expressed in natural law, as it seems to me that it is the strand in Aquinas's thought that most clearly complements that of Bulgakov. Furthermore, his concept of natural law was, perhaps, conditioned somewhat by the medieval cosmology of the time. However, I will be returning to consider the possible significance of Aquinas's concept of natural law in subsequent chapters.

For Aquinas the life of virtue was only possible through friendship, interpreted as charity. Such friendship enfolds the life of every Christian in relationship with God and others. For him 'charity must be seen not so much as an individual virtue, but as a communal and ecclesial practice characteristic of those striving each day to practice the ways of God in the world'.[91] As John Milbank has pointed out, since the Enlightenment and the rise in capitalism, there has been a radical shift in our sense of self-identity.[92] The concept that our selfhood is constituted by love and friendship has been replaced by the need for control and ownership in a way that extends from possessions to persons. While feminists have argued that patriarchal cultures have always fostered a sense of control over women and nature, Milbank seems to be suggesting that this need to control has become so dominant that it has eclipsed

---

[91] P. J. Wadell, 'Growing Together in the Divine Love: The Role of Charity in the Moral Theology of Thomas Aquinas', in G. S. Harak (ed.), *Aquinas and Empowerment*, Washington: Georgetown University Press, 1996, 135.
[92] J. Milbank, *Theology and Social Theory*, Oxford: Blackwell, 1990, 12–13.

all other ways of relating. Aquinas's idea of friendship is relevant in that it counters this trend in contemporary society. Furthermore, once the idea of friendship is reinstated, this can then be extended to include friendship to all living creatures, even though the nature of such friendship will follow a different dynamic from that between humans. I will come back to this idea of extending friendship again later. For the moment it is relevant to see the practical way Aquinas considers the issue of wisdom, namely that wisdom finds its self-expression through charity and that this charity is expressed through friendship.

Aquinas's understanding of friendship goes beyond that of Aristotle in that he suggests that our chief vocation is to be in a relationship of friendship with God. Such friendship is no easy romantic attachment, but a gradual transformation of the human heart so that we can enter more fully into the life of God.[93] Our true and lasting happiness comes from discovering the good that God intends for us and this can only ultimately be found in God. The ultimate good for Aquinas is not Aristotle's *eudaimonia*, a life of flourishing, but *beatitudo*, that is partaking and reflecting on the beauty, goodness and holiness of God. This distinguishes human activity from that of other creatures. Such friendship is only possible by divine gift, given by the grace of God. Receiving such a gift heals wounds and allows us not only to love God but also to live a new kind of life that is in keeping with the desire of God. Moreover, such a life of friendship with God is inseparable from a life in Christ, who both mediates for us and is an example of perfect friendship with God. That life in Christ includes participation in the ecclesial community and the sacraments of the Church.

The search for wisdom: towards a rapprochement of East and West

Teilhard's quest to find a mysticism that mediated between East and West reflected his search for a science that was no longer detached from faith alongside a faith that was relevant

---

[93] Wadell, 'Growing Together', 148–63.

to science. Yet it is in his mystical, poetical theology that we can discover an almost inadvertent resonance with the Sophiology of Vladimir Solovyov. Teilhard's poem *The Eternal Feminine* is significant in its synthesis of scientific cosmology available in the early twentieth century with evolutionary ideas of progress. The unifying principle in creation becomes expressed through the idea of world-soul and the Eternal Feminine. Yet it seems to me that his attention to the Virgin Mary as the locus of Wisdom ultimately restricts her to the realm of creaturely nature, rather than divine agency. Furthermore, while he does suggest that she is active in calling love into being in the incarnation, her main role seems to be a passive one that is in response to the Logos who is Christ. The net result is that the vocation of humanity in science is affirmed in a way that seems to lead to a lack of criticism of its aims and goals. Sophia becomes just the inspiration for even greater achievements in technology. We do, nonetheless, find a nascent ethic in his suggestion that in trying to grasp after pleasures sin corrupts wisdom into folly. The skill to distinguish between wisdom and folly is only possible for Teilhard after the coming of Christ. No longer are we faced with a mirage of Wisdom, rather she draws those who follow her into the light of truth and freedom.

Teilhard's grand schema for the cosmic role of the Eternal Feminine echoes that of the cosmic Christ, but his vision remains a mystical one, rather than one spelt out in dogmatic terms. While it is important for mysticism to be included in any systematic theology, it is only really in Bulgakov's theology that we find a clear attempt to bring together the philosophical, poetic, mystical and theological aspects of Wisdom. While his ideas bear some resemblance to the cosmic Christology of the earlier Church Fathers, such as Maximus the Confessor, he takes Sophia into the very heart of who God is – the very *ousia* of God. Such a move is significant theologically as it means that Wisdom is at the very centre of theology, not just an attribute of God, but the core of who God is in God's-self. The relationship between Wisdom and Love is a very intimate one, wisdom is the 'loving of Love' and as such included in the dynamic perichoretic community of the Trinity. Wisdom becomes the means through which creation and Creator are related to each other – she is at the frontier between the two, but comes to expression as creaturely Wisdom in the created order. A theology of creation is inseparable from the concept of Wisdom.

Such a vision of the relationship between God and creation seems to me to be highly relevant today. If we love God, then we will search for wisdom. If we love God, then we will find God in the creaturely Wisdom of creation. Perhaps, too, we need to remember the dark side of creaturely Sophia that Bulgakov mentions, that it is always possible for this good creation to be distorted or marred by sin. Indeed the development of the idea of the shadow in creaturely Sophia is necessary if we are to begin to appreciate the possibility that there are negative cosmic forces at work in addition to those caused directly by humanity.

Yet such recognition of good and evil is enlarged once we reflect on wisdom as it is understood in the theology of Thomas Aquinas. His location of all true wisdom as being ultimately in the being of God hints at a Sophiology, though this is never really spelt out. He is more practical in his discussion of wisdom, separating wisdom that is learned through reason from wisdom that is given as a gift of the Holy Spirit. Hardy suggests that Aquinas is partly responsible for translating wisdom into knowledge.[94] Eventually this leads to a separation of wisdom from goodness. However, it seems to me that Aquinas's understanding of wisdom is intricately connected with the idea of the good as the aim of a virtuous life. The pursuit of wisdom leads not just to goodness, but also to beauty, hinting at the theme we find in Bulgakov and Teilhard. Hardy also suggests that for Aquinas wisdom is beyond the world in a metaphysic that is out of reach of worldly knowledge in such a way that worldly wisdom becomes severed from its source in divine Wisdom. However, I suggest that some distinctions between divine and earthly wisdom are necessary to sustain, even if such distinctions encourage, which I doubt,

---

[94] D. Hardy, 'The God Who Is With the World', in F. Watts (ed.), *Science Meets Faith*, London: SPCK, 1998, 139–42.

a forgetting of the divine Wisdom. Aquinas clearly affirms the search for wisdom through the intellect, but he also sees wisdom as a gift of the Spirit. The two are mutually related and need to inform each other. The Spirit is not an unreasoning spirit any more than intellectual wisdom is detached from goodness. Rather, a holistic view of wisdom, which Hardy rightly supports, is only possible if some distinctions are sustained. It is through acknowledgement of such distinctions that divine Wisdom can transform the wisdom of the world. It seems to me that Teilhard married human wisdom too closely to wisdom that comes from God and by doing so lost the transformative characteristic that is latent in the idea of wisdom.

Aquinas, in developing the link between wisdom, prudence and charity, presents a model that is relevant to the complex situations facing us in application of modern biology to technology. Difficult decisions about practical issues connected with genetic engineering of crops, animals and humans involve a delicate balance of interests of all parties concerned. Secular approaches seem to rely on risk/benefit analysis in a way that ultimately leads to a stalemate. The risks themselves seem hard to define, as they are often as yet unknown. The very testing of such risk or benefit imposes further risk. Instead, a more fruitful avenue to pursue is the idea of a wisdom ethic, one that is rooted in the idea of the development of wisdom as a virtue in the search for goodness, both for individuals and the community. While Aquinas's idea of wisdom is intimately connected with that of love understood as friendship, in particular friendship with God, ultimately it is Christ who serves as the model of such friendship.

The possibility of friendship is fostered by participation in a eucharistic community. Hence while Aquinas's understanding of wisdom is practical, it is also ultimately sacramental. Hardy suggests that wisdom may be reopened through the practice of worship.[95] In other words, that it is in the context of a liturgical community that we are best able to discover where wisdom may be found. This coheres with Catherine Pickstock's suggestion that true meaning is ultimately to be found in the

[95] Hardy, 'The God Who Is', 144–9.

language of the liturgy.[96] As we might expect for an Orthodox theologian, for Bulgakov the Divine Liturgy is the means through which both creaturely and divine Wisdom become manifest in the world. For him above all it is in the eucharistic change in the bread and wine that the created wisdom of the human nature in Christ comes to bear the likeness of glorious Wisdom hidden in it. This parallels an understanding of Christ as having both a human and divine nature. Yet such a change has its foundation in the unity of all created nature, whether glorified or not.[97] The incarnation links Christ with the whole world in a way that affirms the unity of all creation. For Bulgakov, 'The full significance of this link will be disclosed only at his second and glorious coming; till then it is manifested sacramentally, and, to fleshly eyes, invisibly, in the Eucharist, the primary effect of which, indeed, is to give us a personal union with Christ.'[98] Hence, while for Aquinas the link between wisdom and charity, and the Eucharist is mediated through the notion of friendship, in Bulgakov we find in the Eucharist a mirror of his theological understanding of wisdom as both creaturely and divine. Both writers in some sense point to the importance of the worshipping community in order to build up wisdom. For Aquinas, the life of the sacraments is necessary in order to live the moral life that puts love of God at the centre. For Bulgakov, the Eucharist joins us with the very Wisdom of God and in so doing allows the progressive penetration of the world by Wisdom.

Hence while there is some convergence of ideas in both Aquinas and Bulgakov, the unravelling of wisdom and its meaning for creation needs insights from both writers. But how can wisdom be appropriated specifically in a theology of creation? How might we understand more clearly the relationship between Wisdom and the Holy Spirit? How might an understanding of the feminine become incorporated into our perception of God? An exploration of possible answers to these questions will be the subject of the next chapter.

---

[96] C. Pickstock, *After Writing: On the Liturgical Consummation of Philosophy*, Oxford: Blackwell, 1998.

[97] Bulgakov, *Sophia*, 96–7.

[98] Bulgakov, *Sophia*, 96–7.

4

The Spirit of Holy Wisdom

In Chapter 3 I showed how the Eastern tradition of wisdom which allowed a flowering of Sophiology, particularly in the theology of Sergii Bulgakov, complements the more practical Western theological tradition of wisdom as discernment, as found in Aquinas. The task in the present chapter is to examine specifically how wisdom can become incorporated into a theology of creation. I hope to show that not only are there biblical and traditional precedents for such a development, but also that this contributes to a theology that makes sense in our contemporary scientific cultural context. Furthermore, it allows a rapprochement between the feminist critiques of science and science itself in pointing to ways forward in the dialogue between science and religion.

Colin Crowder has strongly criticised the enthusiasm for wisdom by some theologians as stretching the tradition beyond its original purposes, so that by implication it becomes not only an inexhaustible resource, but also 'a knowledge above knowledge'.[1] It seems to me, however, that it is entirely justifiable to draw on wisdom in order to delineate an adequate theology of creation. Such a theology makes sense in terms of the wisdom tradition of the Old Testament which is firmly rooted in a theology of creation. A focus on creation theology should serve to prevent the kind of Gnosticism that Crowder

---

[1] C. Crowder, 'Wisdom and Passion', in S. C. Barton (ed.), *Where Shall Wisdom be Found?*, Edinburgh: T&T Clark, 1999, 375.

seems to be implying in his critique of modern post-liberal interpretations of wisdom. That wisdom can be misused is surely not an adequate reason for removing wisdom from theological discourse. The issue, rather, is how far wisdom can become a creative tool in a constructive theology of creation that gives further insights into the dynamics of the relationships between God, humanity and the cosmos. The fact that wisdom has many faces, that it can include insights into both systematic theology and practical ethics is an advantage, rather than a disadvantage. For it encourages theology to be brave, rather than timid, to move beyond the safety of a narrow discipline and explore the boundaries with other disciplines and other areas of research. In doing so it becomes richer, fuller and more in touch with the practical realities facing us in our decision-making and policy.

Beyond a Wisdom Christology

I have argued earlier that one of the earliest Christologies was a Wisdom Christology. Furthermore, Wisdom Christology can show us how Christ is related to creation in a way that serves to unite themes of creation and redemption. This is a cornerstone in the construction of a Wisdom creation theology. However, I intend to argue here that this is not the end of the story as far as the significance of Wisdom theology for creation is concerned.

Colin Gunton has suggested that Wisdom Christology informs the relationship between Christ and creation. However, Wisdom Christology goes beyond this in specifying the Wisdom of God in the world. For Gunton, Wisdom is 'a form of divine action in which the relation between Creator and creation is realised in a highly particular way'.[2] This form of divine action is Christological, so that 'we can and must read christologically passages like that from Proverbs which speak of the ministerial action of Wisdom in the creation and upholding of the world'.[3] I am in full agreement with Gunton's

---

[2] C. Gunton, 'Christ the Wisdom of God', in Barton, *Where Shall Wisdom*, 254.
[3] Gunton, 'Christ', 259.

recognition of the importance of Wisdom Christology for linking themes of creation and redemption. I also agree that Wisdom Christology is a vital reminder of the humility of God as expressed in the incarnation. However, I am more cautious about his Christological interpretation of Wisdom in Proverbs. He strongly criticises Matthew Fox for 'a reduction of all divine action to creation'.[4] It is ironical, perhaps, that Fox also develops a cosmic Christology and includes a reflection on the wisdom tradition, but in a way that radically reinterprets the doctrine of the Fall so that the movement of redemption is simply a return back to the original creation. It is true that through identification of Logos with Wisdom in John, all the actions of Wisdom in the Old Testament could be said to find their expression in Christ. However, to read back into this passage a purely Christological reference seems to me to ignore other biblical references to Wisdom which show close identification with the Spirit of God. I have my doubts, then, that Wisdom can be contained within a Christological motif, even though this is a vital strand in any view of theological wisdom that claims to be Christian.

Given the above, how might the identification of Logos and Wisdom be interpreted? If, as I will argue below, Wisdom is a characteristic primarily of the Holy Spirit, but also informs all persons of the Trinity, how can this be reconciled with the strong identification of Christ and Wisdom? I suggest that once we see Wisdom as primarily associated with the Holy Spirit, then any identification with the Logos also makes more sense. For it is only in the power of the Holy Spirit that the Logos can become the Wisdom of God. Christ becomes God incarnate through the power of the Holy Spirit, as the story of the annunciation makes clear. It is only through the Holy Spirit that the cross of Christ expresses the Wisdom of God. It is only through the dynamic involvement of the Holy Spirit that Christ is raised from the dead in the resurrection. The identification of Wisdom with Logos does not mean that the two are indistinguishable, rather one cannot be thought of without the other.

4 Gunton, 'Christ', 259.

The cosmic Spirit and Wisdom

A cosmic pneumatology

While there has been a growing impetus towards the development of a cosmic Christology in contemporary theology, there has been less discussion of the cosmic scope of the work of the Holy Spirit, especially in the Western Church. This is likely to be related to the importance attached to the New Testament witness of the work of the Holy Spirit in the Christian community. While the Old Testament speaks clearly of the work of the Spirit in creation, this is dwarfed by the importance attached to new-creation themes, especially inner liberation in the hearts and minds of the disciples. Eduard Schweizer, for example, suggests that the New Testament takes it for granted that God and the Holy Spirit are everywhere in creation.[5] Unlike many writers on the Holy Spirit he acknowledges the presence of the Spirit in natural events, as recorded in the Old Testament, such as Exodus 15.8, 10; 14.21 or Genesis 8.1. He also recognises that the Spirit is thought of as a creative power in Genesis 1, so that it is the 'wind or Spirit of God which stands behind the act of creation'.[6] The Spirit, too, is a life-giving power, as expressed in Psalm 104.29–30. Here the source of life is ascribed to the 'spirit of God'. Even the animals are given the spirit of life, as recorded in Genesis 6.17; 7.15; Zechariah 12.1. The Spirit is also the source of knowledge and the gift of reason. However, a distinction begins to appear between the Spirit of Life and the Spirit of God in the work of the Spirit in the prophets. A special endowment of the Spirit from God gives right judgement in politics (Isa 30.1). Furthermore the prophets saw the Spirit working in ways that were quite different from that derived from commonsensical observations of the world. Joel 2.28–32, for example, looks forward to a time when God's Spirit will be poured forth on 'all flesh'. How can we reconcile the idea that the Spirit is the source of all life with the belief in

---

[5] E. Schweizer, *The Holy Spirit*, trans. from the German by R. Fuller and I. Fuller, London: SCM Press, 1981, 118.
[6] Schweizer, *Holy Spirit*, 16.

the New Testament that the Holy Spirit is primarily at work in the human community?

There are two possible reactions to this dilemma. One is to widen the idea of God so that all the activities of God become Spirit, as in Geoffrey Lampe's theology of *God as Spirit*.[7] Even bolder is Peter Hodgson's notion that the Spirit is 'an emergent persona of God, generated in the act of outpouring, dependent on worldly activity for its actualisation. Thus Spirit is the final and consummate figure of the divine life, the mediation of identity and difference, of God's primordial self-relatedness and worldly other-relatedness.'[8] In these cases the immanent Spirit seems to substitute for the incarnate Son.

The other possible reaction is to restrict the work of the Holy Spirit so that it is narrowly confined to the work of the human community, as in Charles Moule's *The Holy Spirit*.[9] In general, the tradition of the Western Church has tended to follow this route, that is to restrict the action of the Holy Spirit, which may partly explain the overreaction to this deficiency in Lampe and Hodgson cited above. George Hendry, for example, considers the relationship between the Holy Spirit and Christ, God, Church, Word and humanity, but gives no space for a discussion of the Spirit in creation.[10] Michael Ramsey points out that the term 'Holy Spirit' is never used of the activity of God in the wider created world in the New Testament, even though the Old Testament language about the action of *ruach* in the world is not denied.[11]

Yves Congar points to a further difficulty, namely that the Holy Spirit has not had the attention it deserves in the history of the Church.[12] Substitutes for the Holy Spirit include the Eucharist, the Pope and the Virgin Mary. His monumental work includes a detailed study of the history of interpretation

[7] G. Lampe, *God as Spirit*, Oxford: Oxford University Press, 1977.
[8] P. C. Hodgson, *Winds of the Spirit: A Constructive Christian Theology*, London: SCM Press, 1994, 324.
[9] C. F. D. Moule, *The Holy Spirit*, London, 1978.
[10] G. S. Hendry, *The Holy Spirit in Christian Theology*, London: SCM Press, 1957.
[11] M. Ramsey, *Holy Spirit: A Biblical Study*, London: SPCK, 1977, 122–3.
[12] Y. Congar, *I Believe in the Holy Spirit*. Published in three volumes. Vol. 1, trans. D. Smith, London: Geoffrey Chapman, 1983, 159–64.

of the doctrine of the Holy Spirit. Vatican II went a long way towards a recovery of the importance of the Holy Spirit. However, the Christological reference remained strong and the Spirit was identified with the person of Christ and the Church as the Body of Christ.[13] Congar's second volume on the Holy Spirit is dedicated to an examination of the work of the Spirit in the Church and in the personal lives of believers. The acquisition of the Spirit becomes the aim of the Christian life. While he acknowledges that the Spirit of God is everywhere in the universe, there is very scant treatment of this theme. Furthermore, he concludes that the Church can express the doxology of the universe.[14]

Geiko Fahrenholz argues that the Spirit of God is more than just Pentecost, placing a firm emphasis on the 'core energy of creation itself'.[15] He suggests that the Spirit as cosmic power can be thought of as the 'soul of the world'; the Spirit as psychic power as 'soul of my soul' and the Spirit as social–ecclesial power as 'soul of Christian communities'. He rejects the idea of 'fallen creation', suggesting that the real sin is to refuse the rightful place of the Spirit. Nonetheless, while this theology is suggestive, it is too reminiscent of the Neoplatonic concept of world-soul. It also fails to distinguish between the work of the Spirit in creation, re-creation and in the human community.

Jürgen Moltmann's *Spirit of Life* at least recognises the cosmic dimensions of the Spirit at work in creation, though it is the particular work in the human community that is still the focus of his attention.[16] He notes the discovery of the cosmic breadth of the divine Spirit in his introduction, but his prime purpose is to show how the Spirit is the Spirit of *creative life* in the human community as well as redemption. His recognition that the life of the Spirit has its roots in the natural world prevents his theology of the Spirit becoming detached

---

[13] Congar, *I Believe*, Vol. 1, 167–73.
[14] Congar, *I Believe*, Vol. 2, 222.
[15] G. M. Fahrenholz, *God's Spirit: Transforming a World in Crisis*, New York: WCC, 1995, xii.
[16] J. Moltmann, *The Spirit of Life*, trans. M. Kohl, London: SCM Press, 1992.

from or even hostile to the material world. He draws on the distinction in Judaism between the general presence of God's Spirit in creation, the *ruach* and the more restricted meaning of the Holy Spirit in early rabbinic literature as the 'spirit of the sanctuary'.[17] He suggests that Christian usage of the Holy Spirit is more closely related to the Hebrew idea of Shekinah, the descent of God in time and space. However, it is here that any distinction between the work of the Spirit in creation and in redemption seems to be blurred. For Moltmann there seems to be no such distinctions, both are likened to the presence of Shekinah in the world and in the human community alike:

> With every bit of self-seeking and self-contradiction which we surrender to the will of the Creator who loves us, the Shekinah comes close to God. If we live entirely in the prayer 'Thy will be done', the Shekinah in us is united with God himself . . . We become sensitive to the Shekinah in us, and equally sensitive to the Shekinah in other people and in all other creatures . . . We encounter every other created being in the expectation of meeting God.[18]

The creative action of God's Spirit, the suffering of all creation and humanity and the longing for the new creation are all expressed through the Shekinah. However, while this all-embracing synthesis is inspiring, how far is it valid to conflate the creative and redemptive movements of the Spirit? It is hard in Moltmann's scheme to include a Christological reference, even though it is apparent from his other works that Christology has a central place in his theology of redemption. Even though he includes this reference to Shekinah in all creation, it is in relationship with the work of the Spirit in the human community. The bulk of his discussion is still primarily on the work of the Spirit in humanity, even though he rejects any sense that this means a detachment from the material world.

More cosmic elements in the work of the Holy Spirit can be found scattered in Moltmann's other major works on the

[17] Moltmann, *Spirit of Life*, 47.
[18] Moltmann, *Spirit of Life*, 50–1

doctrines of creation and eschatology, such as *God in Creation* or *The Coming of God* respectively.[19] As one might expect, the former puts more emphasis on the work of the Spirit in the initial creation, while the latter focuses on the work of the Spirit in the new earth. Once more, however, there is a blurring of any distinction between the work of the Spirit in creation and re-creation. The only distinction between the work of the Spirit in creation and that in glorification seems to be in his idea of the subject of the Trinity, while in the former case the Father is subject, in the latter case the Spirit is subject.[20] However, the idea of the Spirit as subject seems to be toned down in his other works where the cosmic Christ becomes dominant.

Patrick Sherry, by drawing on the aesthetic tradition, succeeds in broadening the scope of the work of the Holy Spirit.[21] He suggests that the Spirit of God communicates God's beauty to the world and this beauty is both a sign of divine glory and an anticipation of a transfigured world to come. He distinguishes between the work of the Spirit in creation and that in human minds by the notion of inspiration, which is unique to humanity. His views echo the work of Bulgakov, where the glory of God is related to beauty. He suggests that the restriction of the work of the Spirit to the human community may account for the lack of adequate reflection on the relationship between beauty and the Spirit. He acknowledges that poetic or metaphorical speech about the beauty of God may be more appropriate than philosophical exactitude.[22] He is particularly anxious that the idea of beauty should not be attributed simply to Platonic terminology. Like Moltmann, he is keen to retain the Jewish tradition of humanity as a psychosomatic unity, so that divine likeness includes the body.

[19] J. Moltmann, *God in Creation*, trans. M. Kohl, London: SCM Press, 1985; J. Moltmann, *The Coming of God*, trans. M. Kohl, London: SCM Press, 1996.
[20] For further discussion see, C. Deane-Drummond, *Ecology in Jürgen Moltmann's Theology*, Lampeter: Edwin Mellen Press, 1997.
[21] P. Sherry, *Spirit and Beauty: An Introduction to Theological Aesthetics*, Oxford: Clarendon Press, 1992.
[22] Sherry, *Spirit and Beauty*, 134.

While Sherry's work is important in recovering a forgotten tradition, an emphasis on beauty as the work of the Holy Spirit does not yet answer the question: What becomes of the terrors and sorrows of the natural world? In what sense is the beauty of God different from our own understanding of aesthetics? In other words, the language of beauty seems to encourage a romanticism about creation that may not do justice to the idea of creation groaning in travail. Such a reminder can only really come if there is a link with Christology. I will argue below that wisdom is a more adequate metaphor for the action of the Holy Spirit for this reason, namely that it can never be severed from the wisdom of the cross. Furthermore, wisdom and the Spirit are associated, as Sherry recognises. It seems to me that the gift of wisdom comes *prior* to the gift of illumination and inspiration, which Sherry links specifically with beauty. But what evidence can we find for linking wisdom with the Holy Spirit? In order to address this question I will examine both the biblical literature and the work of Irenaeus.

The Spirit of Wisdom in biblical literature

In general there has been reluctance among theologians to identify wisdom with the Spirit. This may be related to the fact that Spirit of God is more often associated with the prophetic tradition, which is seen to be far apart from the Hebrew tradition of everyday, more domestic wisdom that could be seen to align itself with more 'secular' traditions.[23] Wisdom is more like a habit of thought, while the Spirit is associated with spontaneity and suddenness of appearance. Rees argues that to keep wisdom and the Spirit in watertight compartments fails to do justice to elements in the Old Testament which seem to bring both together in a quite deliberate way.

Outside the wisdom literature the Spirit of God is at times associated with practical common sense normally associated with wisdom. Examples include Exodus 28.3 where those

---

[23] T. Rees, 'The Holy Spirit as Wisdom', in *Mansfield College Essays*, presented to A. M. Fairbairn, London: Hodder & Stoughton, 1908, 20.

making priests' garments are given the Spirit of wisdom, and
Exodus 31.3; 35.31, where the builder of the tabernacle is
filled with the Spirit of God in wisdom, understanding and
knowledge. Similarly, the rule of Joseph over Egypt is one
governed by the Spirit of God and characterised by wisdom
(Gen 41.38–40), and Joshua can lead the people because he is
full of the Spirit of wisdom (Deut 34.9; Num 27.18). Isaiah
11.2 similarly characterises the Spirit of the Lord as also the
Spirit of wisdom and understanding in a way that echoes
Proverbs 8.14–15. More indirect references specifically to
creation include the way the Spirit of God hovers over creation
in God's initial creative act in Genesis 1.2 in a manner that
is reminiscent of the co-operation of Wisdom in Proverbs
8.30. It is a matter for detailed exegesis as to how far such
associations represent a direct influence of the wisdom
literature itself on the Pentateuch. The source of ideas is less
significant than the fact that ideas about wisdom are not kept
separate from other literary traditions that speak of the Spirit
of God.

In addition, the wisdom literature itself brings Wisdom into
association with God's Spirit. The characterisation of the Spirit
of God as vague and undefined, but as also having personality
is also true of Wisdom, who becomes personified in Proverbs
8. Moreover, in Wisdom 7.25–7, Wisdom is described as the
'breath of the power of God, pure emanation of the Glory of
the Almighty . . . She is a reflection of the eternal light, un-
tarnished mirror of God's active power, image of his goodness
. . . she makes all things new' (JB), in a manner that parallels
description of the Holy Spirit. In Wisdom 1.6–7 Wisdom is
mentioned in parallel with the Spirit of God, so that 'Wisdom
is a spirit . . . the Spirit of the Lord, indeed, fills the whole
world'. In Wisdom 7.27 Wisdom is said to inspire the prophets,
which is also the work of the Spirit of God, as 1 Samuel 10.6
suggests. The functions of kingship are given to those who
have Wisdom, as in Wisdom 8.14, 9.7; such an attribute is
also a function of the Spirit of the Lord (1 Sam 16.13). Geyer
has also noted these connections, though, perhaps surprisingly
he suggests that 'when the reader reads about Wisdom, he
will be reminded not only of the Holy Spirit, but also of Jesus

Christ, the Son of God'.[24] However, it seems to me that to jump too quickly to a Christological reinterpretation refuses to allow for an association of the Spirit with Wisdom that is part of the biblical tradition.

The acquisition of Wisdom in both Hellenistic and Palestinian Judaism 'is consistently attributed to a Spirit sent by God, or God's own Spirit'.[25] Roman Catholic theologian Yves Congar comments that in Hellenised Judaism

> Wisdom is brought so close to the Spirit that the two realities are almost identified, at least if they are viewed in their action . . . In Wis.1.7 and 8.1 she – or the Spirit – even has a cosmic function, similar to the part that Wisdom played in Stoicism in holding the universe together. The real function of Wisdom, however, is to guide men in accordance with God's will.[26]

Larcher, too, notes the close connection between Wisdom and the Spirit, though he is more insistent than Congar that Wisdom as well as the Spirit has the power to transform. Hence Wisdom

> has the power at her disposal and the various functions of the Spirit in the Old Testament are attributed to her . . . Wisdom and Spirit are identified in so many respects that Wisdom appears above all as a sublimation of the part played by the Spirit in the Old Testament. This explains why some of the Fathers of the Church regarded Wisdom as prefiguring, not the Word, but the Holy Spirit.[27]

While the New Testament commonly associates Christ with wisdom, as I have discussed in Chapter 2, there are other strands which link the Holy Spirit with wisdom. For example, in 1 Corinthians 12.8, the Spirit gives the gift of preaching

[24] J. Geyer, *The Wisdom of Solomon*, London: SCM Press, 1963, 34.
[25] J. A. Davis, *Wisdom and Spirit: An Investigation of I Corinthians 1.18 – 3.20 Against the Background of Jewish Sapiential Traditions in the Greco-Roman Period*, Lanham: University Press of America, 1984, 142.
[26] Congar, *I Believe*, Vol. 1, 10.
[27] C. Larcher, *Etudes sur le Livre de la Sagesse*, Paris, 1969, cited in Congar, *I Believe*, Vol. 1, 10. The Fathers of the Church who are noted for making this connection between Wisdom and the Spirit are Theophilus of Antioch, Irenaeus and Clementine Homilies. I will be returning particularly to Irenaeus's contribution again below.

with wisdom. Luke 21.15 describes the wisdom that Christ gives the disciples in similar terms to that noted by Matthew 10.20 as coming from the Spirit of God. Rees suggests that the old antithesis between the free workings of the Spirit and the ordered and regulated course of wisdom is overcome in the religious experience of the Christian community. Hence, 'the purpose and reason, the consistency and unity which were intimated in vague outline in the idea of Wisdom, are realised and fulfilled in every factor and function of the Spirit-filled life'.[28] It is also important to note that Paul identifies Christ with Wisdom, but also Christ as exalted with the Holy Spirit (2 Cor 3.17). The Gospel of John, too, demonstrates not just an association between Christ and the Logos, but also between Christ and the Holy Spirit (see, for example, John 1.1; 14.17, 18, 26, 28).

A Trinitarian shape for Wisdom

The Spirit of Wisdom in Irenaeus

Irenaeus was among the earliest theologians of the Church who recognised an association between wisdom and the Holy Spirit. He wrote his book *Against the Heresies* as a response to the prevailing Gnostic traditions that, in general, claimed to have access to a 'higher wisdom' by their own human powers.[29] He ascribed different functions to Logos and Wisdom in the creative action of God, identifying the former with Christ and the latter with the Holy Spirit. Hence he can speak in the following way:

> For with him were always present the Word and Wisdom, the Son and Spirit, by whom and in whom freely and spontaneously, He made all things, to whom also He speaks saying, 'Let us make man after our image and likeness'.[30]

[28] Rees, 'Holy Spirit', 300.
[29] H. Urs von Balthasar (ed.), *The Scandal of the Incarnation: Irenaeus Against the Heresies*, trans. J. Saward, San Francisco: Ignatius Press, 1990, 30.
[30] A. Roberts and J. Donaldson (eds), *Translations of the Writings of the Fathers Down to AD 325*; Irenaeus, *Against the Heresies*, Vol. 1, Edinburgh: T&T Clark, 1874, IV.20.1.

the 'book of the Father' is only known by the Lamb, taking Rev. 3.7: 'receiving power over all things by the same God who made all things by the Word and adorned them by [His] Wisdom'.[31]

I have largely demonstrated, that the Word, namely the Son, was always with the Father; and that Wisdom also, was present with Him, anterior to all creation. He declares by Solomon 'God by Wisdom founded the earth, and by understanding hath established the heaven . . .'[32]

Wisdom is also a characteristic of the Father working in creation, so that God's creation comes 'from the wisdom and power of the Father' and 'subsists by the power, the skill and the wisdom of God'.[33]

However, the distinctive roles of the Father, Son and Spirit in the creation of the universe come out more clearly in passages such as the following:

In this way it is shown that there is one God, the Father, uncreated, invisible, the creator of all, above whom there is no other God and after whom there is no other God. And because God is rational, he therefore created what is made by his Word, and as God is Spirit, so he disposed everything by his Spirit, just as the prophet says: 'By the word of the Lord the heavens were established, and all their power by his Spirit' (Psalm 33.6). Therefore, since the Word establishes, that is gives body and substance, but the Spirit disposes and shapes the variety of powers, the Son is rightly called Word, while the Spirit is called the Wisdom of God.[34]

It seems, then, that Spirit/Wisdom makes beautiful what is established by the Son/Logos. The work of Word and Wisdom are complementary. Hence, the one who 'strengthens all things

---

[31] Irenaeus, *Heresies*, IV.20.2.

[32] Irenaeus, *Heresies*, IV.20.3.

[33] Roberts and Donaldson (eds), *Translations*; Irenaeus, *Against the Heresies*, Vol. 2, Edinburgh: T&T Clark, 1874, V.18.1.

[34] Irenaeus, *Demonstration of the Apostolic Teaching*, translated from the Armenian with introduction and notes by J. A. Robinson, London, 1920, Chapter 5. Denis Minns notes that similar passages are to be found in *Heresies* I.22.1; II.30.9, III.8.3; 24.2; IV.20.1–4; 38.3; 39.2; V.1.3; 9.4, D. Minns, *Irenaeus*, London: Geoffrey Chapman, 1994, 54 n. 22.

by his Word and holds all things together by his Wisdom is
the one true God'.[35]

Minns suggests that Irenaeus's identification of the Spirit
with the Wisdom of God and his description of both as the
'two hands of God' comes from Theophilus.[36] The idea of
two hands of God serves to emphasise that the Word and
Wisdom are not separated from God, but the work of creation
and salvation is the work of the one God revealed as Father,
Son and Spirit. Theophilus believed that God begat both Logos
and Wisdom as distinctive entities that echoes God making
humanity in God's image as male and female. However, he
then seems to subsume the Wisdom of God under the Logos,
so that 'He (the Logos), then, being the Spirit of God, first
Principle, and Wisdom, and Power of the Highest'.[37]

Writers after Clement not only identified Wisdom with
the Logos or the Son, but also ignored the association of
Wisdom and the Spirit. The strong focus on the Son eclipsed
the possible contribution of the Holy Spirit. It becomes
dualistic, rather than Trinitarian. Rees suggests that this form
of Greek theology

> thinks only in terms of God and the Logos; and if the tradition
> and experience of the Holy Spirit still claim recognition, the system
> can only admit it as a shadowy repetition of the Logos, with no
> independent and effective function or principle of its own.[38]

Wisdom and the Trinity

In the section above I have suggested that Irenaeus acknowledged a place for associating Wisdom and the Spirit, but did
so in a Trinitarian framework. A major concern of Irenaeus
was to counter those who speculated on the inner workings
of God. Hence his understanding of the Trinity was never
detached from creation and the economy of salvation.[39]
Nonetheless, while he insisted that the Father has Wisdom, he

[35] Irenaeus, *Heresies*, Vol. 1, III.24.2
[36] Minns, *Irenaeus*, 51.
[37] Theopilus, 'Ad. Autol.' II.10.18, cited in Rees, 'Holy Spirit', 303.
[38] Rees, 'Holy Spirit', 304.
[39] Rees, 'Holy Spirit', 52.

more often linked Wisdom specifically with the work of the Spirit. I hope to show here that Augustine's theology allows for a more explicit Trinitarian understanding of Wisdom. The problem now is how can the distinctive role of the Spirit be expressed? Furthermore, how might Augustine's view be reconciled with the stronger pneumatological approach of Irenaeus? Further, how might this contribute to interpretations of the both the Holy Spirit and the Trinity as Love?

Augustine viewed the Spirit as the Bond of Love between the Father and the Son. It is this interpretation of the Spirit that seems to have dominated Western Christian thought, thereby weakening the *specific* role of the Spirit in the economy of salvation.[40] What is forgotten is that Augustine similarly spoke of the Spirit of God as characterised by Wisdom, but he suggests that Wisdom finds its fullest expression in the Trinity. Augustine's proposal that both Love and Wisdom were characteristic of all persons of the Trinity becomes clear in the following:

> I know not why the Father and the Son and the Holy Spirit should not be called Love, and all together one love, just as both the Father and the Son and the Holy Spirit is called Wisdom, and all together not three, but one wisdom. For so also both the Father is God and the Son God and the Holy Ghost God, and all three together one God.[41]

Similarly he suggests: 'the Father is Wisdom, the Son is Wisdom, and the Holy Spirit is Wisdom, and together not three Wisdoms but one Wisdom'.[42]

He also likens Wisdom to the light of God the Father and the Son in a similar way:

> Therefore both the Father himself is wisdom and the Son is called the wisdom of the Father in the same way as he is called light of the Father; that is in the same manner that the Son is light from light and yet both are one light, so we are to understand wisdom from wisdom, and yet both one wisdom and therefore also one

[40] See Sherry, *Spirit and Beauty*, 108–9.
[41] Augustine, *On the Trinity*, in M. Dods (ed.), *The Works of Aurelius Augustine, Bishop of Hippo*, Vol. VI, Edinburgh: T&T Clark, 1873, XV.27.28.
[42] Augustine, *Trinity*, VII.3.6.

essence ... the Holy Spirit is also wisdom proceeding from
wisdom.[43]

Augustine's understanding of both Love and Wisdom in
the Trinity seems more essentialist compared with the more
personified view of divine Wisdom in the biblical tradition.
Jürgen Moltmann has argued that Augustine's strong emphasis
on the unity of the substance in the one God is the foundation
for his view of the Trinity.[44] He suggests that the unity instead
needs to emerge from the unity of the three persons, rather
than the other way round. He argues that it is the procession
of each person in the other through loving perichoresis that
should be the basis for the triune unity. Nonetheless, it seems
to me that Augustine's recognition of Love and Wisdom in
the Trinity does not necessarily need to be overshadowed by
his stress on the prior unity of God. Both 'love' and 'wisdom'
are *relational* terms, and as such encourage the perception of
the Unity of God and the Trinity of God together, rather than
separately. Furthermore, Wisdom as personified encourages
the perception of God as actively involved in relationship with
the world. Too much emphasis on the social Trinity can have
tritheistic overtones. Instead, by keeping the dialectic of tri-
unity and unity the extremes of either monism or tritheism
are avoided. It is true that, as Moltmann suggests, there is
always a danger that the unity of God might 'drive out' the
tri-unity, but there is an opposite danger as well, the *social*
Trinity might eclipse the Unity.

How might the wisdom motif in the Trinity be understood
in the light of contemporary notions of the Trinity as Love?
Anthony Kelly, for example, uses the analogy of Being-in-Love
to describe more fully the idea of communion between the
persons.[45] He believes that it is necessary to look for an
analogical understanding of the meaning of Love in order to
avoid tritheistic overtones and emphasise the unity in God.
For him:

[43] Augustine, *Trinity*, VII.1.2; XV.7.12
[44] J. Moltmann, *The Trinity and the Kingdom of God*, trans. M. Kohl, London:
    SCM Press, 1981, 16–20; 148–50.
[45] A. Kelly, *The Trinity of Love; A Theology of the Christian God*, Wilmington:
    Michael Glazier, 1989, 181.

God is originatively Love as Father, expressively Love as Son and communicatively Love as Spirit; three subjects in the one conscious infinite act of Being-in-Love. Each divine person has a distinct meaning in the self-constitution of the Divine Mystery; each is Love in a distinctive manner . . . the three are intelligible as Trinity only insofar as they manifest the Divine Mystery as Sheer Being-in-Love.[46]

The Trinity is not so much a social process as a reality that makes history through Trinitarian loving. Kelly argues that the self-transcending Love overcomes the split between the economic and immanent Trinity. Furthermore, the idea of person today has become much more readily understood in terms of relationships, both with others and with the earth.[47] He insists, further, that it is the *procession* of Love between the persons that gives rise to the process of creation. The kenotic relationship between God and the world is expressed through the refusal of God to become anything else but Love in history, 'by refusing any other mode of action or presence'.[48]

How might these ideas impinge on the idea of the Trinity as Wisdom? It seems to me that Kelly is correct to insist on Love as being at the heart of our understanding of the Trinity. An adequate view of the Trinity cannot exclude Love. However, to suggest that *all* other modes of action or presence are automatically refused takes the analogy a little too far. In Chapter 2 I argued that the wisdom of the cross expresses in the fullest sense the Love and Wisdom of God. Hence, the Wisdom of God is never apart from Love. Similarly, Love is never apart from Wisdom either.

I suggest, further, that the idea of the Trinity as Being-in-Love needs Wisdom if it is to break free from a purely psychological analogy. Kelly's identification of the Father as the origin of Love seems to give priority to the Father over the Son and the Spirit. Rather, God as Trinity is the origin of both Love and Wisdom. The distinction of the Father is as One who is related to the Son and the Spirit through Love and Wisdom. The Son is distinct in expressing this Love and

[46] Kelly, *Trinity of Love*, 182.
[47] Kelly, *Trinity of Love*, 188.
[48] Kelly, *Trinity of Love*, 196.

Wisdom in history in physical, material form and the Spirit is distinct in creating Life in Wisdom and Love, but also re-creating and perfecting Life in the Spirit of the Wisdom of Christ.

Is this interpretation compatible with Irenaeus's under-standing of the distinct roles of the Logos and Wisdom in the Son and the Spirit? Other theologians have taken up the idea of this complementary action in the creative action of God. Moltmann includes the idea of Wisdom in the creative process, but the concept is never really developed. He views Wisdom Christology as a form of Spirit Christology, as Wisdom and the Spirit are associated in the Israelite tradition.[49] Further-more, he feels justified in using Spirit, Word and Wisdom interchangeably, so that 'All things have their genesis in a fundamental underlying unity, which is called God's Wisdom, Spirit or Word'.[50] He does, nonetheless, distinguish the creative action of God through the Spirit and the Son in the following way:

> A better image is the song of creation. The word names, differ-entiates and appraises. But the breath is the same in all the words, and binds the words together. So the Creator differentiates his creatures through his creative Word and joins them through his Spirit, who is the sustainer of all his words.[51]

The possible role of Wisdom is not mentioned, possibly because Wisdom can be identified either with the Logos or the Spirit.

In what sense, then, can Irenaeus's association of the Spirit and Wisdom be of relevance in the present discussion? It may help to focus attention on the complementary roles of both Word and Wisdom in the initial creative act of God. I suggest that if Wisdom becomes fused with the divine Logos too readily, then the full significance of Wisdom becomes lost. In particular, it is the *feminine face* of God that is demonstrated through the Wisdom motif that becomes suppressed. It is perhaps surprising that Moltmann, for all his empathy with

---

[49] J. Moltmann, *The Way of Jesus Christ*, trans. M. Kohl, London: SCM Press, 1990, 74.
[50] Moltmann, *Way*, 288.
[51] Moltmann, *Way*, 289.

feminist theology, has failed to spot the potential significance of the wisdom tradition in bringing together insights both from Orthodoxy and contemporary feminist writing. Furthermore, fuller reflection on Wisdom allows the distinction between the work of the Spirit in creation and in the human community to be preserved, without any claim that the two movements are unrelated. It is to these functions of Wisdom that we will turn next.

Wisdom as the feminine face of God

Wisdom has become a popular vehicle for reflection among feminist theologians because of its rich association with feminine divinity. The biblical tradition speaks of Lady Wisdom in contrast to the Wicked Woman Folly or Temptress. In Proverbs the figure of a woman is used in order to elucidate more fully the meaning of wisdom.[52] In the cultural context of the time women were considered to be subordinate and had no recognised authority in the public realm, even though they had considerable influence in the domestic realm. It is striking, then, to consider the lack of maternal imagery in the personification of Wisdom as portrayed in the Old Testament. In addition, close study of the literary, historical and sociological contexts of wisdom suggests that the authority of the figure of Wisdom over humanity expressed in Proverbs is not based so much on the model of political treaties, but on the covenant love as that expressed between man and woman.[53]

Negative imagery, that views the folly of the harlot, serves to contrast covenant love with sexual temptation and thereby the breaking of covenant love. In this sense Wisdom has a positive role in fostering human wisdom that finds at its heart covenant love. This goes beyond any suggestion that Lady Wisdom is just a reaction to goddess worship common among Israel's neighbours. In the context of post-exilic Israel mighty acts of God in history no longer seemed possible, so

---

[52] C. V. Camp, *Wisdom and the Feminine in the Book of Proverbs*, Sheffield: The Almond Press, 1985.
[53] Camp, *Wisdom*, 109.

a return to images of God's action from everyday life naturally took precedence. Camp argues that the figure of Wisdom
is a personification, rather than simply a divine attribute.
Furthermore, the fact that she is portrayed as a woman gives
her particular qualities:

> Personified Wisdom is able – by virtue of her multifaceted presen-
> tation as a woman – to point to the human wisdom tradition as a
> crucial source of knowledge . . . The appeal and effectiveness of
> personified Wisdom lies not only in her alluring female qualities,
> but also in the very structure of the literary device in which she is
> presented. In literarily uniting the general and particular, the
> abstract and the concrete, personification theologically unites the
> human and the divine.[54]

Wisdom portrayed as feminine deity recurs in a range of
cultures in addition to those of the Judaeo/Christian tradition.
Her appearances in a range of cults, including those that use
ceremonial magic, are, according to Caitlin Matthews, valid
paths of exploration.[55] However, such portrayals do not do
justice to the particular way wisdom can be taken up and
explored in a distinctive Christian framework.

Elizabeth Johnson is one author who has made a concerted
effort to rehabilitate the idea of Wisdom from a Christian
feminist perspective. Her book, *She Who Is: The Mystery of
God in Feminist Theological Discourse*, explores the dynamics
of Wisdom in the person of the Trinity.[56] All three persons are
re-described in the light of Sophia. However, she is reluctant
to name God as Father, rather the third person of the Trinity
is Mother Sophia. The approach of traditional Orthodoxy is
to confine the feminine in God to the Holy Spirit. However,
she argues that if we allow ourselves to take this route then
the Holy Spirit still remains the 'faceless' person of the Trinity,
so that we end up with two masculine images and an 'amorphous third person', who as third person is subordinate.[57]

[54] Camp, *Wisdom*, 222.
[55] C. Matthews, *Sophia: Goddess of Wisdom. The Feminine Divine From Black
Goddess to World Soul*, London: Mandala/HarperCollins, 1991.
[56] E. A. Johnson, *She Who Is: The Mystery of God in Feminist Theological
Discourse*, New York: Crossroad, 1992.
[57] Johnson, *She Who Is*, 50.

Sarah Coakley makes much the same point when she suggests that the feminine needs to be thought of in a Trinitarian way, rather than a restriction to the person of the Holy Spirit or the Virgin Mary.[58] Both Johnson and Coakley reject any essentialist view of God as female, rather the feminine in God resists stereotypical views of women. Johnson is highly critical of process theologian John Cobb, for in identifying the Logos with novelty, order, agency and transformation and the Spirit with empathy, receptivity and preservation he seems to have reduced the Spirit to stereotypical female categories.[59] Moreover, if men and women are in the image of God, then both female and male metaphors need to be included. She suggests further that 'Female imagery by itself points to God as such and has the capacity to represent God not only as nurturing, although certainly that, but as powerful, initiating, creating-redeeming-saving and victorious over the powers of this world.'[60]

She also suggests that all talk of 'feminine dimensions' reduce the impact of female imagery. However, it seems to me that too strong a notion of female imagery can exclude important elements that are worth retaining. This comes out most clearly in her re-presentation of God as Mother Sophia. For her, 'Holy Wisdom is the mother of the universe, the unoriginate, living source of all that exists. This unimaginable livingness generates the life of all creatures, being itself, in the beginning and continuously, the power of being within being.'[61] She is the generative source of all that exists, including the Spirit in the world. For her, the maternal image points not just to God's immanence, but a new understanding of God's transcendence as well. Yet this transcendence is not one of power, but is hidden in the profound, lasting relationships, such as in the human experience of a mother who remains mysterious to her young child.

[58] S. Coakley, 'Femininity and the Holy Spirit', in M. Furlong (ed.), *Mirror to the Church: Reflections on Sexism*, London: SPCK, 1988, 130–2.
[59] Johnson, *She Who Is*, 51.
[60] Johnson, *She Who Is*, 54.
[61] Johnson, *She Who Is*, 179.

While I welcome the concept of complementing male imagery of God with female imagery, I believe that Johnson has, in places, taken this too far to be convincing. It is Johnson's insistence on the total replacement of all images of Father by Mother and Son by Child that removes any idea of male imagery. This seems to imply *matriarchy* as a substitute for patriarchy, rather than a richer view that insists on both images being present simultaneously. While, as I discussed above, I am fully in favour of using Sophia-Wisdom as a means of re-imaging the Trinity, I would prefer a *transforming* role of Wisdom, so that she becomes the *feminine face of God*. This need not amount to a stereotypical notion of male and female attributes, which Johnson rightly rejects. Rather, the feminine serves to transform images of God as Father and Jesus as Son and even the Spirit as neutral or male. In speaking of the feminine face of God I am quite deliberately not suggesting that Wisdom fosters a distinct goddess imagery. Rather, it allows feminine imagery to be incorporated into God as Trinity in a way that serves to present a richer, fuller and more holistic understanding of the nature of who God is. There is a sense, then, that God can be thought of as having the character of both Mother and Father. This goes beyond Moltmann's suggestion of a 'Motherly Father', while refusing to go as far as Johnson in her proposed image of God as Mother.[62]

In what sense is the idea of the feminine Sophia relevant for a discussion of the male Jesus as Logos? In other words, has the replacement of Sophia, a feminine term, with Logos, a male term, further reinforced the patriarchal presentation of Christianity in the manner that Johnson suggests?[63] Fiorenza is sharply critical of the dominance of the Father/Son language in John, which she believes excludes the idea of woman Wisdom. She suggests that the 'Fourth Gospel . . . marginalises and "silences" the traditions of God as represented by Divine

---

[62] J. Moltmann, 'The Motherly Father: Is Trinitarian Patripassionism Replacing Theological Patriarchalism?', trans. G. Knowles, in J. Metz and E. Schillebeeckx (eds), *God as Father?* Concilium 143, Edinburgh: T&T Clark, 1981, 51–6.
[63] Johnson, *She Who Is*, 152.

Woman Wisdom'.[64] Martin Scott has investigated the significance of the gender of Sophia for the Johannine portrayal of Jesus as Logos/Sophia.[65] He criticises the portrayal of Sophia in much biblical scholarship for not giving sufficient treatment to the question of the feminine aspect of Wisdom. He suggests that Sophia is highly significant for our understanding of God, for 'she is not merely a means of talking about God, who is really male, but rather an expression of who God is in her very being'.[66] He suggests that since Logos and Sophia had already been established as a synonym prior to John's Gospel, the Logos idea gave John the opportunity to use Logos as a way of expressing Christ as the embodiment of Sophia. The Logos formula also solved the problem of how to relate the male Christ with the feminine Sophia.[67]

If this is the case, then the original purpose of John's use of the Logos was not so much to reinforce patriarchy, but rather to show links between Jesus and Sophia. The significance of this is that it shows John's Christology is a *Sophia Christology* that takes precedence over the *Logos Christology*. This would imply that any identification of Sophia with Logos is not to replace Sophia, but to strengthen her imagery, in the manner akin to Johnson's interpretation above. In other words, characteristics such as rationality and order, normally associated with Logos, become part of the imagery of Sophia as well. In this context it is worth emphasising that the incarnation of Wisdom in Christ comes through the power of the Spirit, so that it is through Spirit-Sophia that the Logos becomes transformed. Later interpretations of John forgot the root of this Christology and replaced Sophia with a purified and rarefied Logos. Such interpretations have not only distorted the image presented to us by John, but have forgotten the deepest meaning of the incarnation, that is for Christ to become incarnate in the earthly, material world.

---

[64] E. Schüssler Fiorenza, *Jesus: Miriam's Child; Sophia's Prophet*, London: SCM Press, 153.
[65] M. Scott, *Sophia and the Johannine Jesus*, Sheffield: Sheffield Academic Press, 1992.
[66] Scott, *Sophia*, 80.
[67] Scott, *Sophia*, 114.

The notion of Jesus as pure Logos incarnate can give the impression that God is still detached from the world of living, created beings. While the image of Sophia can also be subject to a similar Platonising tendency, at least Wisdom is also rooted in the everyday life of the Hebrew world. The Logos formula never had this grounding and so is always in danger of failing to stress the immanence of God in creation. Mary Grey suggests that the character of Logos can foster images of a logo-centric, profit-based and competitive ethic in contrast to the character of Sophia that is non-dualistic, ecological and relational.[68] It is this lopsided view of Logos alone that can dominate. If we follow Scott's interpretation of John's intention in using Logos to describe Christ, then Logos needs to be transformed through the concept of Sophia. Logos is not so much eliminated as put in a wider context of Wisdom. This suggestion parallels the development in philosophy that I discussed in the first chapter. Where Wisdom becomes pure rationality, as in the replacement of Sophia by Logos, then distortions are bound to follow.

Another area pertinent for the present discussion is Johnson's interpretation of Sophia-Spirit. She has no trouble in viewing the work of the Spirit in the natural world as well as in humanity. The Spirit is present in the wonder we experience as we view the beauty of the earth, but also in the pain as we view the devastation of the earth. The work of the Spirit includes creativity in the human community and the amorphous quality of the Spirit can serve as an advantage. For Johnson this quality 'allows a particular openness to being appropriated in female images; that the Spirit's traditional concentration on the human race and its individuals hides an alternative stream of cosmic and community activity waiting to be rediscovered . . .'[69]

While I agree with her inclusion of a cosmic interpretation of the work of the Spirit, her conflation of the work of the Spirit in the human community and in the natural world is problematic. I discuss a possible outline of how these two movements might be distinguished in the section below.

[68] M. Grey, *The Wisdom of Fools? Seeking Revelation for Today*, London: SPCK, 1993, 2.
[69] Johnson, *She Who Is*, 132.

Furthermore, while it is important to include the suffering of the Spirit in the world as a corrective to more romantic portrayals of God's presence in creation, it needs to be set in a Christological context. The suffering of the Spirit in the pain and frustration of creation finds expression in the wisdom of the cross, through a cosmic Christology. In other words it is through the *Spirit of Christ* that God identifies with the victims of the devastation of the human community and the victims of the natural world. Once we reject this Christological referent, then the suffering of the world could seem a *necessary* part of the process. I will return to this idea again in the next chapter.

Creation through Wisdom

Given this framework for a theology of creation based on wisdom, how can this be elaborated further? In particular how can the strands of wisdom elucidated encourage a particular creation theology that is distinct from other models of the relationship between God and the world? First of all the metaphorical and poetical language of the wisdom literature suggests that an interpretation of the relationship between God and creation based on wisdom needs to be seen in a metaphorical way.[70] It is one way of perceiving the creative acts of God in a way that seems to cohere with the biblical witness, the early Church and contemporary concerns. I will return to the issue of modern science again in the next section.

I have argued for a Trinitarian view of Wisdom, rather than one narrowly conceived in terms of either the Logos or the Spirit. This serves as a framework for a doctrine of creation. The advantage of a Trinitarian basis for creation theology is that it preserves a sense of both the immanence and the transcendence of God. Moltmann finds in the social Trinity an ecological motif that reinforces the notion of God's immanence.[71] The sense of God's transcendence seems to be pushed to the future, so the glory of God is from ahead, rather than

---

[70] C. Deane-Drummond, 'Sophia: The Feminine Face of God as a Metaphor for an Eco-Theology', *Feminist Theology* 16 (1997), 11–31.
[71] Deane-Drummond, *Jürgen Moltmann's Theology*.

from above, as in classical theology. Wisdom also encourages a relational view of the world that resonates with ecological ideas. However, it also retains a sense of God's transcendence in a way that is difficult for purely ecological models. Wisdom is realised in an ontological way in the Godhead, in a similar way to Love. In other words Wisdom is part of the being of God. However, such ontology is not divorced from epistemology. We know God through Love and Wisdom expressed in dim reflections in the created world. Moltmann's strong rejection of all natural theology effectively seems to evacuate the presence of God in creation, except as hints of the eschaton, the new creation and the new earth.[72] While he does acknowledge the work of the Trinity in the creation of the world, the dynamic of creation and re-creation is never really clarified. By contrast, the wisdom Trinitarian framework does allow for a limited natural theology, though not at the expense of a theology of revelation. The Old Testament witness speaks of the Wisdom of God manifested in the order of creation. While it is clear, as I suggested earlier, that the authors themselves were not arguing for a natural theology, in a limited sense the presence of Wisdom in the world can serve as a reminder of the presence of God.

The image of Wisdom's involvement in creation challenges the view that God's action can be portrayed in the language of male images alone. The feminine face of God comes out clearly in the Wisdom motif. However, the vehicle commonly used by eco-feminists to describe the action of the feminine divine in creation is *Gaia*, rather than *Sophia*.[73] I discussed the problems associated with Gaia as science in Chapter 2. The image of Gaia is popular among eco-feminists as a way of expressing the dynamics of interrelationships on earth. Nonetheless, the idea that the earth is a living organism is taken up in an uncritical way. Gaia is also an evocative reminder of Gaia the ancient Greek goddess of the earth. Ruether associates Gaia with an inner divine voice 'that speaks

---

[72] Moltmann, *God in Creation*, 57–60.
[73] See, for example, R. Ruether, *God and Gaia: An Eco-Feminist Theology of Earth Healing*, London: SCM Press, 1992; A. Primavesi, *From Apocalypse to Genesis*, London: SCM Press, 1992.

from the intimate heart of matter'.[74] She associates Gaia as feminine with the sacramental tradition of the Church. She suggests that divinity has another voice as well, that coming from the covenantal tradition, a voice of power that also paradoxically identifies with the powerless and weak. In doing so she seems to have reinforced the association of maleness with the transcendent God and femaleness with the immanent God in a way that I find far from satisfactory. She adds to this stereotype the concept that the 'law' needs a 'heart' and so must listen to the voice of Gaia.

It is hard to distinguish Ruether's particular view of Gaia from pantheism. The image of Wisdom is, by contrast, more effective than Gaia for a radical eco-feminism. Wisdom has its roots deep in the biblical tradition and the tradition of the Church. She can become an effective metaphor for transformation since her influence reaches right back to the earliest Judaeo-Christian tradition in a way that is impossible with Gaia. Ruether's suggestion that Gaia is biblical seems to come from her own imposition of the term 'sacrament' on to Gaia. Ruether may be avoiding any stronger use of Gaia as she is reluctant to reclaim the image of Gaia as goddess in its entirety. However, the biblical personification of Wisdom allows her to be taken up into an understanding of God in a way that would be impossible for the Gaia image. Unlike Ruether's Gaia, Wisdom is not restricted to the realm of nature, but is part of who God is in the Trinity. Wisdom is not divorced from the Word, but they both work together in love to build a new community. Wisdom is inclusive of reason in a way that is difficult with the image of Gaia that Ruether presents.

How might this presence of God as Wisdom come to be expressed? In the first acts of creation in the beginning the form of this expression seems to be primarily a pneumatological one. The Spirit moving over the waters of creation is also the Spirit of Wisdom. However, this is the same Spirit that is in communion with God as the Trinity of Love. In other words the creative activity of God as Trinity is an outpouring of this Love for creation. Any separation of the

[74] Ruether, *God and Gaia*, 254.

immanent Trinity and the economic Trinity is not really
relevant here. Such speculations go beyond what we know of
God, that God in Love and Wisdom created the world.
Creation is then in Love, but through Wisdom.

Drawing on Irenaeus's idea of the complementary action of
Word and Wisdom in the creation it is clear that both are
engaged in God's interaction with the world. Is it possible to
suggest, along with Irenaeus, that the Word establishes the
world, while Wisdom shapes and perfects it? While I would
agree with Irenaeus that both Word and Wisdom are involved
in the creative process, I am less happy with the priority
that he seems to give to the Word in his schema. This also
seems to be the implication of Patrick Sherry's view that the
Spirit is the perfector of creation, expressing the beauty of
God. Although this goes some way to restoring the Spirit in
the cosmic process of creation, the Spirit still seems to take
second place, at least in a chronological sense. It seems, thereby,
to weaken the role of the Spirit in creation. In some places
Irenaeus does suggest that Wisdom is the source for the
foundation of the world, so his views are not really consistent.
Instead, I suggest that it is the co-operation of Word and
Wisdom together that establishes, shapes and perfects the
world. One cannot be considered without the other, but the
two are not synonymous either.

The joint action of Word and Wisdom in creation is
expressed in the incarnation of the Son. In the person of Jesus,
the Son becomes both Wisdom incarnate and Word incarnate.
This is a unique interpenetration of the Godhead with the
material world. Whereas in the act of creation Word and
Wisdom serve together to shape the creative process, in the
incarnation of the Son both Word and Wisdom become part
of the fabric of creation itself. Furthermore, it is through the
Holy Spirit that the Son becomes incarnate as Jesus Christ in
history. This is a fundamental affirmation of creation by God,
namely that God enters fully into the material world in the
history of Jesus of Nazareth. The significance of Christ for
creation is this ultimate act of love and humility.

However, in looking for traces of God in creation, while we
might see signs of love, wisdom and beauty on the earth, we

can also find disease, trauma and suffering. Such suffering is evident in the evolving universe where the process itself is an ambiguous one. For, as Moltmann suggests, 'in the same process milliards of living things fall by the wayside and disappear into evolution's rubbish bin. Evolution is not merely a constructive affair on nature's part. It is a cruel one too.'[75] The love of God is not indifferent to this suffering. Such love of God for creation goes deeper still in the crucifixion of Christ. Christ identifies not just with the victims of human tragedy, but with nature's victims also. It is in this sense that Christology can be said to be cosmic in scope.

I am less convinced that Christology can be read into the initial act of creation in the manner that Moltmann seems to suggest. As I mentioned earlier, Gunton also proposes a strong Christological perspective on Wisdom that re-reads the passages describing Wisdom in Proverbs according to a Christological referent. It is also surprising that while Gunton affirms a triune creator, he does not mention Wisdom in the context of his Trinitarian doctrine of creation.[76] Like Irenaeus, he views the Spirit as the perfector of creation, though he does not make the link with Wisdom in the way Irenaeus suggests. However, it seems to me that Wisdom in Proverbs is more closely aligned to the action of the Spirit in the world, rather than any stronger Christological reference. It is true that the Word is involved in creation in the manner I suggested above, but this is in the context of a Trinitarian understanding of who God is.

I am also cautious about Moltmann's identification of the groaning of creation described in Romans 8.18–23 in a Christological way in order to support a cosmic Christology.[77] Rather, it is through the *Spirit* that the suffering of all creation comes to be identified with Christ's death and through the *Spirit* that creation finds hope in Christ's resurrection. The cross displays the wisdom of God by showing forth a means

---

[75] Moltmann, *Way*, 294.
[76] C. Gunton, *The Triune Creator*, Edinburgh: Edinburgh University Press, 1998.
[77] See, for example, Moltmann, *God in Creation*, 189. For further commentary, see Deane-Drummond, *Jürgen Moltmann's Theology*.

through which creation can become glorified. In other words the wisdom of the cross brings redemption into creation.

In what sense can we distinguish the movement of the Spirit in creation from that in the human community? This is a difficult problem that has variously been avoided either by restricting the work of the Spirit to the human community, transforming an understanding of God so that God is pure Spirit, or encouraging an understanding of Spirit as world-soul, with little reference to the Christological context. Any suggestion at this juncture is bound to be somewhat speculative. However, I believe that the idea of wisdom does give some pointers as to the way this problem can be approached.

I have suggested above that the work of the Spirit in creation is the work of Holy Wisdom. Wisdom does not enter into creation in a pantheistic way, rather Wisdom, along with God's Word, serves to shape creation along distinctive lines. The importance of Wisdom is that she does not force creation according to a rigid formula. Rather, Love allows the freedom of creation to be preserved in a manner that admits the possibility of pain and suffering. Wisdom is both humble, but persuasive, she challenges, but at the same time is never divorced from Love. This is not the same as the process model where God urges the world into completion. For process theology, God becomes through the world process. God as Wisdom does not need the world in order to be God. Rather, God chooses to express Love and Wisdom in the creation of the world. God identifies fully with the world, but only in a literal, material sense in the incarnation. The world is enfolded in the triune God in a pan-en-theistic way, rather than through pantheism. In other words while the movement of Wisdom in creation can be thought of predominately as through the Spirit of Wisdom, it makes most sense in a Trinitarian context.

When we come to consider the particular role of the Spirit in the human community, it seems to me that Wisdom has to adopt a more prophetic stance. Wisdom is now not so much urging as challenging change and transformation. In this sense Wisdom only makes sense in terms of a Wisdom Christology. Hence the work of the Holy Spirit in the human community refers to the Christ event and emerges fully following Christ's

death and resurrection. The Holy Spirit in the human community is synonymous with the Spirit of Christ, the two cannot
be considered apart from the other.

As creatures created in the image of God humanity is always
struggling to show forth this image. Even apart from the
Wisdom of Christ, humanity expresses something of the
Wisdom of God, as the Spirit of Wisdom is present in all creation. Furthermore, Wisdom reminds humanity that it cannot
think of itself as apart from creation. Hence, while it is possible
to distinguish the movement of the Spirit in the natural world
and that in the human community, the lines must not be drawn
too sharply. The human community is part of and integral to
the whole of the created world. Any separation is for the
purpose of greater clarity, rather than suggesting a radical
disjunction between human and natural worlds. Indeed, if the
separation is taken too far this could encourage human domination of nature in a way that would be destructive of the
need for community and communion. However, if there is no
separation at all then humanity becomes just a passive observer
in the natural world. The movements of Wisdom in the natural
and human worlds can encourage a deeper empathy for the
natural world, but a realistic appreciation of the distinction
of humanity as well.

A further way that this unity in distinction between
humanity and the natural world can be clarified is through
Rahner's notion of nature and grace. Rahner suggests that in
the case of humanity, nature is never 'pure nature', but nature
existing in a supernatural order that has a potency for the free
grace of God. This lends to creation an inner openness to
God, so that there is 'within the concrete order of total creation,
an inner openness to grace and a real crying need for grace'.[78]
He suggests that the orders of creation and redemption can be
thought of as distinct, but in each other as well. Hence 'the
redemptive order must develop within the created order as its
all-informing, healing and divinizing principle', but also 'the
created order remains included in the redemptive order . . . in

---

[78] G. A. McCool (ed.), *A Rahner Reader*, London: Darton, Longman & Todd,
1975, 194.

so far as it is a distinct, necessary factor in the redemptive order'.[79] Rahner's concept of nature and grace is a welcome shift towards the affirmation of the natural world compared with the extrinsic medieval views of grace that he rightly criticises. However, he does retain a sharp distinction between humanity and 'beasts', suggesting that the latter are 'utterly incapable of elevation to the supernatural order. When God made them he could have had no intention of giving them a supernatural end'.[80] In the light of a greater understanding of the commonality between humanity and creatures such a sharp division seems unacceptable today. We are not in a position to know how far the grace of God moves beyond the human community. Nonetheless, it is clear that the receptivity to grace reaches its zenith in the community of human persons. The possibility of rejection of this grace remains, along with dire consequences for both humanity and the earth.

The problem for environmentally aware models of creation is that the relationship between God and nature becomes the focus at the expense of consideration of the human community. A theology of creation based on Wisdom is significant not just for a systematic theology, but also for guidelines as to how to engage in a practical way with the problems to hand. I showed in the last chapter that while the Eastern traditions have highlighted the significance of wisdom for systematic theology, Aquinas has shown the importance of wisdom for ethics as well. Wisdom challenges the human community, both at the level of thinking about creation as expressing the Wisdom of God, but also at the level of practice. I will be returning to this question again in the chapters that follow.

Wisdom in the dialogue with science

As long as we remember the history of the biblical emergence of Wisdom, then the language of Wisdom can become a valuable link between the sacred and the secular. I have shown that Holy Wisdom can be thought of as having a divine origin. However, there is a distinction between the all-pervasive Spirit

[79] McCool, *Rahner*, 195–6.
[80] D. L. Gelpi, *Light and Life: A Guide to the Theology of Karl Rahner*, New York: Sheed & Ward, 1966, 51.

of Wisdom in the life of creation and that given as Gift to
the human community in the Spirit of Christ. The former
begins with the creation and the human community, eventually
becoming incarnate in a unique way in the person of Christ.
The latter follows the death and resurrection of Christ and
leads to the renewal of the Christian community and eventually
the renewal of the whole earth, as I will discuss in the next
chapter.

In the Old Testament some were endowed with a special
outpouring of God's Spirit in such a way that there seemed
to be a distinction between sacred and secular wisdom. The
presence of the Spirit of Wisdom was so strong that she became
personified into Lady Wisdom, taking on divine characteristics.
However, a tension existed in the portrayal of Wisdom. Did
she come through education and learning, in common with
the secular cultures of the time; or was she given as divine
gift? Both strands seem to be present in the Old Testament
wisdom literature. Hence wisdom becomes a way of linking
the secular and the sacred. Wisdom affirms that traces of
wisdom can be found in the secular world, but ultimately it is
divine Wisdom that is critical of all human wisdom. Such a
paradox emerges most forcefully in the wisdom of the cross in
1 Corinthians which I discussed in Chapter 2. The fact that
biblical wisdom literature shared some common insights with
other surrounding cultures was one reason why this body of
literature was ignored in twentieth-century biblical scholarship.
It was not considered to be distinctive enough to warrant
serious study and reflection. The resurgence of interest in this
literature in more recent years has uncovered both the distinctive and common characteristics. The fact that the search
for wisdom is so universal and that wisdom has universal
characteristics is an advantage, rather than a disadvantage,
as far as a theology of creation is concerned. It allows
insights from human activities, such as science, art, literature
and philosophy to be included in the discussion. However,
the criteria for true wisdom is always measured against
divine Wisdom as revealed through the life of the righteous
in covenant relationship with God. While the covenant is
not spelt out in much of the biblical wisdom literature, it is

presupposed. Eventually this wisdom becomes identified with the Torah, and then with the Logos. However, this narrowing need not weaken the broad basis for wisdom, wisdom's many faces, as I discussed in Chapter 1.

For the wisdom writers, also, there was little distinction between the cultural wisdom of the human community and the natural wisdom emerging from observations of the natural world. In other words the split between nature and history was not as clear cut as it seems today, the human and natural communities were considered to be part of a unified whole.[81] While it would be impossible to regain this sense of an undivided world in a post-Enlightenment culture, the wisdom literature at least tries to foster an inner attitude that seeks areas of common ground between the natural realm and that of history. In the Old Testament literature, 'Creation is the basis not only of regularity, but of a meaningful and satisfactory order of events in the world, a purposefulness of created beings and things'.[82] Attempts to use ecological wisdom as a model for human behaviour might seem to draw on this perspective. Examples include that of John Carmody who suggests that the source of wisdom is 'ecological'.[83] He believes that the sense of the sacred in nature is an important corrective to modern technological lifestyles. Other authors use Gaia as a way of introducing an interdependent paradigm for human behaviour.[84] The idea of purpose in the universe emerging from the Old Testament witness is an important theological concept that needs to be retained, even though science itself in practice rejects any teleology. It is also essential that humanity regains a sense of communion with the natural world. However, to suggest that ecology can be a *guide* to

[81] H. J. Hermisson, 'Observations on the Creation Theology in Wisdom', in J. G. Gummie, W. A. Bruggeman, W. L. Humphreys and J. M. Ward (eds), *Israelite Wisdom: Theological and Literary Essays in Honour of Samuel Terrain*, Missoula, MT: Scholars Press, 1978, 43–57.

[82] Hermisson, 'Observations', 46.

[83] J. Carmody, '"Ecological" Wisdom and the Tendency Toward a Re-mythologization of Life', in J. B. Metz and E. Schillebeeckx (eds), *No Heaven Without Earth*, London: SCM Press, 1991, 94–103.

[84] See, for example, E. Sahtouris, *Gaia: The Human Journey From Chaos to Cosmos*, New York: Pocket Books/Simon & Schuster Inc, 1989.

moral behaviour seems to me to go too far. Even the wise of the Old Testament 'were far from explicitly seasoning their moral teachings each time by referring to the orders of creation'.[85] Furthermore, there is a tendency for eco-feminist authors to be sharply critical of science, even while drawing on the science of ecology to support their critique.[86] I will be returning to the feminist critique of science in the next chapter. My purpose here is to show how there are ways of thinking about science that are compatible with the wisdom perspective outlined above.

In the wisdom literature there is a sense that the activity of the Creator is not just in the beginning, but is continuous, so that even the orders of creation themselves are flexible rather than rigid.[87] There is a temptation to assume that the more rigid cosmology of the earliest civilisations has little to say in the light of modern science. However, the concept of God working in creation in a *continuous way* leaves room for more fluid interpretations of the relationship between God and creation that are necessary in the light of modern cosmology. Ruth Page's theology is important in reminding us of the way God and creation can be affirmed in the light of modern discoveries in science.[88] Drawing on Heidegger's notion of 'Letting-Be', she suggests that God in creation continuously creates the possibilities for creation to emerge. Her belief that there is a free exploration, choice and experiment in the mind of God fits in well with the new physics, even though within such possibilities there is always a propensity for one or other form to emerge in a given situation. The old notion of God and creation in terms of classical cause and effect is no longer acceptable in the light of modern science. This seems a very valid point to make. However, to conclude that all God is doing is creating the possibilities seems to weaken any sense of purpose other than a creation that is entirely free to be itself. Such an interpretation is countered somewhat by Page's

---

[85] Hermisson, 'Observations', 47.
[86] C. Merchant, *The Death of Nature: Women, Ecology and the Scientific Revolution*, San Francisco: Harper & Row, 1983.
[87] Hermisson, 'Observations', 47.
[88] R. Page, *God and the Web of Creation*, London: SCM Press, 1996, 6–18.

elaboration of Heidegger's 'With-Being' as a way of expressing God's relationship to creation as a communion with and in friendship.[89]

Page's notion of God as friendship bears some relationship to Sallie McFague's interpretation of God relating to the world primarily as a friend.[90] However, McFague believes that we need to begin a theology of creation with a discussion of humanity as an earth creature, rather than with the cosmos, in order to emphasise what we know about ourselves as creatures of the earth.[91] Page suggests that humans are capable of giving due attention to God, who is always with creation, as one of the possibilities that exist. Her concept of pansyntheism, God with all creation, clarifies the way God can be described as relating to creation in a way that is more difficult to adopt with panentheism. For example, McFague understands the world as *God's Body*. This is a form of panentheism, the view that the world is in God. Panentheism is popular among many theologians who are scientists and those influenced by process theology.

It seems to me that Page's notion of pansyntheism coheres with the idea of God expressed as the Spirit of Wisdom in creation. The Spirit of Wisdom is a humble Spirit, whispering to the world in its becoming. This echoes the words of Proverbs 8.30 'I was by his side, a master craftsman [or little child], delighting him day after day, ever at play in his presence'. The idea of playfulness of Wisdom in the creation of the world encourages a more poetic appreciation of the relationship between God and the world that resists simple constriction to particular physical events. While the question of 'Exactly how does God do this?' is of concern to a scientist, I am less convinced that this will be problematic for the theologian, who is used to more metaphorical ways of speaking about God.

[89] Page, *Web*, 40–6; 52–8.
[90] S. McFague, *Models of God: Theology for an Ecological, Nuclear Age*, Minneapolis: Fortress Press, 1987, 157–67.
[91] S. McFague, *The Body of God: An Ecological Theology*, Minneapolis: Fortress Press, 1993.

Tentatively we might say that when God's whisper is heard it leads to flourishing and fullness of life, while when it is ignored this leads to death. It is like a resonance, perhaps a pattern-forming quality on a different plane of reality than has been so far discoverable by science. If we identify God with the events themselves, such as quantum events, this opens the door to pantheism. I am *not* saying that God is simply fitted into the gaps in our understanding. In other words God as Wisdom is not detached from the physical and biological processes either, but instead hints at the way to fullness. Moreover, the incarnation of Christ reminds us of the possibility of the total interpenetration of God in the material world. Human life becomes more conscious of this whisper of God and so can respond in love, friendship and worship. This is distinct from process theology where God becomes identified with the world process. The difference in the view I am suggesting is that God is far greater than these events in creation; the physical world of nature as we know it is, instead, contained in God. Wisdom helps us to delineate the boundaries of this pansyntheist model of the way God relates to the world.

As I have indicated above, Page's notion of pansyntheism is an excellent way of describing the work of the Spirit of Wisdom in creation and focusing on the immanence of God. However, I am less convinced that this is an adequate means of portraying the rich tapestry of God's relationship with the created order, in particular God's transcendence and Trinity. For Page, God's transcendence just means that God is independent of limited human thought and action. She criticises any belief in transcendence in terms of a God removed from the world in a 'distant heaven' that she attributes to Moltmann.[92] Nonetheless, for Moltmann heaven is not as remote as she implies. Rather, heaven means God's potentiality for the earth, it is the storehouse of the possibilities for the earth in both time and space.[93] He distinguishes the field of potencies in God from

[92] Page, *Web*, 44.
[93] Moltmann, *God in Creation*, 164–8. See also C. Deane-Drummond, 'Jürgen Moltmann on Heaven', in A. Lane (ed.), *The Unseen World*, Exeter: Paternoster, 1997, 49–64

that of the earth itself, which allows a greater emphasis on the transcendence of God.

Page's interpretation of Christ is also significant in this context. For her, Jesus Christ is the exemplar of human behaviour in his mutuality of relationship with God. He was one who truly listened to God in his inner being. He becomes incarnate 'because in his words and actions (his concurrence) that possibility and presence become visible and effective'.[94] However, this seems to remove any possibility that the relationship between God and creation is a triune relationship. If God is thought of in a unitary monistic way, then ironically the relational aspects of the Being of God are lost even within a claim of friendship. By contrast, God as Wisdom and Love in the Trinity retains this relationality in the heart of who God is. Furthermore, the commitment to creation is expressed more forcefully through God's intention to become God incarnate, meaning Christ is not just humanity in tune with God, but God entering the human and biological realm in a fully physical sense as well. Only in Christ does the distinction between God and creation becomes fused. A Wisdom Christology retains the classic sense of God entering into creation in a unique way in a single human life.

Wisdom also allows for 'bottom up' causation described by scientists as existing at the dawn of existence alongside a complementary 'top down' approach without being identified with either. There is freedom in creation as expressed in human freedom that is not compromised by divine Wisdom. Indeed human wisdom at its best becomes a mirror of divine Wisdom. We learn to listen to the created world around us in a way that lets it speak, to discern *goodness* where it exists. Wisdom is not just about knowledge, about information, but it *includes* these in an organic relationship to the whole. Above all this view allows for the apophatic tradition that admits that we can never discover the full Wisdom of God or fully understand life in all its complexities. It refuses to allow science to dictate the details of the way God works in the world, reducing God to a modern empiricist. The alternative 'top down' approaches,

[94] Page, *Web*, 62.

while they avoid this dilemma, can easily slide into a modern form of deism. While they can explain the interaction of the world in its complexity, they are weaker when it comes to the question of origins.

Conclusions

I have suggested in this chapter some of the ways in which Wisdom can inform and reform a theology of creation. I have argued that the significance of Wisdom for creation moves beyond a narrow Christological referent and includes participation in the work of the Trinity. In particular, a cosmic pneumatology emerges in a way that challenges previous attempts to confine the work of the Spirit to the human community. I suggest that there is a strong biblical basis for aligning the work of the Spirit with Wisdom. The early theology of Irenaeus also makes connections between the Spirit and Wisdom in a way that helps to clarify the joint work of Wisdom and Word in the work of creation. I argue that the work of Wisdom makes most sense once it is considered to be integral to the Being of the divine Trinity. Such a view, which echoes the theology of Augustine, can include an understanding of the Trinity as Love. In addition, I suggest that Wisdom can become the means through which we can image God according to feminine metaphors. This is a necessary corrective to the dominance of male images in the history of Christian theology. Nonetheless, I consider that these male images are not so much replaced by female images, as allowed to exist alongside in a complementary manner. Drawing on the above insights, I suggest, further, that the dynamics of God's involvement with creation can be described through use of Wisdom language. Creation is through Wisdom, but in Love. In particular I show how the creative process can become the work of the whole Trinity, distinguishing the particular roles of the Spirit of Wisdom and the Christ, as Wisdom incarnate. I argue against finding evidence for a cosmic Christology in the initial acts of creation, rather Christology reaches creation through re-creation in the Spirit of Christ. Finally, I suggest ways in which the language of creation through Wisdom can take account of modern science, especially cosmology. Drawing particularly on Page's idea of pansyntheism, I show how this model can be used to describe God's immanence in the world through the Spirit of Wisdom. Nonetheless, creation is never static, but always dynamic, moving forward to completion. How can this future be compatible with God creating the world in freedom? In particular how can the future of humanity be reconciled with the future of the earth? I begin to explore possible answers to these questions in the chapter that follows.

5

The End of Creation

I suggested in the first chapter that if science is to be true to itself then it needs to be a search for wisdom. In one sense the contribution of theology is a reminder of the high calling of scientists to seek after wisdom, understood as an interpretation of knowledge that is not separated from the ethical claims of truth and goodness. Theology, too, may offer its own interpretation of the meaning of wisdom. However, wisdom is more than just a heuristic tool for relating science and theology. An idea that I have developed throughout this book is that the dynamic of God's interaction with the world is in Love through Wisdom. The significance of this understanding of a theology of nature has a bearing on pneumatology, as I discussed in the last chapter. This brings us to the theological language of wisdom as a dynamic interpretation of God's immanence in the world. While the Russian sophiologists' visionary interpretation remind us of the mediatory role of wisdom between God and creation, Aquinas's understanding points to a practical task of humanity. Furthermore, wisdom is significant for feminist theology in suggesting a language about God that develops feminine metaphors. But how is our present understanding of creation to be related to the future of the earth? In particular, what has the language of wisdom to contribute to an understanding of the dynamic between creation and new creation? How might we envisage the end of creation?

Wisdom and apocalyptic

For scholars of the Old Testament the initial idea that wisdom literature could be related to the apocalyptic tradition has proved to be something of an enigma. I explored a similar problem in the last chapter, where the possibility that wisdom could be related to the activities of the Spirit seemed at first sight to be somewhat surprising. Wisdom is more often associated with the activity of the sage, while the Spirit is associated with that of the seer. The contrast seems striking.[1] While for the sage the meaning of life is immanent and is accessible through the present mundane experiences of the world; for the seer meaning is to be found in the future, the transcendent realm. A sage seeks meaning in proper conduct of life now, through social relationships, personal integrity and so on. By contrast, the seer seeks meaning in divine activity that will occur in the future. Wisdom is available to all earnestly seeking her; while for the seer revelations are given to the few from mysteries coming from another world. A sage expresses confidence in the order, harmony and balance of God's creation and the place of humanity within it; while the seer despairs of all order this side of the eschaton; there seems to be no justice meted out in this world. Yet there are pointers in another direction as well. Just as wisdom can be associated with the Spirit, so too it can become linked with prophecy and mysticism, as Mary Grey suggests.[2]

The issue of relating wisdom to the apocalyptic tradition is complicated further by the fact that the term 'apocalyptic', like eschatology, is a somewhat slippery, ill-defined category.[3] Christopher Rowland argues against conflating apocalyptic and eschatology. While a popular interpretation of the eschatology of apocalypses could suggest that they point to a future

---

[1] E. E. Johnson, *The Function of Apocalyptic and Wisdom Traditions in Romans 9–11*, Atlanta: Scholars Press, 1989, 70–1.
[2] M. C. Grey, *Prophecy and Mysticism: The Heart of the Postmodern Church*, Edinburgh: T&T Clark, 1997, 61–80.
[3] For a sharp critique, see T. F. Glasson, *Jesus and the End of the World*, Edinburgh: St Andrew Press, 1980. Also relevant is J. Carmignac, *Le Mirage de l'Eschatologie*, Paris: Letouzey et Ané, 1979.

that is ahistorical, it is significant that 'their authors expected a vindication of their righteousness within the world of men, not in some intangible existence beyond the sphere of history'.[4] Furthermore, the eschatological expectations within apocalyptic literature are neither uniform nor confined to this genre alone. Hence to use the term 'apocalyptic' to describe a particular kind of eschatology is not really justified.[5] The possible connection between wisdom and apocalyptic becomes less surprising once apocalyptic literature is no longer perceived simply in terms of a particular eschatological framework. Overall, both wisdom and apocalyptic literature concerned themselves with problems of human existence in this world. In certain wisdom texts, such as Job, the answer to the problem of innocent suffering comes through divine revelation. Rowland concludes that wisdom is one of the constituents of apocalyptic literature, 'indeed probably the most important of all, the quest for knowledge and the belief that some answers at least could be found'.[6] Rowland critiques von Rad's suggestion that wisdom is a source for apocalyptic literature. However, while there is little evidence for a developmental link, there is a relationship between both types of literature.[7]

Stone explores the relationship between wisdom and apocalyptic literature through a detailed analysis of their parallel lists.[8] The subject matter of the apocalypses is catalogued through these lists. He notes that wisdom and the secrets of nature are included in the subject matter along with astronomy, meteorology, cosmology and uranography. Many elements of the lists present in 4 *Ezra* and 2 *Baruch*, for example, have their parallels in Job 28 and 38, especially with reference to creation themes. He also notes the presence of interrogative

[4] C. Rowland, *The Open Heaven*, London: SPCK, 1982, 38.
[5] Rowland, *Open Heaven*, 26–9; 37.
[6] Rowland, *Open Heaven*, 208.
[7] Rowland, *Open Heaven*, 204. See G. von Rad, *Old Testament Theology II: The Theology of Israel's Prophetic Traditions*, trans. D. M. G. Stalker, Edinburgh: Oliver & Boyd, 1965, 306–8.
[8] M. E. Stone, 'Lists of Revealed Things in the Apocalyptic Literature', in F. M. Cross, W. E. Lemke and P. D. Miller (eds), *Magnalia Dei: The Mighty Acts of God, Essays on the Bible and Archaeology in Memory of G. Ernst Wright*, New York: Doubleday & Co., 1976, 414–52.

lists more often associated with wisdom literature. For example, the form of rhetorical questions that pose the inaccessibility of Wisdom and the greatness of Wisdom, found in passages such as Sirach 8.4–5 or Wisdom 9.13–18, is also expressed in 2 *Baruch* 14.8–9. A similar passage is found in 4 *Ezra* 4.10–11.⁹ These examples support Rowland's conclusion that there is an integration of wisdom language and ideas into apocalyptic literature.

Stone notes an even more striking development in the pseudepigraphon known as *1 Enoch (Ethiopic Enoch)*. In *1 Enoch* 93.11–14 rhetorical questions about wisdom are replaced by rhetorical questions about the heavenly secrets. However, the context of this passage is one where, in *1 Enoch* 93.10 the elect will receive 'sevenfold instruction concerning all His creation'.¹⁰ Stone believes that this implies that the possibility of such knowledge of the heavenlies does exist, but *only* the righteous will receive it. He argues that both the form and the language of wisdom have been reinterpreted and reused for the purposes of the apocalyptic writing. In this case at least, wisdom is invested with a *new meaning*. The unknowability of creation, as expressed in the wisdom literature, is now proclaimed as accessible to the seer through divine revelation.

The above survey suggests that wisdom and apocalyptic are not as disparate as we might have thought, indeed wisdom is readily taken up and used in a way that enlarges and clarifies the apocalyptic tradition. Wisdom is relevant, then, not just for theological reflection on creation, but also reflection on the end of creation as well. Furthermore, as I will show below, wisdom in the book of *Enoch* provides a way of relating creation and its ultimate end in a way that provides a rather different model from the linear progression model that has characterised much Christian reflection on the history of humanity and the cosmos. I will explore the way this might be related to the more linear models of the history of creation later in this chapter.

---

⁹ Stone, 'Lists', 421–3.
¹⁰ Stone, 'Lists', 425, see 423–6.

The wisdom of 1 Enoch

The language used in *Enoch* is somewhat bizarre to our modern ears, a heady mixture of stories about fallen angels, corruption of kings and references to links with stars, alchemy and the like. However, the mythological world of this writer would have been familiar to those in the early Christian Church and gives a more profound basis on which to understand the apocalyptic imagery of the New Testament. Writers in the early Christian Church, including Irenaeus, used the Book of *Enoch*, but it soon fell out of favour and was eventually declared outside the canon by Augustine of Hippo in the fifth century.

The narrative of *Enoch* is interesting, not just because of the connection between wisdom and apocalyptic, but because of the way it points to the links between creation, Fall and new creation. The early part of *The Book of Watchers*, which makes up the first section of *1 Enoch*, retells the creation story of Genesis, but more details are included about the Fall. The Fall of humanity now is intricately connected with the fall of angels. One angel, known as Asael, brought heavenly knowledge to the earth, that of metallurgy for weapons of war for men, 'adornments', precious metals and cosmetics for women, and it was this that corrupted the earth by encouraging human beings to crave for forbidden knowledge and abuse women. It seems then, that the Fall amounts to a misuse of power and abuse of wisdom, which 'manifests itself on earth in an exactly parallel form, the abuse of women and the corruption of creation'.[11] The gift to the elect is the gift of both the earth and of wisdom, as 5.7 and 5.8 suggests:

> And for the elect there will be light and joy and peace, and they will inherit the earth: but for you the godless, there will be execration (5.7).

> Then shall wisdom be given to the elect, and all of them shall live and sin no more, either through sinning unwittingly or from pride: but those who have wisdom will be humble. In an intelligent

[11] M. Barker, *The Lost Prophet: The Book of Enoch and Its Influence on Christianity*, London: SPCK, 1988, 38.

man it [wisdom] is illumination, and to a prudent man it is understanding; and they shall not err (5.8).[12]

It is significant that human wisdom is lost through ungodliness
and pride, the sin most commonly attributed to fallen angels.

Yet it is clear that Enoch, who is counted as wise before
God, is given access to the secrets of the creation of the world
through a heavenly journey.[13] This seems to contradict the Book
of Job, where the understanding of the creation of the world
is declared as too difficult for him, such knowledge belonging
to God alone. For Enoch, the gift of knowledge made him like
one of the angels and brought him into the presence of God.
Margaret Barker believes that this seems to suggest a lost
tradition in the early Jewish literature. She suggests:

> This association of the vision of God and scientific knowledge
> (what seems strange to us was science to them) is very important,
> not because the scientific knowledge is in any way accurate, but
> because it is entrusted to those who have a special calling into the
> presence of God. Knowledge of the workings of creation is part
> of the vision of God.[14]

On the one hand there is the claim that knowledge opens the
eyes of Adam and Eve and is the root of evil. On the other
hand, knowledge brings Enoch into the presence of God.[15]
Nonetheless, *Enoch*'s account of the Fall connects knowledge
with the pride that desires more knowledge than is given, so
Enoch elaborates ways in which knowledge can, itself, become
corrupting. The outcome is the desecration of the earth and
the abuse of women. While the secrets of creation are known
for those wise in the eyes of God, those who become self-
inflated by their knowledge fall back into mortality and are
no longer gifted with wisdom.

The second section of *Enoch* (37–71), known as *The
Parables* or *The Similitudes*, is a vision of wisdom. It is a

---

[12] M. Black, *The Book of Enoch or I Enoch: A New English Edition*, Leiden:
E. J. Brill, 1985, 27.

[13] Enoch went on this journey after Asael, the fallen angel, pleaded with him to
intercede on his behalf, a remarkable role reversal. See chapters 13–16 and
17–36 for an account of his journeys. Black, *Enoch*, 32–42.

[14] Barker, *Lost Prophet*, 53.

[15] Barker, *Lost Prophet*, 24.

book about judgement on the kings of the world and the fallen angels, presided over by the Son of Man, and identified with Enoch himself. Parables were used to describe correspondences in the world of both heaven and earth as a basis of teaching, but also as a way of identifying where such correspondences went awry and could become the basis of healing and magic.[16] *Enoch*'s vision of creation is apocalyptic, but one that led to an understanding of the secrets of this present earthly and material existence. It is like a hidden agenda in reality that has lasting relevance. *The Parables* speak of a covenant or oath that binds all creation (*1 Enoch* 41; 69). This covenant secures the order of creation, harking back to ancient mythology that had common currency in the ancient world. Such an oath reflects the idea of promise between all parties, but may also have hinted at the binding of destructive forces that would destroy creation. Such ideas of precariousness in the order of creation and the ongoing restraint of evil forces are only hinted at in the Genesis account, where the idea of chaos is mentioned almost in passing. The covenant idea in the Old Testament included both natural and moral laws, interwoven together rather like a spider web.[17] The judgement follows from the breaking of covenant, portrayed as disasters in war or in the realm of nature. This parallels accounts in Isaiah 24.4–6; 21–22. The future of creation is now portrayed as a healing of that which is broken and damaged, rather than progress towards a known goal.

The third section of *Enoch* (72–82), known as *The Astronomy Book*, is a revelation to Enoch of all the laws of heavenly bodies, given by the angel Uriel. The bulk of this is a detailed description of the movement of the sun and moon, understood loosely in terms of the science of the time and the way the movements of both affect the months and seasons. Much of this sounds curious and strange, for example the sun is named as the same size as the moon, but seven times as bright (*1 Enoch* 72.37). Barker is optimistic about the accuracy of this text, believing that this shows the writer of *Enoch* knew

---

[16] Barker, *Lost Prophet*, 66.
[17] Barker, *Lost Prophet*, 83.

about the secret calendar of the day and was well versed in current scientific ideas of the time.[18] Otto Neugebauer is more sceptical, believing that the discussion on the lunar year in chapter 74 is a later addition and that the scribe only had a vague idea about the lunar cycle, confusing Alexandrian years with those recorded in *Enoch* and ending up with some spurious numerical identities.[19] Similarly, the idea that some winds bring prosperity and others calamity is presented in such a way that it seems to have lost all touch even with known empirical data of this period.[20] Again, the geographical data described in chapter 77 has a mystical agenda, rather than containing an accurate portrayal of features. Nonetheless, whatever the accuracy of the science, even according to the standards of the day, the message is clear: there is a proper time and season for all things, and we alter the calendar at our peril.

In the Old Testament we find a parallel tradition where those who abuse wisdom become mortal and no longer live forever, like the angels.[21] In *Enoch* the language of the stars seems to be a reference to angels.[22] The link between angels and stars echoes a passage in Daniel 12.4, where the wise are described as those who shine like stars forever. Margaret Barker suggests that 'Wisdom was a key factor in the apocalyptists' picture of transformation, even though it is not clear whether wisdom effected the change, or was the result of it'.[23] However, the wisdom suggested as necessary was not a crude dualistic speculation, since the apocalyptic tradition sees the potential unity between heaven and earth. Hence:

> Upper and lower, future and present were not essentially separate, but could only be described in terms of each other. The visible world was described in terms of the invisible, and vice versa.

[18] Barker, *Lost Prophet*, 24–5.
[19] O. Neugebauer, 'Appendix on the Astronomical Chapters (72–82)', in Black *Enoch*, Notes to chapter 74, 399–401.
[20] Black, *Enoch*, Notes to chapter 76, 405.
[21] See Genesis 3, Psalm 82 and Ezekiel 28.
[22] M. Barker, *The Older Testament: The Survival of Themes from the Ancient Royal Cult in Sectarian Judaism and Early Christianity*, London: SPCK, 1987, 29.
[23] Barker, *Older Testament*, 29.

Thus the *māsāl*, the characteristic teaching form of the wise men, can describe the heavenly world to teach about the earth, as in the Similitudes (Num 24.3; Isa 14), or the natural world to teach about the heavenly, as in the Gospels. It is a great mistake to read apocalyptic as a dualistic system; nothing could have been more completely integrated.[24]

The question of how to relate the wisdom of the apocalyptic writers to that in the Old Testament is made more difficult by the fragmentary nature of pre-exilic sources. The theme of wisdom in *Enoch* does not seem to be dependant on the mantic wisdom tradition, as we might have expected, since it draws on traditional wisdom, such as that found in Proverbs.[25] Nonetheless, the portrayal of wisdom in *Enoch*, which is linked to heavenly images, is very different from that of wisdom in post-exilic traditions, such as Ben Sira, where wisdom is associated with the Torah. In *Enoch* wisdom comes by a mystical revelation and is related to the Son of Man, who as yet has not come to earth.

Wisdom and apocalyptic in the New Testament

Additional examples of an interweaving of strands of wisdom and apocalyptic ideas can be found in the New Testament. Romans 1.18–32 is apocalyptic in speaking of the divine wrath anticipated for those who refuse to acknowledge God. Their claim to be wise is confounded by their wickedness. As Johnson points out: 'Paul employs language that can be said to stand at the very hearts of both apocalyptic and wisdom contexts: God's eschatological wrath on idolatry, on the one hand, and the foolishness of idolatry on the other.'[26] The well-known passage in Romans 8.14–23 speaks of all of creation, groaning as in travail, waiting for future redemption. As I discussed in Chapters 2 and 4, it is often used to support a cosmic

---

[24] Barker, *Older Testament*, 29.
[25] J. C. Vanderkam, *Enoch and the Growth of an Apocalyptic Tradition*, Monograph Series No. 16, Washington: *Catholic Biblical Quarterly*, 1984, 172.
[26] E. Johnson, 'Wisdom and Apocalyptic in Paul', in L. G. Perdue, B. B. Scott, W. J. Wiseman (eds), *In Search of Wisdom: Essays in Memory of John G. Gammie*, Westminster: John Knox Press, 1993, 273.

Christology, though I have argued that it is more relevant for a cosmic pneumatology. In the present context, the background influence is more likely to be the traditions aligned with *Enoch*, envisaging an ordered, but precarious creation. Barker suggests that this tradition is more ancient than the Genesis account, which tended to render passive the great threats to creation. The binding of evil forces, casting out of demons and the restoration of creation speaks of a world where magicians, healers and wonder-workers were common. She suggests that *Enoch* in particular may be the background influence on Romans 8.[27] In the light of *Enoch* we can interpret Romans as suggesting that the new sons of God, who have acquired angelic status by the gift of the Spirit, will release the binding of creation.

Wisdom is again portrayed in apocalyptic guise in the Book of Revelation. In this case wisdom *is* revelation. The revelation includes commentary that relates not just to the human community, but to the whole cosmos, symbolically depicted as the heaven, earth and sea. The secrets of the end time are revealed, but for a purpose, so that appropriate action can be taken now.[28] In Revelation 5.12 and 7.12 hymns are sung to the throne of wisdom, but only God and the Lamb are worthy recipients of wisdom. In Revelation 5.13 the circle of worship includes the whole creation, a doxology of praise addressed to God and the Lamb, who represents Christ. Tina Pippin suggests that the personification of Sophia in different figures of Mother of the Messiah, the Son of Man and the Spirit that we find in Revelation leads to Sophia's disempowerment in comparison to the figure of Lady Wisdom in Proverbs.[29] However, it seems to me that Sophia, in being identified with God, Jesus and the Spirit, reinforces the idea that she is of *divine* origin. I will return to her identification with Mary again below.

While the specific dependence of Revelation on *Enoch* is difficult to prove, it seems likely that there was a shared literary

[27] Barker, *Lost Prophet*, 89–90.
[28] T. Pippin, 'Wisdom and Apocalyptic in the Apocalypse of John', in Perdue, Scott and Wiseman (eds), *In Search of Wisdom*, 285–95.
[29] Pippin, 'Wisdom', 293.

tradition in both Jewish and Christian literature.[30] Many apocalyptic texts, including *Ezra* and Job, speak in mythological language of monsters such as Leviathan or Behemoth. In Revelation the sea monster and the earth monster are not supernatural powers, but political powers opposed to God that will be ultimately overthrown with the coming of God's reign. Supernatural forces of evil are focused on the figure of the Dragon. The defeat of the Dragon is identified with the slaughter of the Lamb. There seems to be no Jewish precedent for representation of ultimate evil in the form of a Dragon.[31]

The ultimate future of the Church, portrayed as the ideal Bride in the final chapters of Revelation, anticipates the Church at the consummation of history.[32] The prayer of the Church for the coming of Christ anticipates the coming of the Bridegroom. Revelation 22.17 promises the water of life of the new creation, yet in some sense it is available in the present, as living in the context of the New Jerusalem. The vision of the Woman in the Sun, described in chapter 12, is commonly interpreted as a reference to the people of God giving birth to the Messiah. However, as one might expect, Orthodox and Roman Catholic traditions associate her with the Virgin Mary, who ultimately anticipates the pure Bride at the close of the age. The Bride is given the task of 'leading the whole Church, and together with it the whole redeemed world of Creation, into that perfect union of the created body with its Divine Head which can be described only as the Marriage of the Lamb, understood as the *skopus*, the final goal of Creation itself'.[33] Père Louis Bouyer suggests that the personified Wisdom of God is ultimately identified with the glorified creation, redeemed through the blood of the Lamb. In the early Middle Ages, liturgical texts composed in Moscow applied the themes of biblical Wisdom to Mary, seen in the

---

[30] R. Bauckham, *The Climax of Prophecy: Studies on the Book of Revelation*, Edinburgh: T&T Clark, 1993, 39.
[31] Bauckham, *Climax*, 186–93.
[32] Bauckham, *Climax*, 167–8.
[33] P. L. Bouyer, 'An Introduction to the Theme of Wisdom in the Tradition', in *Le Messager Orthodoxe* 98 (1985), 149–61, citation 160.

light of Revelation 12. As Mother of God she becomes the eschatological icon of the final glory of the Church and the whole creation. It is significant, perhaps, that this vision of Mary is also a feature of the Western Church. For example, in Chartres Cathedral, dedicated to Our Lady, one of its most significant stained-glass windows shows the influence of the Sophiology of Bernard Silvestrus.[34] Yet worship at the throne of Wisdom is reserved for God and the Lamb, implying a distinction between the presence of Sophia in Mary and that in God and Christ. This distinction is important, as it allows for an elevation of Mary as the icon of divine Sophia, but not as divine Sophia incarnate.

Apocalypse and eco-feminist theology

Given this Sophianic interpretation of the future of creation, it is worth considering how this contrasts with the future of the earth envisaged in feminist eco-theologies, such as the theology of Rosemary Radford Ruether and Grace Jantzen. As Brenda Meehan suggests, it is true that ideas, such as cosmic interconnectedness and a valuing of nature, are common to both McFague's and Ruether's eco-theology and resonate with Sophiological interpretations of creation.[35] However, I shall argue that it is the understanding of wisdom in redemptive categories, particularly that of the apocalyptic tradition, that highlights the distinctive nature of this tradition compared with eco-theologies based on Gaia or images of the world in terms of the body of God.

Ruether's writing is sensitive to the particular theological categories that have become dominant in Western culture, locating a form of dualism in the themes of creation and redemption. In *Gaia and God* she tries to keep different aspects of the Christian story intact, even while reinterpreting the concepts in a radical way. The idea of God becomes transformed in a revised understanding of covenant, so that the ancient jubilee laws provided a corrective to exploitative practices, either between humans or against the earth. The

---

[34] Bouyer, 'Introduction', 151–2.
[35] B. Meehan, 'Wisdom/Sophia, Russian Identity, and Western Feminist Theology', *Cross Currents* 46 (1996), 162.

special task of humans becomes that of caretakers of the whole community of creation.[36] Nonetheless, humans are ultimately accountable to God for their actions.

The idea of Gaia seems to be related to a recovery of the sacramental tradition, in particular a reworking of the early cosmological images of the presence of the divine. Drawing on Matthew Fox, Teilhard de Chardin and process theology, she develops an interpretation of Gaia, understood as the feminine voice in the heart of matter itself. She admits that a simplistic return to the Goddess is not really adequate, what we need is a 'coincidence of opposites' in the manner that we find in subatomic physics.[37]

However, in her more recent eco-theology she reinforces the idea of divine immanence so that any notion of transcendence understood as immortality seems to disappear completely from view. In particular, she insists that mortality itself is not sin, but needs to be embraced as part of life. She suggests that humanity needs to see itself as part of an organic community, one that accepts that following death it will rise up again in new forms.[38] Similarly, she suggests that our bodily matter

> lives on in plants, animals and soil, even as our own living bodies are composed of substances that once were once part of rocks, plants and animals, stretching back to prehistoric ferns and reptiles, before that to ancient biota that floated on the first seas of the earth, and before that to the stardust of exploding galaxies.[39]

Acceptance of our material, earthly nature and its ability to be taken up into the processes of the cosmos is all that apparently we can hope for in the future. While she admits that this 'spirituality of recyling' also 'demands a deep conversion of consciousness', it is less certain how far this can be

---

[36] R. Radford Ruether, *Gaia and God: An Ecofeminist Theology of Earth Healing*, London: SCM Press, 1993, 226–7.

[37] Ruether, *Gaia*, 247.

[38] R. Radford Ruether, 'Ecofeminism: Symbolic and Social Connections of the Oppression of Women and the Domination of Nature' in R. S. Gottlieb (ed.), *This Sacred Earth: Religion, Nature, Environment*, New York/London: Routledge, 1996, 332–3.

[39] R. Radford Ruether, *Introducing Redemption in Christian Feminism*, Sheffield: Sheffield Academic Press, 1998, 119.

thought of as a Christian interpretation of future redemption. It certainly has moved away completely from the apocalyptic tradition that anticipates a new creation radically distinct from the old, even if signs are still available in the present. It is as if the death of Christ on the cross is acceptance of mortality, so we surrender to the 'Great Matrix of Being' that is renewing life through regrowth following death. Redemption seems to collapse into creation in a way that seems unable to live with the tension between God and Gaia that she outlines in her earlier work. While the strong dualism that Ruether is keen to rebut is not an option, the collapse of distinctions that her cyclical view seems to imply could lead to resignation, rather than hope. As the book of *Enoch* showed, the idea of creation as a web is not incompatible with the notion of a new future, one where significant transformation takes place in the light of such an anticipated end.

The concept that the earth is God's body as a way of re-imaging the relationship between God and creation is spelt out formally in Grace Jantzen's *God's World: God's Body* and then in Sallie McFague's *The Body of God*.[40] Jantzen insists that it is the universe, rather than the earth as such that is the body of God. But what is the ultimate future of creation according to this view? She suggests that dualism serves to justify controlling attitudes towards the other, be it sexuality, feelings, women, other races or the earth.[41] The idea of sin as misuse of power towards women and the natural world echoes the concept of the Fall in *Enoch*. However, redemption for Jantzen is not through a mysterious Son of Man figure who intercedes with God. For her the solution is to heal the fear by tapping into the Spirit of God understood as one who brings liberation and healing.

It seems to me that Jantzen is correct to identify fear as a key factor in motivating oppression, especially in the human

---

[40] G. Jantzen, *God's World: God's Body*, London: Darton, Longman & Todd, 1984; S. McFague, *The Body of God: An Ecological Theology*, London: SCM Press, 1993.

[41] G. Jantzen, 'Healing our Brokenness: The Spirit and Creation', in M. H. MacKinnon and M. McIntyre (eds), *Readings in Ecology and Feminist Theology*, Kansas City: Sheed & Ward, 1995, 284–98

community. I have more reservations about whether fear encourages a rapacious attitude to the earth, though the habit of control no doubt spills over into all our attitudes. Yet if we examine more closely her understanding of Spirit in creation, it seems that this is not Spirit in the traditional sense of the Trinity, but rather the Spirit *is* God, understood as immanent in the world.

In *Becoming Divine*, her most radical book so far, she suggests that pantheism is the most fruitful way of considering who God is.[42] Moreover, she locates the fear of pantheism as the fear of a loss of identity, defined as the maintenance of boundaries. She believes that once we see God as in the world in a pantheistic way, this leads to a new vision for the future of the earth. Now: 'Instead of the mastery over the earth which is rapidly bringing about its destruction there would be reverence and sensitivity; instead of seeing domination as godlike we would recognise it as utterly contradictory to divinity.'[43] Yet it seems to me that there is no reason to believe that pantheism would lead to this change in attitude. She suggests, quite rightly, that it is not enough simply to valorise categories such as women, earth, bodiliness at the expense of men, intellect and spirit. Yet her pantheistic approach inevitably tries to collapse one into the other, just as dualism forces their separation.

Even though, as she claims, the divine cannot be reduced to the earth, it seems that her idea of transcendence is located primarily in the linear notion of becoming. Following the French feminist philosopher Irigaray, she suggests that transcendence is 'the projected horizon for our embodied becoming'.[44] Rejecting panentheism as too close to dualism leaves her vulnerable to the charge of reinstating the idea of the goddess. For the transcendental mode of God is the female divine. She argues that if anyone rejects this view, this simply comes from the elemental fear of being swallowed up in the maternal womb, a fear of loss of boundaries. Yet it is hard to

---

[42] G. Jantzen, *Becoming Divine: Towards a Feminist Philosophy of Religion*, Manchester: Manchester University Press, 1998.
[43] Jantzen, *Becoming Divine*, 269.
[44] Jantzen, *Becoming Divine*, 271.

understand what this transcendence means other than the notion that the person is more than the body. Furthermore, it is a future that seems to be emerging from the present conditions of the world without any reference to the final end, understood in terms of a new coming. For her all eschatology seems to be collapsed into the present, so that the 'pantheist symbolic in which that which is divine precisely is this world and its ceaselessly shifting bodies and signifiers, then it is this which must be celebrated as of ultimate value . . . a pantheist symbolic supports a symbolic of natality, a flourishing of the earth and those who dwell upon it'.[45] Thus all worship must be directed earthwards in celebration of the interconnectedness of life. It seems, then, as if eschatological themes as expressed in the idea of *parousia* are now lost from view. The idea flourishing is earth-centred, and while a welcome corrective to the arrogant control of the natural world, is unlikely to contain the spiritual resources needed to combat the forces of evil that threaten the life of the cosmos.

Science and the end of creation

Given the reluctance of some eco-theologians to speak in categories of redemption, it is worth asking what kind of future might be envisaged from the perspective of science. What is the final fate of the earth according to modern cosmology? Such projections into the future are inevitably speculative. However, like the science of beginnings, the science of the end does need to be taken into account by contemporary theologians. There is a tendency to be so obsessed with the ideas surrounding the origin of the universe that its possible fate slips quietly from view. Yet it seems to me that it is only in the light of a careful consideration of this future that theology can have something meaningful to say to our present world.

The threat of a nuclear holocaust and ecological collapse has forced us to consider the real possibility that the earth will end in a way that was not true for earlier generations. Yet apart from this, modern science points to a final destiny of the earth in language that echoes that of the apocalyptic

---

[45] Jantzen, *Becoming Divine*, 274.

writers. The fate of the earth is intricately related to the fate of the sun. The first stage is the increase in the sun's temperature, accompanied by an increase in brightness, but eventually the sun becomes a giant red sphere.[46] The heat in itself will destroy much of known life, ice caps will melt causing floods, deserts will increase and even the oceans will boil, effectively incinerating all life as we know it today. The final fate is worse still, for 'the Earth will be slowly but inexorably vaporised and will then probably be engulfed by an expanding sun'.[47] In the sun itself, nuclear reactions will fuel an even greater rise in temperature, even after the earth as we know it has come to an end. Eventually it will take on a bluer colour, but when all the nuclear fuel is exhausted it will become a 'black dwarf'. Stars other than the sun follow the same sort of fate, disappearing into black holes or becoming black dwarfs.

While serious discussions of the end of the universe are still far more limited compared with those about its origin, there are some signs that interest in this area is increasing. An important question relates to whether the universe is an open or closed system. If there is insufficient matter, then the universe is expanding indefinitely. The fate of the universe is one known as 'heat-death', rather like the description that I outlined above. An open universe will continue to expand indefinitely until it runs out of energy. The German physicist, Hermon von Helmholtz, predicted the so-called heat-death of the universe as early as 1854.[48] However, if the universe is closed, then there is enough matter to halt its gradual expansion and bring it back into a 'big crunch'. Calculating the amount of matter is very difficult, especially since much exists as unseen, 'dark matter'. Such matter is 'visible' indirectly by distortions in light caused by gravity. Recent data on the total amount of matter in the universe seems to suggest that the universe is more likely to be a closed, rather than an open system.[49] The

---

[46] See A. R. Peacocke, *Creation and the World of Science*, Oxford: Clarendon Press, 1979, 320.

[47] Peacocke, *Creation*, 325.

[48] M. W. Worthing, *God, Creation and Contemporary Physics*, Minneapolis: Fortress Press, 1996, 160–75.

[49] Worthing, *God*, 162ff.

two alternatives to the obliteration of matter that science seems
to present is either an ever expanding universe or an implosion
of galaxies in a 'big crunch'. Even if the universe went through
cycles of expansion and contraction, eventually the fate of
matter is the same, that of total obliteration.

Alongside this very gloomy scientific picture of the fate of the
earth, more recently much more optimistic portraits
of the fate of intelligent life have appeared in the writings of
contemporary physicists such as Freeman Dyson and Frank
Tipler. Freeman Dyson bases his model of the future of life
presupposing that the universe is an open system. He suggests
that given the adaptation of life to the present conditions in
the lifetime of the planet, there is every reason to suppose that
intelligent life on other planets might be able to evolve from
present-day humans.[50] Indeed, it is faith in the ability of this
intelligent life that gives him the optimism to suggest that life
may be able to guide the universe for its own purposes. He
resists the current theories of matter that seem to suggest its
ultimate instability, so that protons eventually disappear into
radiation. Such instability would inevitably lead to the dis-
appearance of life. Even then he believes that patterns of life
and consciousness may be able to be transferred from one
medium to another.[51] He argues against the classical idea that
an open universe leads inevitably to an equilibrium state at
constant temperature and entropy, according to the second
law of thermodynamics. If the universe is closed rather than
open, we still have 10^{10} years to find a way out! Dyson admits
that intelligent life as we know it will not survive, rather it
needs to become embodied in new forms, so that 'the preferred
embodiment for life in the remote future must be something
like Hoyle's black cloud, a large semblance of dust grains carry-
ing positive and negative charges, organising itself and com-
municating with itself by means of electromagnetic forces'.[52]
Yet does such a vision give us any more cause for hope when
compared with the earlier accounts of a slow heat-death?

[50] F. Dyson, 'Time Without End: Physics and Biology in an Open Universe', in
   Reviews of Modern Physics 51:3 (1989), 447–60.
[51] F. Dyson, *Infinite in All Directions*, New York: Harper & Row, 1988, 110ff.
[52] Dyson, 'Time', 454.

Frank Tipler's portrait shows some similarities to that of Dyson, though he uses theological language to support his views.[53] Unlike Dyson, Tipler assumes that the universe is a closed system. His position is a curious one, in that while claiming to be an atheist, he wraps his physical models in the language of God. He suggests that the future does make an imprint on the present, since the physical laws do not change with time. However, it is by no means clear how this might be an imprint from ahead, in the way Christian eschatology would suggest. Furthermore, immortality for Tipler seems to mean simply information processing. Such processing is dependent on increasing availability of energy as the 'final singularity' approaches. While proper time will inevitably come to an end in a closed universe, he suggests that time could exist for infinite subjective time. His speculations that probes loaded with genetic information will be able to reproduce humanity in other far-flung locations seem both far-fetched and dehumanising. For him distinctions between living and non-living no longer exist, until life so pervades and controls the system that it reaches what he terms the 'Omega Point'.[54] While he borrows the language from Teilhard de Chardin, he modifies his theology in important ways. While Teilhard understood God as immanent in an evolving universe and yet transcendent through a form of pan-en-theism, Tipler cannot ultimately avoid pantheism. For Tipler such an 'Omega Point' means total omnipresence and omnipotence and omniscience, the final convergence of space and time through which a new resurrection is made possible, one that is envisaged as the Person, who is God. Such a resurrection of past humanity seems to be in the forms of light rays, extracted as information to be used at the very instant of the Omega Point.[55]

---

[53] See F. J. Tipler, *The Physics of Immortality: Modern Cosmology: God and the Resurrection of the Dead*, Basingstoke: Macmillan, 1994.

[54] The idea of the Omega Point appears in earlier publications, see J. Barrow and F. Tipler, *The Anthropic Cosmological Principle*, Oxford: Clarendon Press, 1986, 676ff.

[55] F. Tipler, 'The Omega Point as Eschaton: Answers to Pannenberg's Questions for Scientists', *Zygon* 24:2 (1989), 217–53; Tipler, *Physics of Immortality*, 220ff.

What is left of the reality of human life in such speculations? If this is a scientific eschatology, it is an apocalypse indeed. Yet it is one with no real hope of transformation and new life. It is in stark contrast to the biblical view of the end where ultimately, following immense struggles, all creation is caught up in praise and worship of God. In the models of both Dyson and Tipler, science has refused to let go of intelligence and turned this into a god to be perpetuated *ad infinitum*. Such pride is more likely to accelerate the fate of the destruction of the earth, rather than allow its perpetuation. Indeed, equating knowledge with information emerging from the pride of humanity is the ultimate sin of the angels, described in the apocalypse of Enoch. Far from being a cosmological vision of the future, it is one that rests ultimately with human abilities alone, even though such abilities are recast in theological language. In this it fosters the idea of control and domination of humanity over not just this earth, but far into the outer reaches of the galaxy as well.[56] Given these major differences, it is somewhat surprising that Wolfhart Pannenberg seems to welcome Tipler's eschatology, though it is hard to see how it is really compatible with his own position. Pannenberg believes that we should welcome Tipler's eschatology as at least it opens the window for dialogue, when compared with the earlier position in science that envisaged a totally bleak future. He believes that:

> The situation offers a new and exciting prospect for an intellectually serious development of the Christian doctrine of creation, but on the condition that theologians sacrifice their emotional subjectivity as well as the splendid isolation of a supposedly self-sufficient doctrine in order to participate in a pilgrimage of interdisciplinary discussions on conjectural interpretations of our world.[57]

While he is correct in believing that we need to take into account the latest speculations of scientists on the future of

---

[56] C. J. S. Clarke, 'Review of F. Tipler, *The Physics of Immortality*', *Theology in Green* 5:2 (1995), 45–7.

[57] W. Pannenberg, 'Theology and Science', *Princeton Seminary Bulletin* (1992), 299–310, citation on 310.

the universe, it seems to me that we need to be very careful not to endorse their theologies just in the name of inter-disciplinary harmony. He also may have misunderstood Tipler in his belief that for him the resurrection of the dead means simulation of an earlier existence. It is clear that this is not simulation in the common sense of the word, it is rather, as I have outlined above, continuation of information as energy.

Developing a cosmic eschatology

Given this pessimistic view of the future of the earth as expounded in scientific eschatology, it seems that all attempts to root eschatology just in the present conditions of this world are bound to offer little consolation. The apocalyptic language of a new coming and new beginning needs to be born in mind when constructing an adequate contemporary eschatology. The temptation to think of the future narrowly in terms of the future of human life is not confined to contemporary physics. Theologians, especially those in the Western tradition, have focused almost exclusively on the future of the human com-munity. Karl Rahner, for example, defines eschatology as 'the doctrine about man insofar as he is a being who is open to the absolute future of God himself'.[58] He believes that eschatology is not concerned with human life in isolation, but in com-munity, and the world is simply the milieu in which this community is situated.[59] He seems to understand the future as that which emerges from present human experience of grace. As Mary Grey suggests, salvation conceived in terms of community needs to be inclusive of the well-being of the whole community of the earth.[60]

---

[58] K. Rahner, *Foundations of Christian Faith: An Introduction to the Idea of Christianity*, trans. W. V. Dych, London: Darton, Longman & Todd, 1978, 431.

[59] Rahner, *Foundations*, 432.

[60] M. Grey, 'Salvation in Community: From Holy Well to Holy Waitrose', in M. Grey, D. Ford, R. Bauckham and T. Hart, *The Scope of Salvation: Theatres of God's Drama, Lincoln Lectures in Theology 1998*, Lincoln: Lincoln Cathedral Publications, 1999, 9–22.

The future of creation in Moltmann's eschatology

Jürgen Moltmann's eschatology is worth considering here, as he has consistently argued for the value of a contemporary eschatology that has a broad basis. His bold attempt to translate all of theology into the eschatological key does demonstrate a willingness to envisage the future in cosmic categories, though the focus in his earlier work *Theology of Hope* was still on history, rather than nature.[61] Moltmann distinguishes between secular and religious hope. He suggests that science on its own is powerless to decide the direction of its own future. Hence, it can only talk in terms of a world of possibilities. Moltmann speaks of the possibilities emerging from the present as *futurans*, everything is potentially there in the present, it is the future of what has already come.[62] Another way of perceiving the future is a 'coming to', or *adventus*, that is a coming of something new and different. The present is then an anticipation of this new coming. Translated into Greek *adventus* becomes *parousia*. It is prophetic in the sense of meaning the coming of God and the coming of Christ. For Moltmann the starting point for eschatology is the anticipation of God's *adventus* in the death and resurrection of Christ.

In view of this perspective it is therefore not surprising that Moltmann rejects Teilhard's absorption of evolution into salvation history.[63] In one sense Teilhard's eschatology can be welcomed as it offers a future hope that is cosmological in scope. However, the way this hope becomes expressed as the Omega Point through the elevation of humanity sets up a tension in his theology and serves to weaken the cosmic dimension at the expense of anthropology. I have already discussed how Frank Tipler has developed his ideas: the Omega Point now seems to be devoid of all contact with creaturely creation and redefined as pure information-processing. While I am sure that Teilhard would have objected to his theology

---

[61] J. Moltmann, *Theology of Hope*, trans. J. W. Leitch, London: SCM Press, 1967.

[62] J. Moltmann, *The Future of Creation*, trans. M. Kohl, London: SCM Press, 1979, 29–30.

[63] J. Moltmann, *The Way of Jesus Christ*, trans. M. Kohl, London: SCM Press, 1990, 294ff.

being used in this way, it does show a fundamental flaw implicit in his thought, namely far too great an optimism about the possibility of human achievement. His recognition of evil is certainly present, but it is dwarfed by his vision of the future. Moltmann believes that Teilhard has not recognised adequately the real ambiguity in the evolutionary process:

> Evolution always means selection. Many living things are sacrificed in order that 'the fittest' – which means the most effective and most adaptable – may survive. In this way higher and increasingly complex life systems, which can react to changed environments, undoubtedly develop. But in the same process milliards of living things fall by the wayside and disappear into evolution's rubbish bin. Evolution is not merely a constructive affair on nature's part. It is a cruel one too.[64]

In other words, by baptising the process, Teilhard's Christ seems to allow suffering as part of the process, instead of identifying with the victims. Moltmann is concerned, furthermore, that Teilhard constantly sought to find positive reasons for terrible acts of destruction. Hiroshima did not promote horror in his mind, so much as enthusiasm both for the achievement of science and for the way atomic power might promote the evolution of humanity. For Moltmann the only identification that Christ could possibly have is with the victims of Hiroshima, not with its inventors.

In this context Moltmann is surely correct to seek to install the redemptive role of Christ. Christ as redeemer is not so much associated with the complex labyrinth of evolution, as with its final redemption, a movement from the future to the past. It is possible, then, to discern in the present 'tendencies in the evolution of nature and in human history as being also parables and hints, anticipations and preparations for the coming of the messianic new creation'.[65] What might this future look like? The sabbath is the feast of creation, but is only manifested clearly at the end of creation, showing the meaning of creation in the beginning.[66] The advantage of the sabbath

[64] Moltmann, *Way*, 294.
[65] Moltmann, *Way*, 304.
[66] J. Moltmann, *God in Creation: An Ecological Doctrine of Creation*, trans. M. Kohl, London: SCM Press, 1985, 276–96.

metaphor is that it links the experience of the present with that of the future, while still pointing to a future that is yet to come.

Yet the sabbath metaphor is not intended to imply that the future of creation is simply a restoration of the pristine creation at the beginning. Moltmann believes that the eschatology of those creation spiritualities that draw on the idea of an eternal return is such that the removal of sin is now all that is required for the future redemption of the earth.[67] However, it seems to me that this is an oversimplification. Freedom from sin can *also* be associated with redemption in a more linear model of eschatology. What seems to be the most important issue is the possibility of the consummation of creation, either in the eternal present, or projected into the future. Moltmann believes that eco-feminism has reminded us to bring eschatology down to earth, so that 'there is no earthly life without death'.[68] I would concur with his critique of Ruether's attempt to find God purely in the cycles of life and death in an eschatology of the present, as I discussed earlier.

Moltmann argues that the initial creation fails to speak of creation infused with the glory of God, such as we can expect at the consummation. His notion that creation is *completed* in the new eschaton as well as simply redeemed from sin is a significant aspect of his theology.[69] The newness of the new creation echoes the apocalypse of John in the book of Revelation. Yet this is in tension with the idea that nothing is lost, but rather is brought back together in a new form, one that is able in some sense to contain the glory of God. He rejects the Lutheran theology of the seventeenth century, which envisaged a total annihilation of the earth, where only the saved will survive in heaven. Instead, he draws on the Orthodox idea of deification of the world, where it is the Spirit who transforms all of created reality. Moltmann takes a further

---

[67] J. Moltmann, *The Coming of God*, trans. M. Kohl, London: SCM Press, 1996, 261–7.

[68] Moltmann, *Coming*, 275.

[69] M. Volf, 'After Moltmann: Reflections on the Future of Eschatology', in R. Bauckham (ed.), *God Will Be All in All: The Eschatology of Jürgen Moltmann*, Edinburgh: T&T Clark, 1999, 248.

step in suggesting that at the consummation the whole world becomes the image of God, freed from transience and mortality. But what does freedom from mortality and transience mean? It appears that for him the possibility of sin no longer exists in the new creation, and this includes freedom from mortality.[70] This idea sits rather uneasily with his suggestion that in the new creation humanity continues to have human needs and dependencies, including sexual relationships and dependence on nature.[71] His portrayal of the future of nature sounds rather too idealised and I fear will be ignored by most biologists and those influenced by science.

In other words the way this earth relates in a concrete way to the life of the new earth remains something of an enigma in Moltmann's theology. Hence, he suggest that 'This earth, with its world of the living, is the real and sensorily experienceable promise of the new earth, as truly as this earthly, mortal life here is an experienceable promise of the life that is eternal, immortal.'[72] In what sense might this earth show forth the promise of the new earth? His attempt to combine nature and history in the idea of the sabbath is suggestive, but does not really tell us much about how the present creation can become linked with this motif, other than through the human community.[73] More recently he has suggested that the sabbath includes the wisdom of the fallowing principle, but this does not seem to me to take us very far.[74]

John Macquarrie's discussion of Christian hope is relevant to a cosmic eschatology as he suggests that hope must not deny human freedom. If all events are predetermined then this encourages passive waiting, rather than an active hope.[75] The problem with apocalyptic images is that, by their focus on the final annihilation at the end of creation, they could lead to a

[70] J. Moltmann, 'Can Christian Eschatology Become Post-Modern?', in Bauckham (ed.), *God Will Be*, 262–3.

[71] Moltmann, *Way*, 250–62.

[72] Moltmann, *Coming*, 279.

[73] For further discussion, see C. Deane-Drummond, *Ecology in Jürgen Moltmann's Theology*, Lampeter: Edwin Mellen, 1997, 250–3.

[74] J. Moltmann, 'The Liberation of the Future and Its Anticipations in History', in Bauckham (ed.), *God Will Be*, 284.

[75] J. Macquarrie, *Christian Hope*, Oxford: Mowbray, 1978, 8–10.

passive resignation in the present. Nonetheless, another strand in apocalyptic literature exemplified by the book of *Enoch* demonstrates a view of time that encourages interpretation of present events as having their counterpart in the heavenly realm. This leads to the image of the new creation as a healing of the web of life, rather than a progression to the new. Both images have their difficulties. While the linear image seems to detach the future from the present by being too remote from present experience, the circular one seems to suggest a muted hope for the future, one that is simply a myth of the 'eternal return'. While the first is related to nineteenth-century ideas of modern physics, that life on this earth will inevitably come to an end, the second is related to nineteenth-century ecology, that the world and its systems are part of a stable network of relationships. Both views have since proved to be too simplistic. The bleak view of the final heat-death of the universe has now been questioned. On the other hand, the realisation that all our ecosystems are in dynamic interrelationship with each other shatters the image of a stable unitary system to which we can ultimately return. It is the possibilities of the future of the earth and our engagement with it that seem to be relevant to consider. In particular, how can human hope that includes freedom encompass the hope for creation?

Eschatology and the new genetics

Given the cosmological basis for hope that I have outlined above, it is worth considering how geneticists have reinterpreted an understanding of what re-creation means. Their particular vision for the future has practical and ethical outcomes. Their focus is on the present achievements of science and how this may impinge on the future of nature.

Ronald Cole-Turner first mooted the idea that genetic engineering could be thought of as co-creation over a decade ago.[76] For him the power of genetic technology is one that can be welcomed, for 'Unlike brute power to destroy (as for instance with nuclear weapons), genetic engineering offers us

---

[76] R. S. Cole-Turner, 'Is Genetic Engineering Co-Creation?', *Theology Today* 44 (1987), 338–49.

power to create'.[77] Like most other research on this area, the
focus of his concern was on the possible medical benefits of
genetic technology. For him, the only possible ethical objections
to genetic engineering lay in the presently illicit human germ-
line therapy where the genetic change would be passed to the
next generation.

Cole-Turner recognises that if we are to think of ourselves
as co-creators we must have some idea of what God intends.
He believes that it is inevitable that we think of ourselves as
co-creators, once we see God as being distinct from creation
in the traditional sense of God 'standing over' the processes of
nature. For him 'God's creative intent is evolutionary, or in
more traditional theological language eschatological. Its goal
transcends any present achievement and its progress is marked
by continuous achievement'.[78] Drawing on Arthur Peacocke's
idea of humanity as co-creator and even co-explorer, he suggests
that technology can even add something new to the creative
powers of God, since 'we will offer God a new way to influence
the creation'.[79] This argument is faulty on two counts. First of
all Peacocke never intended his ideas to be used to justify genetic
engineering, rather he spoke in bold terms of the possibility of
technology in a general sense in the context of a twin desire
for humans to act as trustees and preservers of nature.
Furthermore, he suggests that human intervention must always
be sensitive to the world's eco-systems.[80] Cole-Turner's claim
that genetic engineering is simply 'finding power within nature
for creation's aims', rather than 'power over nature for our
aims', seems to be a distortion of Peacocke's proposal.[81] Instead,
it amounts to a theological rationalisation of human intentions.
There is no attempt to distinguish what God might intend
compared with human volition, since humans are offering the
possibilities to God as co-explorers.

Philip Hefner, similarly, believes that as created co-creators
we enable the systems of nature to go beyond what is naturally

[77] Cole-Turner, 'Co-Creation', 339.
[78] Cole-Turner, 'Co-Creation', 347.
[79] Cole-Turner, 'Co-Creation', 348.
[80] Peacocke, *Creation*, 300–6.
[81] Cole-Turner, 'Co-Creation', 349.

possible. This is not a retrograde step, rather it is an enabling of the systems of nature to 'participate in God's purposes in the mode of freedom'.[82] Non-human nature is exalted to participate in transcendence and freedom by the action of humans. For both Hefner and Peters, it is freedom that is the defining quality of being human. Through these processes we open up new futures for the whole natural world and ourselves. The eschatological view expressed here is clearly both optimistic and fully realised. The

> purpose of human being and human culture is to be the agency for the birthing of the future of the nature that has birthed us – the nature which is not only our own genetic heritage, but also the entire human community and the evolutionary and ecological reality in which and to which we all belong – at least the nature that constitutes planet earth.[83]

This highly optimistic anthropology is embedded in an eschatology that is realised through human interventions and technology. While Hefner rejects scientism, it seems to me that his transcendent dimension arises out of science and seems to baptise its efforts in the transformation of nature.

I suggest that the power unleashed by genetic engineering has the potential to transform the world to an even greater extent than atomic energy. While the latter is necessarily confined to the wealthier areas of the world, genetic technology spreads into the very fabric of life on earth, transforming in days and weeks species that have taken millions of years to evolve. While the limited use of genetic engineering for medical purposes is not called into question, the spread into common agricultural use raises particular ethical issues that need to be addressed. The possibility of the military use of genetic engineering as a form of biological warfare raises once more the spectre of even more drastic misuse of power.[84]

---

[82] P. Hefner, 'Biocultural Evolution and the Created Co-creator', in T. Peters (ed.), *Science and Theology: The New Consonance*, Oxford: Westview Press, 1998, 174.
[83] Hefner, 'Biocultural Evolution', 181.
[84] W. Barnaby, *The Plague Makers: The Secret World of Biological Warfare*, London: Vision, 1999, 136–43.

Given this potential, we can now ask ourselves how far any of these are adequate Christian theologies in their description of the future of the earth, the future of creation. I suggest that the theology of Jürgen Moltmann is particularly relevant in this context. Like the eschatology of Dyson or Tipler, the portrayal of the future according to Hefner or Cole-Turner is couched in terms of *futurans*, rather than *adventus*. Even in his earlier reflections, Moltmann was aware of the danger that humankind's will to power over the world through science and technology can become close to humans attempting to attain self-assurance from their works.[85] The most relevant issue here, however, is not so much soteriology as eschatology.

For Moltmann none of the creatures of the earth have 'been destined to be "technologically manipulated"'.[86] Such false dreams of humanity lead to an aggressive ethic that is ultimately destructive. He suggests that a right attitude towards the natural world is one that respects the dignity of all God's creatures. God's love for all creation, Christ's self-offering for them and the indwelling of the Holy Spirit in them all add up to confer on every individual creature rights in an all-comprehensive community of creation. However, it seems to me that conferral of rights on nature will do little to curb the growing impetus towards genetic engineering. Furthermore, do we need to ban all genetic engineering outright or critique its objectives? Genetic technology has developed and we cannot put the genie back in the bottle. What we need to do now is to find ways of approaching genetic engineering that offer a thorough critique that makes some sense to both the public and the scientists themselves. I will be returning to this issue again in the next chapter.

Creation and new creation through the lens of wisdom

The tendency in our response to the new genetics or, for that matter, the future according to the new physics, is to swing back and forth between apocalyptic fears and utopian dreams. We need instead what Moltmann has called realistic

[85] Moltmann, *Hope*, 64.
[86] Moltmann, *Way*, 307.

hope.[87] Similarly, Hans Urs von Balthasar believes that we must not think of the future as an abyss or utopia, an escape from reality, rather it leads to a practical sharing of responsibility, and is given meaning by the coming of Christ into history.[88] But how can we find such a hope in the midst of actual problems facing us in genetic engineering? How can we envisage the new creation in such a way so as to give us a guide to present dilemmas in our relationship with the earth?

The first clue comes from consideration of wisdom as translated into eschatological categories by those writing at the time of the dawn of the early Church. Those who suggest that humanity can become co-creators with God need to bear in mind that while it is true that knowledge can lead us to God, it can also be a source of corruption as well. Once knowledge is distorted through pride, then all wisdom disappears. The Apostle Paul makes a similar point in his first letter to the Corinthians (1.18), which I discussed in Chapter 2. This letter seems to have been set in the context of over-arrogant confidence in human abilities. Righteousness implies covenant, which leads to sanctification and redemption. Furthermore, if we explore the idea of covenant we find at its heart the love of God. The covenant mentioned in the book of *Enoch* is a covenant with the whole of creation. Such a promise is portrayed in mystical terms in the vision of John in the book of Revelation, where he speaks of a new heaven and a new earth made possible through the blood of the Lamb. Such a covenant perspective suggests that we need to take a more careful look at the way we are using the knowledge we have gained and ask, Is such a change a fitting development?

The way we might begin to make such judgements is assisted by the theology of Thomas Aquinas and his theory of natural law. While his theology has been much maligned because of its seemingly static view of cosmology, I suggest that elements of his theology are retrievable today. Moreover, they give us a means of linking creation and new creation through the

[87] J. Moltmann, *Religion, Revolution and the Future*, trans. M. D. Meeks, New York: Charles Scribner's Sons, 1969, 196ff.
[88] H. Urs von Balthasar, *Elucidations*, trans. J. Riches, London: SPCK, 1975, 55–8.

perspective of wisdom in a way that is much more difficult in the cosmic eschatology of Jürgen Moltmann. Furthermore, it seems to me that we can modify his concepts in the light of current scientific knowledge in a way that is true to his original intention, namely to bring the insights of rational thought into theological reflection.

Aquinas's understanding of both natural law and moral law is that it in some way reflects the eternal law or wisdom of God. He suggests that it is impossible for any of the verbal formulations of these laws to encompass the divine wisdom. It is in the nature of wisdom itself to admit that such a task is beyond human grasp.[89] For him the universe is an ordered one, created through the wisdom of God. Yet while he believed that God gave this order, it was also still under the influence of God's creative power and subject to an open future.[90] In other words, the concept of order for Aquinas is a dynamic one, responding to both emanation from and return to God.

Aquinas suggests that the role of humanity is not just to accept the order in creation, but to work to bring order into it. The idea of ordering, then, is not just related to the ecological ordering of different species, 'according to their kinds', but also their final destiny or *telos*. He assumes that the ordering in the universe is present as given, rather than simply imposed by human intelligence. The tendency today is to reject all notions of ordering as projections of the human mind. However, for Aquinas acknowledgement of our ability to understand the order is certainly both provisional and partial. This seems to me to be consistent with the workings of modern science, which admits the reality of ordering in the natural world, while acknowledging that human understanding remains provisional. In a postmodern culture any such admissions of order can seem idealistic or 'foundational'. However, Aquinas's search for intelligibility in the moral sphere at least is not the same as predictability, for the activity of the Spirit presents the unexpected situation that demands a particular response. Hence, 'What wisdom brings is not an ability to see

---

[89] Aquinas, *Summa Theologiae*, Vol. 28, London: Blackfriars, 1963, I–II, 96.6; 91.3; 93.3.
[90] Aquinas, *Summa Theologiae*, I–I 73.1.

into the future, but the openness to see into the present, and
to recognise the Spirit in the present in whatever manner he
manifests himself'.[91]

What Aquinas's understanding of natural law brings to a
doctrine of creation is the idea of the intrinsic dignity of all
life and life to come. How does this account relate to the
creation story recorded in the book of *Enoch*, which implied
the precariousness of life? It seems to me that the two accounts
are not necessarily as incompatible as they might appear. Once
we cease to think of Aquinas's understanding of order as rigid
stability, but instead as the partial reflection of the wisdom of
God, then its vulnerability to change and destruction remains
a real possibility. The medieval world in which Aquinas lived
was only too aware of the presence of evil forces, as well as
angelic ones. It is essential to recognise that the cultural context
in which Aquinas developed his idea of natural law was one
where the precariousness of life was much more keenly felt
than it is today. If we see natural law in a theoretical way in
isolation from this, then the dynamic possibilities within it
become obscured.

Another aspect of his thought that is significant for
eschatology is his understanding of the final goal of creation
as beauty. As I mentioned in Chapter 3, the ultimate good for
Aquinas is not Aristotle's *eudaimonia*, a life of flourishing,
but *beatitudo*, that is partaking and reflecting on the beauty,
goodness and holiness of God. This seems to be related to
Moltmann's idea of the final consummation of creation, where
God will be all in all. While Mary Grey's suggestion that
flourishing is implicit in salvation seems a valid one, it seems
to me that an eschatological vision has to go beyond this and
consider the idea of beauty as well.[92] This need not necessarily
imply an escape from this world in the way some feminists
have suggested. Aquinas suggests that this goal of *beatitudo*
serves to distinguish human activity from that of other
creatures. His eschatology remains, ultimately, an anthropological one. For him the ordering of the animal and plant

[91] J. Mahoney, *Seeking the Spirit: Essays in Moral and Pastoral Theology*,
London/Denville: Sheed & Ward, 1981, 94–5.
[92] Grey, 'Salvation in Community', 22.

kingdom is for the sake of their benefits to humanity. This anthropological concentration seems to be related to his idea of the friendship that he suggests is only possible between God and humanity, understood as charity, rather than wisdom as such. Moreover, he was undoubtedly influenced by the attitudes to nature that were common at the time, which viewed animals as designed with human needs in mind.[93]

However, it seems to me that the friendship of which he speaks can become extended to include all creation, even if these friendships are expressed in a rather different way from that between God and humanity. Indeed the Noachic cosmic covenant and the cosmic themes throughout the biblical tradition suggest that God's love and friendship is far more cosmological than Aquinas implies. This is not the same as simple naturalism, rather the new earth is inclusive of a redeemed creation. It is the new heaven and new earth which reflect the beauty of God, as Bulgakov's theology would imply. Such beauty is, moreover, only made possible because of the death and resurrection of Christ. Wisdom, as the wisdom of the cross and resurrection, and filled with the Spirit of Wisdom, becomes the means of linking creation and new creation in a way that avoids both the annihilism of Lutheran eschatology and the docetism that Moltmann suggests is implied by the idea of deification in Orthodox theology.[94] As Oliver O'Donovan suggests, 'the resurrection of mankind apart from creation would be a gospel of a sort, but of a purely gnostic and world-denying sort which is far from the gospel the apostles actually preached'.[95]

Yet O'Donovan is correct to admit that there is some generic ordering present in the community of this creation, for to pretend otherwise is a denial of the ordering that is apparent in ecological systems. I will return to this point again later. The relationship between generic ordering and

[93] See K. Thomas, *Man and the Natural World: Changing Attitudes in England, 1500–1800*, London: Penguin, 1983, 19.
[94] Moltmann, *Coming*, 274.
[95] O. O'Donovan, *Resurrection and Moral Order: An Outline for Evangelical Ethics*, 2nd edn, Leicester: Apollos, 1994, 31.

teleological ordering reflects the tension between creation and new creation. Yet in some sense the new creation makes its stamp on this creation in a way analogous to what scientists have termed 'backward causation'.[96] While on a formal basis scientists reject the idea of purpose in the universe, the concept of progression in Darwin's theory of evolution reintroduced the idea of history into biological concepts. Teilhard de Chardin and his contemporary equivalents, process theologians, married this idea of progression to theological purposefulness. The dynamic flow of creation to new creation now is from behind, with the Omega reached through a process of progressive evolution. Yet while this might seem to allow creation to be open to a range of possibilities, it is still reliant on current understanding of nature in the present. Moreover, Teilhard's model assumed linearity in the evolutionary process that is far from correct, its shape being more like a multiple branched bush, rather than a pyramid.[97] The significance of a recovery of the theological idea of *parousia,* or as Moltmann would put it, *adventus,* is that it allows for a new creation that is unexpected, coming from the Eternal Wisdom of God. Such a dynamic opens up the idea of wisdom in the human community, so that freedom from all determinism is preserved.

As I suggested earlier, the unique gift of freedom in the human community keeps hope alive, but also allows distinctions to open up between the ordering in the natural world and that in the moral sphere. Those who have been tempted to find a basis for moral law in the natural law, be it through the idea of evolutionism, Gaian philosophy or the like, have come across the difficulty that ecological systems are, from a scientific perspective, described by a number of different models. According to the population-community approach to ecology, for example, ecosystems are networks of interacting populations of living organisms, non-living components such

[96] J. Earman, 'Causation a Matter of Life and Death', *Journal of Philosophy,* 73, 1976, 5–25.
[97] G. Schroeder, *The Science of God: The Convergence of Scientific and Biblical Wisdom,* New York: The Free Press, 1997, 88.

as water being external influences.[98] This model focuses on the growth of populations and the structure and composition of communities of organisms and their interactions. An alternative model which draws on biophysical processes examines energy flows in the system as a whole, both living and non-living components. This is more akin to the Gaian approach to the earth, though in this case the processes are not automatic, but regulated by the living components in a regulatory feedback process.[99] A third model is one that conceives of ecosystems according to so-called hierarchy theory.[100]

Hierarchy theory takes special account of the particular way the observations are taken in any given 'observation set'. The particular space-time scales that are used in any given observation set need to be taken into account. Hence, ideas such as equilibrium, local, global or stability are all relative to the particular scale adopted. In this way ecosystems may be described as static or dynamic, fluctuating or in steady state, integrated or a collective of individual components. The complexity of natural systems is overlooked when one observation set is used. Eco-feminists have renamed this 'observation set theory', in place of 'hierarchy theory', which they find offensive because of the implied idea of domination.[101] The theory suggests that the context of observations is crucial in coming to certain conclusions in ecological theory. Furthermore, to envisage the natural world as either totally disordered or ordered is a mistake, since the complexity of the system is such that both aspects are apparent, depending on the perception of the observer.

These results in themselves caution against trying to extrapolate from natural systems to those in the human community. Nonetheless, it seems to me to suggest that natural systems

---

[98] K. J. Warren and J. Cheney, 'Ecological Feminism and Ecosystem Ecology', in K. Warren (ed.), *Ecological Feminist Philosophies*, Indianapolis/Bloomington: Indiana University Press, 1996, 244–62.

[99] For a further discussion of different scientific models of Gaia, see C. Deane-Drummond, 'Gaia as Science Made Myth: Implications for Environmental Ethics', *Studies in Christian Ethics* 9:2 (1996), 1–15.

[100] R. V. O'Neill, D. L. De Angelis, J. B. Waide and T. E. Allen, *A Hierarchical Concept of Ecosystems*, Princeton, Princeton University Press, 1986.

[101] Warren and Cheney, 'Ecological Feminism', 246.

are far more complicated than we have previously suspected. A description of the order that we do find in terms of wisdom seems appropriate, since such wisdom allows for both the possibility of change, without denying that patterns and dynamic interrelationships do exist. Wisdom admits that we are still a long way from understanding the full story. As long as natural law is perceived in this light, rather than in a rigid way, it can be retrieved.

The mystery of life as we know it urges us to speak in the language of metaphor, rather than through discursive categories. This metaphorical way of speaking seems to be the only way we can portray the ultimate future of the earth in a theological sense. Apocalyptic literature uses such language, but the imagery can sometimes seem strange to modern ears. Moltmann's portrayal of the new earth is not fully satisfying as he presents it in such a way that uses discursive language that is more appropriate to descriptions of life as we know it in the present. However, his speculations sound like the product of an imagination that goes beyond anything imaginable for life on this earth. This tends to sever the connection between this world and the next, which is the opposite of his intention. It seems to me that it is in a discovery of the mystery of life here that we can move into metaphorical language that is the most appropriate for images of life to come. It does not pretend to be any more than a faint picture of what might be ahead, but at the same time affirms that the glory of God is present. I suggest that we find indications of such appropriate imagery for this future creation in the theology of St Hildegard of Bingen.

Creation and new creation in Hildegard

Hildegard (1098–1169) was a German mystic who also, significantly, possessed a wide knowledge of both medicine and the sciences. Her visions allowed her to see the universe as directed by a power that she names Sapientia and Caritas understood as being in dynamic relation to God, Christ, the Church, creation and every individual. She anticipated the Sophiology of Solovyov and Bulgakov, though for her it is through images and pictures that Sophia comes to be expressed.

Her *Liber Divinorum Operum* (Book of Divine Works) consists
of ten visions, the first five concerned with the eternal
relationship between God, humanity and the cosmos and the
last five deal with the history of salvation, culminating in the
Last Judgement. Her second vision portrays Wisdom as co-
creator and mother of the world.[102] This somewhat strange
portrait shows Yahweh as Creator encompassing a woman's
body, which represents Sophia, his Amon or Co-Creator. The
world is contained inside this body, represented as a sphere,
with all of creation encircled and with a figure of a human in
the centre. The imagery suggests that all of creation is in
the womb of Sophia, and she is likened to the mother of the
cosmos.

Her ninth vision shows Caritas and God's Omnipotence
side by side. It seems reasonable to suppose that Caritas is
also Wisdom, since her visions of the glorious feminine figure
are called Caritas and Sapientia in an interchangeable way.[103]
She wears a white silk garment, covered by a green cloak repre-
senting the world of creation, with jewels on this cloak. Green
is representative of both life and hope for creation, its *viriditas*
or 'greenness'. Creation is envisaged as the cloak of Wisdom,
decorated with humanity. Barbara Newman comments: 'The
colors have both a theological and moral significance: green
denotes the fruitful, life giving power of Wisdom; white the
sweetness of divine love in the Incarnation; and golden chains,
the obedience of all nature to its God.'[104] The motif of the
garments combines the sapiential themes of revelation of divine
beauty with co-operation of grace with human effort in the
virtues. For example, in *Scivias*, her ninth vision associates
Wisdom with the virtues of justice, strength, holiness, humility,
self-control and spiritual discernment.[105] Associated with
Sophia in this portrait we find the image of the Holy Spirit,

---

[102] Hildegard of Bingen, *Book of Divine Works*, M. Fox (ed.), trans.
R. Cunningham, Santa Fe: Bear & Co., 1987.
[103] B. Newman, *Sister of Wisdom: St Hildegard's Theology of the Feminine*,
2nd edn, Berkeley/Los Angeles, University of California Press, 1987, 49.
[104] Newman, *Sister*, 73.
[105] T. Schipflinger, *Sophia-Maria: A Holistic Vision of Creation*, trans.
J. Morgante, York Beech: Samuel Weiser, 1998, 153.

bearing six wings and with a garment of fish scales. The fish
scales represent the water of life, while six is the symbolic
number of effusive love. The five spheres in the wings represent
the power of the feminine.[106]

Her tenth vision presents a view of the end of time, where
both time and eternity are portrayed as a whole, depicted as a
wheel with a line across the middle. Love/Wisdom is dressed
in symbolic garments, related to human activity. The colours
on the wheel show different stages in the history of the world
and history of the Church, pointing towards the new beginning in the incarnation. The activities of those who promote
justice and humility are welcomed as the world deteriorates
towards the close of the age, along with persecutions of the
faithful. She anticipates the coming of the Antichrist, though
she perhaps surprisingly does not give us an account of the
Last Judgement itself, or the bliss of the saved.[107]

Images of the future of creation are evident in her fifth vision
in *Scivias*, that Hildegard describes in the following way:

> After this I saw that a splendour white as snow and translucent
> as crystal had shone around the image of that woman . . . and in
> this brightness . . . appeared a most beautiful image of a maiden
> . . .
>
> And I heard the voice from heaven saying, 'This is the blossom of
> the celestial Zion, the mother and flower of roses and lilies of the
> valley. O Blossom, when in your time you are strengthened, you
> shall bring forth a most renowned posterity.[108]

It seems reasonable to suppose that the figure of *Virginitas* is
that of the glorified Church, who, like the Mother of God is
at the heart of the Church. She became like one who longed
for her bridegroom, echoing the imagery of Revelation. Yet in
other images of the Virgin it is clear that she is associated not
just with paradisal Eve or Mary, but with painful and ascetic

---

[106] Schipflinger, *Sophia-Maria*, 149. Schipflinger's identification of the ninth vision
of Sophia with Virgin Mary seems to me to be unjustified.
[107] S. Flanagan, *Hildegard of Bingen: A Visionary Life*, London: Routledge,
1989, 150–1.
[108] Hildegard of Bingen, *Scivias*, trans. Mother Columba Hart and Jane Bishop,
New York: Paulist Press, 1990, 201.

love, expressed in the lives of clergy and nuns. She deliberately excludes the affirmation of maternity from the sphere of the sacred, along with sexuality in both men and women.[109] In this she is clearly influenced by the patriarchal culture of the time.

A further problem that we might pose to Hildegard's visionary portraits of creation is the influence of the concept of an ideal beginning, presenting what seems to be a circular view of salvation history. However, other aspects of her theology show that she was aware of a more historical account of salvation history, including accounts of creation, fall, death, resurrection and final judgement. In these cases the imagery she uses is more masculine, rather than the feminine portrayal of an eternal cosmos.[110] While some theologians have used her visions as a basis for creation spirituality, this ignores her concentration on the incarnation, where she suggests that the feminine divine finds its deepest meaning.[111] For her, it is through the feminine divine that the incarnation becomes possible, and as such this has eternal significance.

Hildegard's writing presents us with a holistic image of the new creation that combines reflection on the eternal present with an unfolding history of salvation. While much of the imagery reflects the presuppositions of her time, there are aspects that may be retrieved in considering the dynamic of the future of creation. In particular, her sapiential theology offers a positive view of creation, while recognising the real possibility of sin, especially that of injustice and pride. She also included in her visions some insights from her knowledge of science and medicine of the time. Like the theology of Aquinas, the relevance of her theology lies as much in her sapiential method, as in the content of her visions.

Conclusions

I began this chapter with a consideration of the biblical image of the end of creation, expressed in apocalyptic literature. I

[109] Newman, *Sister*, 228–9, 251–2.
[110] Newman, *Sister*, 45.
[111] Newman, *Sister*, 250.

proposed that the theme of wisdom need not be eclipsed by
the idea of apocalyptic. On the contrary, the writings of both
the canonical and pseudepigraphal texts show a richness of
wisdom imagery incorporated into ideas about the end of
creation. The description of sin as knowledge distorted into
pride and abuse of nature has particular resonance today. The
book of Revelation presents us with an idealistic image of
Wisdom, portrayed as the ideal Church and represented by
the Virgin Mary. Yet it is surprising, perhaps, that such images
of the future seem to have been ignored by eco-feminist writers,
such as Ruether, who seems to portray the future of the earth
as ending in a cycle of eternal return. Such a future would be
ultimately hopeless, as science predicts an ultimate ending of
all life as we know it on earth. Even for those physicists, such
as Frank Tipler, who insist that there may be indefinite life, it
is a life divorced from any earthly living referent as we know
it today. We are left with a cold image of a detached
intelligence, perpetuating itself to the farthest flung parts of
the galaxy and beyond. Theological eschatology must resist
all attempts to be content with a distorted anthropological
image of the future, even that accredited with the label of
science. Instead a cosmological image of the future can emerge.
Such a cosmology is not a simple progression of the present
into the future, as in Teilhard, but a response to *adventus*,
made possible by the *parousia* of Christ. Such a theology
corrects the distorted eschatology permeating the theology
of some contemporary writers on the new genetics. Yet
Moltmann's theology lacks certain clarity in relating the
dynamic of creation and new creation. What kind of shape
for creation will be found in the new creation? Aquinas's idea
of natural law gives us some clues here, since the idea of both
the natural and moral laws are partial reflections of the eternal
Wisdom of God. The future of creation must ultimately be
found in the indwelling of all creation in the Wisdom of God.
This supports a theology of beauty, not just flourishing. More
recent ecological research warns us against drawing too close
a parallel between the workings of nature and the moral laws
of the human community. Yet this does not deny that there
are some connections that are possible. In particular, Hildegard

presents us with a visionary account of creation in terms of Sophia that is particularly relevant in considering the shape of the new creation. She combines Sophianic images of this created world in an eternal present with more linear images of the world yet to come, where evil is finally conquered by the Lamb. The incarnation of Christ shows that the end of creation has in some sense come now, but it is yet to be finally consummated in the glory and beauty of God. But how can this eschatology give us insight into the present, in particular the future direction of science? In what sense can theology contribute to defining a new shape for science in the next millennium? Possible answers to these questions will be developed in the following chapter.

6

The Future of Science

The future of the earth as envisioned by physicists seems to us a remote possibility in some distant future that is very hard for us to imagine. In this chapter I will be developing an issue that is far more accessible, namely the future of science itself, in particular the biosciences. However, in order to understand how this future may unfold, the shifting culture of the sciences needs to be explored. Yet such a culture is not detached from the cultural environment in which science has emerged, since modern experimental science is itself a product of Western culture. As I discussed in Chapter 3, few would doubt that in pre-modern times the Oriental nations were responsible for considerable advances in science. Joseph Needham suggests that a non-interventionist science would have emerged in China if the prevailing social conditions had allowed it to flourish.[1] More recent research suggests that Needham's thesis is correct, that science in non-Western cultures is less detached from philosophy and religion, though the definition of science differs from the Western version.[2] For the purposes of this chapter I will be focusing on the dialogue between Christian theology and Western science,

---

[1] J. Needham, *The Grand Titration: Science and Society in East and West*, London: Allen & Unwin, 1969, 211.
[2] H. Selin, *Science Across Cultures: An Annotated Bibliography of Books on Non-Western Science, Technology and Medicine*, New York/London: Garland Publishing, 1992.

rather than other versions that have been proposed, such as Islamic science.[3]

Tracing elements of scientific culture

Even allowing for the fact that science is rooted in Western culture, there are aspects to the culture of sciences that render it distinct from other disciplines. It is hard sometimes to distinguish these features, since we have adopted many of them more widely in society at large. However, as Stanley Hauerwas has pointed out, it is those areas which we take for granted in the human condition that are most significant for ethics and, I suggest, for theology as well.[4]

Facts and values

While the dogma that science could separate facts from values was the rallying cry of twentieth-century logical positivists, I will argue here that elements of this attitude remain. For positivism only factual knowledge was verifiable and in this alone we find meaning. In other words, ethical language was relegated to that which is non-verifiable and so rendered meaningless.[5] The influence of scientific approaches to theology through, for example, literary and historical criticism, shows that in method, at least, science as rooted in the verification of facts is making a contribution to the way theology is shaped, whether or not we recognise this process as indebted to science. Even postmodernism, which relies on a hermeneutics of suspicion, is still in some sense a child of modernity. The theoretical physicists Alan Sokal and Jean Bricmont roundly rejected the attempt by French postmodern philosophers, including among others, Irigaray, Lacan and Lyotard to support their views by drawing on their mathematical formulations.[6] They insisted that their work was 'abused' and

[3] Z. Sadar, *Arguments for Islamic Science*, Aligarh: Centre for Studies on Science, 1985.
[4] S. Wells, *Transforming Fate Into Destiny: The Theological Ethics of Stanley Hauerwas*, Carlisle: Paternoster Press, 1998, 137.
[5] A. J. Lisska, *Aquinas's Theory of Natural Law*, Oxford: Clarendon Press, 1997, 62–3.
[6] J. Bricmont and A. Sokal, *Impostures Intellectuelles*, Paris: Odile Jacob, 1997.

distorted, enlarged to support philosophical speculations that were completely unrelated to their original ideas. They even went as far as publishing a hoax article in an American journal called *Social Text*, deliberately offering a parody of the new physics as simply a linguistic construct.[7] It seems likely that the French theorists were unjustified in their particular use of science. However, I will show later that some scientists are quite adept at enlarging their science into myths.

One possible explanation for the hostility of Sokal and Bricmont is that it seemed to them to break what has become a sacred code, that science is purely objective. This is a more acceptable version of the idea that facts must be separated from values, though many scientists would not necessarily use this language today. The sharp critique of social scientists pointing to the value-laden nature of facts has attempted to put an end to such ideas of value neutrality. The aim of most practising scientists is always to be able to adopt as near an 'objective' and value-free position as possible. For Sokal and Bricmont blatant use of certain mathematical facts to support a particular value system seemed to go against the cultural root of science itself, namely its desire for objectivity and by implication value neutrality. Ironically, perhaps, the fact/value distinction is itself beginning to break down with the advent of quantum physics. Those attuned to this new physics recognise that all our observations affect, in some way, what is observed, that the world is one of probabilities. This does not mean, however, that facts in the new physics suffer from the same foibles as values, as some social scientists would have us believe. For practical purposes we still operate according to a Newtonian system, the laws of gravity and motion still have relevance to our everyday existence. An argument can be made for an expansion of Newtonian physics to include more recent research, rather than a simplistic replacement of one by another.[8] In this sense the mythology of the split between facts and values survives, albeit in a more muted form.

[7] S. Hughes, 'The Naked Postmodernists', *The Times Higher Educational Supplement*, 10 October 1997, 22.
[8] J. Brooke and G. Cantor, *Reconstructing Nature: The Engagement of Science and Religion*, Edinburgh: T&T Clark, 1998, 96–101.

Rather than simply showing that there are values in science, a point to which I will return to again later, a more interesting question is to ask, 'Why have scientists been reluctant to let go of this view of science as value-neutral?' I suggest that it is in discovering some of the reasons for this belief that a core aspect of the culture of the sciences comes into view. This is quite apart from the idea that some scientists now have a rather more sophisticated understanding of the nature of science. The origin of the idea that science is value-free can be traced to four key factors:[9]

1. *Ideal of theoria* This is based on Aristotelian principles that science must be detached from practical affairs. In this sense science becomes value-free, as it is more about principles and theory than practice. Francis Bacon was a champion of the idea of the utility of science and the usefulness for human benefit. This tended to weaken the distinction between theory and practice in a way that continues even today. It becomes much harder to sustain a model of freedom from value once science is applied in particular ways. Modern genetic engineering is a case in point. Yet even Bacon was aware of the need to pursue science for its own sake, independent of possible applications.

2. *Scientific method* A core goal of scientific method was to achieve objectivity, with no traces of influence from 'bias' that might be caused by moral or other qualities, such as religious beliefs. Such beliefs would, it is argued, distort any knowledge gained. Such a quest for objectivity has been part of modern biblical hermeneutics, where one of the aims is to search for and eliminate as far as possible presuppositions of the interpreter. The apparent failure in the humanities to achieve such a goal can lead to one of two reactions. One is to assume that this quest must continue and that theology must

[9] For discussion see R. N. Procter, *Value-Free Science? Purity and Power in Modern Knowledge*, Cambridge: Harvard University Press, 1991, 262–70.

become 'theological science'.[10] The other is to admit to subjectivity and use more contextual approaches, which accept the limitations that this brings. As I hinted earlier, the recognition that pure objectivity is ultimately impossible in science as well, as shown by modern physics and some areas of biology, such as ecology, has failed to dent the quest, at least, for objective knowledge.

3. *The nature of value* Prior to Copernicus's revolution, the ancients believed that value is God-given, built into the structure of the cosmos. The idea that value is created by human agency, rather than in raw nature, is presupposed by most scientists. Perhaps surprisingly, Aquinas also views human wisdom as not just an acknowledgement of God's wisdom in the natural world, but an active entering into creation so as to bring order into it.[11] More recently environmental philosophers, such as Holmes Rolston III, have attempted to locate value in the natural world itself, rather than restrict it to human beings.[12] While there is a possible clash here between ecologists/biologists who advocate a form of naturalism and other scientists, for the time being we can assume that most scientists assume an instrumental approach to value, in other words that value is measured by its usefulness to humanity. Accordingly, the world of nature becomes value-free, or 'disenchanted', and no longer organised according to natural harmonies. Science is neutral because nature is neutral, it is just an exploration of the efficient causes of laws in nature, without any reference to the idea of purpose.

4. *The security of knowledge* The dramatist Euripedes believed that knowledge of nature was 'safe', that is free from politics and ethics.[13] Francis Bacon conferred that

[10] This seems to be Thomas Torrance's position, see T. Torrance, *Theological Science*, Edinburgh: T&T Clark, 1996.

[11] J. Mahoney, *Seeking the Spirit: Essays in Moral and Pastoral Theology*, London/Denville: Sheed & Ward, 1981, 94–5.

[12] Holmes Rolston III, *Genes, Genesis and God, Values and Their Origins in Natural and Human History*, Cambridge: Cambridge University Press, 1999.

[13] Procter, *Value-Free Science?*, 263.

knowledge of nature was neutral and a Christian understanding of the Fall is related to the knowledge of good
and evil. He identified moral knowledge as 'dangerous'.
In spite of his protestations of neutrality, he envisaged
science as the herald to a new utopia on earth. By the
nineteenth century a much narrower conception of
science had emerged, where science was specialised and
fragmented into numerous sub-disciplines. Such fragmentation has continued into the twentieth century.
Science was no longer an indulgence for an elite, but a
way of earning a living, especially in its applications to
industry. However, even as the bulk of science became
the servant of industry, the longing of many scientists for
purity of knowledge continued, especially in the universities. Even subjects sometimes considered to be at the
border between science and the humanities, such as
sociology, insisted on value-neutrality as a way of securing
reliable knowledge.

Given these possible reasons for scientists wishing to hold
on to the ideal of value-neutrality, it is worth considering how
such a proposal could serve to promote the interests of science.
It is too simplistic to consider that scientists do not recognise
the importance of values themselves, rather they believe that
in providing a detached approach to the problem this could
be of service in arbitrating between opposing groups in legal
or social disputes. The fact that science itself may be used in a
political way, as by both Greenpeace and the biotechnology
industry in the current disputes over the genetic engineering
of crops, is clearly undermining this ideal of science as secure
knowledge.

Another, related claim is that science is both transcultural
and apolitical. It would be foolish to suggest that certain
experiments in science cannot be repeated in different cultural
and political settings, though it is equally fallacious to suggest
that science policy is an entirely neutral affair. Scientists
themselves are now beginning to acknowledge this as well.
While in Britain the 1960s and 1970s political debates were
primarily about the regulatory bodies that controlled access
to funds, by the 1980s, under the Thatcher government, the

key criterion was commercial utility, an attitude that is still pervasive today. Finally, the 1990s debates are primarily about survival, with the creation of a 'superleague' of 'research' universities.[14] Given this squeeze on funding, it is hardly surprising that scientists in universities have turned more and more to funding from the military or commercial sectors, with their own values and particular vested interests. Scientists in the 1990s were much more on the defensive, lacking their earlier confidence. Yet there are elements of traditional ideals of science that still persist, in spite of the increased fragmentation and specialisation.

I suggest that the practical success of science tended to support and reinforce its ideals. The implication of this analysis is that science becomes not just encultured in the Western world, but a shaper of that culture as well. Yet we might ask ourselves if this model still needs some refinement. The practice of science is not as detached as it seems, scientists work in communities and develop their own narratives, some might even suggest their own wisdom. Before the modern shift to a scientific cultural ethos is cast too quickly in a negative light, it is worth teasing out other elements of what the culture of the sciences might be like, especially those that have potential for engagement with Christian theology.

The search for truth and wonder

While political and other pressures on scientists will diminish their interest in seeking truth as they perceive it in the natural world, it is important to acknowledge the strength of this claim. Hanbury Brown describes science in the following way:

> it acts as our essential link with reality and if we fail to maintain this link, then there is no longer any 'nature's truth', nor is there 'public truth', there is only 'your truth' and 'my truth' and we are in danger of losing the distinction between fact and fiction and science and magic.[15]

---

[14] C. C. Rassam, *The Second Culture, British Science in Crisis: The Scientists Speak Out*, London: Aurum Press, 1993, 196–208.
[15] H. Brown, *The Wisdom of Science: Its Relevance to Culture and Religion*, Cambridge: Cambridge University Press, 1986, 123.

Brown's claim that science is an arbiter of truth can easily slide into scientism. A check on such a development emerges in the new physics. However, the recognition in quantum theory that the observer conditions all observations, does not lead to the opposite extreme of subjective truth. Rather, any objectivity needs to be qualified and not claimed to be final in any sense. This leads to more searching for what David Deutsch has described as the 'Fabric of Reality'.[16] Richard Dawkins points out that, for scientists, fiddling data or lying about the results is, in scientific practice, the one 'unforgivable' sin. For him there is 'something almost sacred about nature's truth'.[17] However, before the search itself is dismissed, it seems to me that such ideals, however misplaced, were necessary in order to foster its achievements. As Michael Polanyi has reminded us, science involves a personal, committed way of approaching the world which bears some resemblance to a faith commitment.[18] Also as Pope John Paul suggests, every truth presents itself as a universal claim, even if it is not the whole truth. He even defines the human being as 'the one who seeks the truth'. Furthermore, for scientists it is the personal confidence that an answer can be found that spurs on the search.[19] The euphoria of the nineteenth and early twentieth centuries about the unlimited possible benefits of science has now faded, but few would wish to live in a world without clean water, electricity, antibiotics and medicines that make human life possible. The search for truth in the theological sense is related to answers to ultimate questions, but also in the context of a human community of faith. While the ultimate truth for a Christian is revealed in Jesus Christ, this is not opposed to the truths found in the natural order of things discovered by scientists. However, not all claims to truth in science are compatible with the Christian vision of truth. Where science

---

[16] D. Deutsch, *The Fabric of Reality*, London: Penguin, 1997.
[17] R. Dawkins, 'The Values of Science and the Science of Values', in W. Williams (ed.), *The Values of Science*, Oxford: Westview Press, 1999, 13–14.
[18] M. Polanyi, *Personal Knowledge: Towards a Post-Critical Philosophy*, London: Routledge, 1958.
[19] Pope John Paul II, *Faith and Reason, Encyclical Letter Fides et Ratio*, London: Catholic Truth Society, 1998, 41–5.

takes on itself the claim to be the Final Truth, then it becomes a metaphysical quest that goes outside its initial aims. I will be returning to the question of scientism again later.

Another aspect of the culture of science that is easy to omit is that of wonder. It is curiosity about life, as well as the search for truth, that often drives scientists. This was particularly true for early modern science, before it became a profession. In the seventeenth and eighteenth centuries the real interest in science came from 'sheer enjoyment that the practice of science brought to its amateurs'.[20] This was a technologically innocent world, having an exuberance that is hard, perhaps, for us to imagine with our popular image of scientists today as terribly serious. The picture of science as unhealthily masculine does not do justice to the real contribution of women to early experimental science. It was, perhaps, the transformation of science into a profession that led to gender issues of exclusion. Seventeenth-century scientists, such as John Ray, celebrated their sense of wonder by pointing to God as the source of all wonder. John Ray sold hundreds of copies of his book *The Wisdom of God Manifested in the Works of Creation*, which stayed in print even up to the next century. I suggest the reason for this was the sense of wonder it seemed to evoke, rather than any sense of detached, cold observation of the natural world. It becomes much harder, though I would argue not impossible, to sustain this vision once experimental techniques are adopted. In other words it is the particular *way* of looking that is significant. Is it a looking with a view to control, or is it a tuning in to the natural world through careful listening?

It is, perhaps, surprising that Richard Dawkins, who is one of the champions of the mechanistic ways of looking at the world, has also declared recently that science is the ultimate source of wonder. He admits that this is a deliberate attempt on his part to shake off the image of someone who has piped too long to the tune of the *Selfish Gene*. For him 'The feeling of awed wonder that science can give us is one of the highest

[20] G. V. Sutton, *Science for a Polite Society: Gender, Culture and the Demonstration of Enlightenment*, Boulder: Westview Press, 1995, 337.

experiences of which the human psyche is capable. It is a deep aesthetic passion to rank with the finest that music and poetry can deliver.'[21] He suggests that science helps us break out of the numbness of the familiar by opening up new worlds in a way that leads to wonder. Related to the idea of wonder is the search for beauty, which is connected with an understanding of the truths of science. In as far as he points to the wonders of creation his book is a kind of proto-theology. However, it is a deliberate attempt to redirect those who search for poetry and mysticism in religion to science and science alone. He is particularly critical of peddlers of astrology and the paranormal and most theologians would similarly reject superstitions of this type. He draws the line, too, where theology is taken up into a scientific view and becomes for him simply 'bad poetic science'. This relates to his idea of science alone as the ultimate source of wonder. Any amalgam with religious concepts distorts, for him, the purity of science. He also rejects holism of all sorts and views co-operation as secondary to the fundamental process of genetics. His affirmation of the role of imagination in science is not new. What does seem strange is the way he aims to redirect all imagination to science itself. It is here that his sense of wonder is ultimately problematic, as it seems to point to the self-glorification of human activities in science alone.

Mechanistic and organic views of nature

Modern experimental science is often stereotyped as viewing nature as a machine, rather than an organism. Feminist critics of science, such as Carolyn Merchant, have been particularly critical of the machine metaphor, believing that this led to both the desacralisation and 'death' of nature.[22] She identifies science, epitomised in the figure of Francis Bacon, as responsible for the domination of both nature and women. However, before concluding too rapidly that a return to an organic approach is all that is required, three issues need to be born

---

[21] R. Dawkins, *Unweaving the Rainbow: Science. Delusion and the Appetite for Wonder*, London: The Penguin Press, 1998, x.

[22] C. Merchant, *The Death of Nature: Women, Ecology and the Scientific Revolution*, London: Wildwood House, 1980.

in mind. The first is that without some sense of nature as 'other', which is characteristic of the Judeo-Christian faith, I have my doubts if any of the benefits of science would have been realised. The second is that one of the key characteristics of experimental scientific method is its claim to search for causes in nature, rather than through reference to a Scholastic 'final cause'. It seems likely that this contributed to a rejection of organic approaches, rather than any deliberate quest for the domination of nature, or for that matter, women.[23] The third issue is that it is too simplistic to think of science as just treating nature as a machine. In practice both the romantic and more mechanistic approaches to science have existed side by side, though it was the mechanistic view that attracted the most institutional support.[24] The organic approach has its dangers, too, in particular that associated with Fascism. The holistic approach to science was very popular in Germany at around the time of the Third Reich. Its positive contribution was a fostering of multilevel discourses.[25] However, the fear of the Fascism that this seemed to support effectively dampened this movement in scientific circles. I am not arguing that organic approaches to nature are necessarily Fascist, rather that there are dangers in both extreme versions of mechanism or organicism. Replacing mechanistic philosophy with an equally problematic holism does not take us very far.

Theology and scientism

One aspect of scientific culture that has been the subject of strong criticism from both philosophers and theologians alike is its attempt to invade all other forms of human activity. Scientism is the name given to the idea that science is the ultimate explanation of reality. I have already discussed in Chapter 1 the way this form of science tries to drown out other voices. Scientism may take different shapes. A common one is as the ultimate source of knowledge. The positivist claim that

---

[23] J. Biehl, *ReThinking Ecological Politics*, Boston: South End Press, 1991, 107–8.
[24] Brooke and Cantor, *Reconstructing Nature*, 96.
[25] A. Harrington, *ReEnchanted Science: Holism in German Culture from Wilhelm II to Hitler*, Princeton: Princeton University Press, 1996, 208.

everything is within the power of science still lingers on today, in writing such as that of Peter Atkins, so that he claims that 'there is no question whose answer is not attainable by science'.[26] Physicists such as David Deutsch and biologists such as Richard Dawkins take this view. Deutsch, like Dawkins, argues that the basis of life is molecular, so that the organism is the environment of the replicators known as genes.[27] For Deutsch life is a 'side effect' of the macroscopic physical processes operating at the molecular level. However, he cannot bring himself to believe that life will ultimately be meaningless, as the logic of such a view might suggest. Rather, if we assume a closed universe, that is a universe ending in a 'Big Crunch', we are only a tenth of the way through history from the early 'Big Bang'. He concurs with Frank Tipler, who suggests an infinite future for intelligent life, a topic I dealt with in some detail in Chapter 5. I suggest that Tipler's vision for the future of the earth amounts to a form of scientism.

Another shape that scientism may take is as the ultimate source of human values. Richard Dawkins's thesis expressed in *The Selfish Gene* might, at first sight, give the impression that he locates our ultimate source of value in our genes alone.[28] However, to be more precise he argues that altruism is 'selfish' as far as genes that code for such *behaviour* are concerned, since evolution is dependent on *conservation* of particular genes. Mary Midgley's initial misunderstanding of this led to some bitter debate, though I think she is right to point out that the language he uses is too suggestive of moral action to be contained in the way that he wants. In other words statements such as 'we are survival machines' are inevitably value-laden. Dawkins himself betrays certain weariness when he says recently: 'I am tired of being identified with a vicious politics of ruthless competitiveness, accused of advancing selfishness as a way of life.'[29] Rather, the Darwinian notion of

---

[26] P. Atkins, 'The Limitless Powers of Science', in J. Cornwell (ed.), *Nature's Imagination: The Frontiers of Scientific Vision*, Oxford: Oxford University Press, 1995, 122–33.
[27] Deutsch, *Fabric*, 171ff.
[28] R. Dawkins, *The Selfish Gene*, Oxford: Oxford University Press, 1989.
[29] Dawkins, 'Values', 19.

nature 'red in tooth and claw' is a lifestyle that he believes we need to vehemently reject. He also rejects the idea of eugenics, though admits that science does not rule it out as a possibility. For him, nothing, not even human values, should deny science its possibilities.

Hence, while he denies that science is an ultimate source of values, he seems to contradict this by elevating the value of scientific knowledge. A second important thread to his work is his belief that science can discover the way values emerge and are transmitted in human communities. He suggests that the behavioural responses to reward and punishment that we find in animals are primitive forms of so-called *primary values*, as they imply goal-directed behaviour. Such values evolve through a process of Darwinian natural selection. He suggests, further, that there is a genetic component to the unique human ability to learn language. However, while natural selection led to the emergence of humans with large brains, our ability to think and have foresight means that we can act against what might seem to be the dictates of our genes. He introduces another concept, namely that of 'memes', which are cultural constructs passed between members of the human community. Such memes compete for survival and, like genes, only some survive. He calls this the 'science of values', that is a particular biological way of interpreting how values are passed from one generation to the next. With some irony he suggests that just like those who dismiss the claims of the Old Testament as a source of values, so too he is entitled to choose not to behave as one governed entirely by his genetic make up.[30] He admits that this leaves us in an 'ethical vacuum' and this is what we should admit to instead of claiming to gain our sense of value from a religious source.

It seems to me that even if biological research suggests that there is a biological component to altruism or even values, then this is not necessarily incompatible with Christian belief. We might choose to challenge its *scientific* basis by pointing to the fact that values emerge in a complex and intricate way in human culture that only has a very tenuous link with

[30] Dawkins, 'Values', 35–7.

genetics. Memes, in particular, sound like an over-extrapolation of what is known in evolutionary theory. It is when sociobiology is claimed to be the only explanation that it becomes particularly dangerous. While Richard Dawkins refuses to accept that he gains his values from science, he denies the possibility of any religious experience as having any value at all. It seems to me that to be logically consistent he would have to admit this as being a possibility, especially as the science on its own has left us in an 'ethical vacuum'. In addition, his system of priorities still comes from scientific analysis, so it is more likely that his values are rooted in science as knowledge in a general sense, even if they are not crudely identified with his particular hypothesis of the selfish gene.

It is ironical, perhaps, that a form of scientism as the ultimate basis for value also comes from those at the organic end of the scientific spectrum. I refer to the Gaia hypothesis of James Lovelock. I do not intend to discuss this hypothesis in detail, except to say that it has become a source of values for those wishing to reconstruct a world-view on more ecological lines.[31] The fact that the hypothesis itself is highly ambiguous ethically is a point ignored by many of its advocates.[32] It is also surprising that Mary Midgley, who has actively campaigned against scientism in all its forms, seems to be quite ready to affirm Lovelock's approach as highly suggestive for philosophy and ethics.[33]

Public attitudes to science

Public attitudes to science are important as they have a direct bearing on the degree of acceptance of certain technologies in a way that helps to foster or stem their development. Public attitudes to science are influenced by the more popular accounts of science. Such popular accounts allow scientism to

[31] See, for example, K. Pedler, *The Quest for Gaia*, London: HarperCollins, 1991; E. Sahouris, *Gaia: The Human Journey from Chaos to Cosmos*, New York: Simon & Schuster, 1989.
[32] See C. Deane-Drummond, 'Gaia as Science Made Myth: Implications for Environmental Ethics', *Studies in Christian Ethics*, Summer 1996, 1–15.
[33] M. Midgley, *Utopias, Dolphins and Computers: Problems of Philosophical Plumbing*, London: Routledge, 1996, 149ff. See also M. Midgley, *Science as Salvation: A Modern Myth and its Meaning*, London: Routledge, 1992.

flourish. However, there are indications that the public is paying little attention to utopian portrayals of science in the context of the new biotechnology. Instead, there is an increased wariness towards genetic engineering and sensitivity to its environmental and health risks. Unilever and a number of non-government organisations sponsored one of the more recent reports, *Uncertain World*.[34] The research is significant in and of itself as it demonstrates the way *some* large companies might be showing a more responsible attitude to the impact of new technologies. A research method known as *focus groups* involved guided discussions with nine small groups of people from different parts of the UK and with different social characteristics. The results overall showed very little public enthusiasm for biotechnology. Public perception identified commercial interest as lying behind many of the new proposed products, especially those related to food. Their concern seemed to be exacerbated by certain kinds of information, rather than reduced. This counters some of the arguments of the Ministry of Agriculture, Fisheries and Food (MAFF) Committee that suggested public anxiety could be allayed by more information.[35] The *Uncertain World* report did not address the question of the religious dimensions to the public concerns over genetic engineering. However, close examination of the original data used to produce the document has revealed the following results.[36]

Almost all respondents were anxious or worried about the idea that genetic engineering amounted to a 'messing about with nature'. Their sense of risk arising from such 'tampering' was related to possible effects on both their own health and damage to the environment. However, their anxiety went

[34] R. Grove-White, P. Mcnaghten, S. Mayer and B. Wynne, *Uncertain World: Genetically Modified Organism, Food and Public Attitudes in Britain*, Lancaster: Centre for the Study of Environmental Change, 1997.

[35] *Report of Ethics of Genetic Modification and Food Use Committee*, chaired by J. Polkinghorne, London: HMSO, 1994.

[36] This research was funded by the Christendom Trust and conducted by the author in collaboration with Robin Grove-White and Bronislaw Szersynski and by kind permission of Phil Mcnaghten, Sue Mayer and Brian Wynne who allowed open access to the original data collected from the focus-group interviews.

beyond a recognition of possible risks, so that for them there seemed to be something fundamentally wrong about interfering with the natural world in this way. This confirms other research by Frewer and others which showed that public concern over genetic engineering is not just about the final products of the research, but the processes involved as well.[37] Their concern was expressed in terms of a strong sense of order in the natural world. Comments included remarks such as 'I don't think we should mess with nature. Nature was designed for specific reasons. We mess with it. We have no right.' 'It's actually broken the natural order.' While most respondents were not Christian in the formal sense of the word, the idea that the natural world has some kind of design that we interfere with at our peril seems to be strongly rooted in their social consciousness. In some cases a more explicit reference to theism surfaces. For example, one respondent believed that interference with nature goes beyond permissible boundaries, for 'I'm not sure whether man should play God and change things for the better, for the lucre, at the end of the day'. For many, the idea of God *as such* is hidden, but the sense of ordering prevails.

Another related theme that surfaced is the idea that what is present in nature as untouched by human interference is good. Overall, the *reason* for changing the natural to something else was questioned. While a form of biotechnology has been going on for centuries in cheese and beer-making, etc. any attempt to try and persuade us that this is the same as genetic engineering was dismissed. The irreversible nature of genetic change is such that the original 'natural' form may be lost and this seems threatening. Most analytical philosophers argue that equating the natural with value, that is what is natural is automatically good, is a weak philosophical argument. It is a form of romanticism whereby the good is seen to be the natural. It is also associated with the so-called 'naturalistic fallacy' where values are read directly from the facts of the

[37] L. J. Frewer, C. Howard and R. Shepherd, 'Public Concerns in the United Kingdom About General and Specific Applications of Genetic Engineering: Risk, Benefit, and Ethics', *Science, Technology and Human Values* 22(1), 1997, 98–124.

natural world, that is an 'ought' from an 'is'. But does the public reaction invite a deeper reflection on the nature of value?

I suggest that some sense of natural order does have precedence not just in philosophy, but in theology as well. Thomas Aquinas's idea of natural law is a good example of how the orderliness in nature can be affirmed, but *without* necessarily committing the naturalistic fallacy. Anthony Lisska has pointed to the recent revival in interest in Aquinas's theory of natural law, both among contemporary philosophers and lawyers.[38] He argues that the idea of natural law can be retrieved even when subject to critical analytical philosophy. One of the questions he asks is whether it is still possible to retain Aquinas's idea of natural law. At the turn of the twentieth century G. E. Moore developed a stinging critique of Mill's work in what has come to be known as the naturalistic fallacy.[39] Moore's thesis seemed to dismiss all forms of naturalism, including natural law, from serious consideration. Moore developed the earlier work of David Hume, who suggested that no value statements could be validly derived from facts. This led to the split between facts and values that has dogged philosophy and the scientific enterprise ever since. Any systems of meta-ethics that took their bearings from the natural world were effectively sieved out through the screen of the naturalistic fallacy. In effect this dismissed both Aristotle and Aquinas from serious consideration, as both seemed to define moral terms from general statements about human nature, which are factual observations about the world.[40]

However, a closer examination of their philosophy shows that for both Aristotle and Aquinas a rather different theory of ontology was presupposed, compared with that taken to be the case in Moore's critique.[41] Moore assumed that ontologically there were simple, discrete natural and non-natural properties. A disposition or potentiality cannot be fitted into a metaphysical system of facts, understood as complete in themselves. Facts, once understood as discrete entities, are

---

[38] Lisska, *Aquinas's Theory*, 1–15.
[39] For more details of this debate see Lisska, *Aquinas's Theory*, 58–62.
[40] Lisska, *Aquinas's Theory*, 196.
[41] Lisska, *Aquinas's Theory*, 197–200.

sharply distinct from values. Aristotle and Aquinas approached moral theory very differently, using an ontology of dispositional essence. Such a scheme breaks down the fact/value distinction, so that it is the disposition of the natural process towards some goal that forms part of its nature. The end or goal is defined as a good in and of itself. In other words the good is not added to the fact about the natural world, but is inherent in it as it progresses towards its goal. The value is the end of the natural process. Hence such a scheme avoids the force of the naturalistic fallacy critique by linking closely the dispositional properties, or formal cause, with the final cause, defined as having value. To put it more simply, the facts evolve into the valuable, rather than value being read off the facts. Alasdair MacIntyre reinforces Lisska's thesis by his suggestion that twentieth-century philosophers have become so entrenched in the naturalistic fallacy issue that other insights from earlier classical texts are effectively dismissed. Like Lisska, he argues for a recovery of some of the insights from Aquinas's understanding of natural law and virtue ethics.[42] I discussed the relationship between Aquinas's view of natural law and his understanding of wisdom in the last chapter.

I have argued so far that the public sensitivity to breaking what is perceived as the natural order is not necessarily committing the naturalistic fallacy if it could be aligned with Aquinas's notion of natural law. I am not suggesting by this that Aquinas's approach be adopted in an uncritical way. Michael Northcott, for example, has discussed ways in which Aquinas's theory of natural law needs revising in the light of contemporary anthropology and current ecological concerns.[43] Rather, the public recognition of the value of natural order should not be dismissed out of hand as philosophically illegitimate. One of the main criticisms of genetic engineering highlighted by the public is that it seems to lack purpose, other than that of commercial gain. The fact that those interviewed

---

[42] A. MacIntyre, *After Virtue: A Study in Moral Theory*, 2nd edn, London: Duckworth, 1985, 59.

[43] M. Northcott, *The Environment and Christian Ethics*, Cambridge: Cambridge University Press, 1996, 226–48; 266–8.

were able to discriminate between different forms of genetic engineering, favouring those forms that had specific medical purposes over those in food production, shows a degree of sophistication that is not usually recognised by the scientists themselves or the government. Scientists involved in genetic engineering find the objection to it on the ground of naturalness highly puzzling. For example, the Nuffield Council on Bioethics makes the following point: 'The 'natural/unnatural' distinction is one of which few practising scientists can make much sense. Whatever occurs, whether in a field or a test tube, occurs as the result of natural processes, and can, in principle, be explained in terms of natural science.'[44] However, it seems to me that the public response shows a higher degree of sensitivity than a simple objection to transgressing particular boundaries. Rather, the natural is linked to a particular purpose; the 'design' is for something in particular. Hence, changing the purpose of a particular creature to another, different end brings in the issue of value. Furthermore, there is an awareness of interconnectedness, so that changing one part could have unforeseen effects on another part. While in theory, at least, some of these changes could be achieved by normal breeding methods, it is the extent and the speed of these changes that seems threatening, as well as the changes themselves. This relates to a greater awareness of ecology and interconnectedness and the environment in our present culture compared with earlier generations, a topic I will return to again below.

A biologist could reinterpret Aquinas's view of dispositional properties by pointing to the developmental aspects of all complex life forms. While teleology is officially rejected by science, I suggest that the idea of latency is not, especially in the light of our current knowledge that different genes are switched on and off at different stages of development of complex organisms. This dynamic understanding of creaturely being is far closer to Aquinas's notion of essence compared with the fixed ontology of Moore.

---

[44] Nuffield Council on Bioethics, *Genetically Modified Organisms: The Ethical and Social Issues*, London: Nuffield Council on Bioethics, 1999, 15.

In addition, the affirmation of the worth of the natural world can be reinforced by consideration of the religious concept that what is created is good. This needs to be qualified by the recognition that not all events in nature are subject to moral approval. Ruth Page suggests that a romantic affiliation of the good with the natural world is unnecessary and at times unhelpful in view of the realities of the harshness of the natural world.[45] Yet it is clear that diseases cannot be described as 'sinful' in any sense and overall there is a 'yes' to creation as a gift from God. Furthermore, given Aquinas's scheme, value is given to the final cause, hence any evaluation of the worth of creatures has to be seen in this light.

Public responses in the study by the Centre for the Study of Environmental Change (CSEC) showed that in almost all cases there was a mixed reaction to the idea of transgenic experiments when human genes were transferred to pigs or sheep. The reaction was particularly strong if *human* genes are proposed to enter the food chain. Common language such as 'it's disgusting', 'horrible', 'cannibalism', 'no, not that', and so on, all reflects an abhorrence with the idea that we might be consuming something of another human being. The MAFF committee suggested that if the public was more aware that a *copy* of the human gene was used and this copy multiplied billions of times before entering the new species, then it would not necessarily cause a problem. Yet it seems to me that the public reaction is not a logical response to facts, but a deep-seated intuition towards the special place of humanity and our distinction from the rest of creation. When one respondent was reminded of the very tiny fraction of material that was of human origin, which might even share the same chemicals as bacteria, the reaction was the same.

Overall the theological notion that humans are made in the image of God prevails, albeit in a hidden form. Nonetheless, some were more prepared to object from explicitly religious grounds. Of fundamental concern was the source of the

---

45 R. Page, 'The Animal Kingdom and the Kingdom of God', in *The Animal Kingdom and the Kingdom of God*, Edinburgh: The Church and Nation Committee of the Church of Scotland and The Centre for Theology and Public Issues, 1991, 7.

human gene; would it have come from a foetus? There was a sense that religious (in this case explicitly Roman Catholic) boundaries had been crossed by other medical research and that it may well happen again. Was this going to lead to an infringement of human dignity, especially in the case of an unborn child?

So far scientific research does seem to have taken some account of the public anxiety over genetic engineering of humans. Human cloning is at present outlawed, even though the Human Genetics Advisory Commission recommended that cloning should be allowed for therapeutic purposes.[46] There is less evidence that scientific research has taken account of public attitudes to genetic engineering of non-human species with human genes. One of the reasons for this reluctance may be the view of scientists that if the public understood the science, then their fears would be allayed. However, public concern goes beyond a simple response to the scientific facts and is more inclusive of other elements, such as particular ethical concerns for particular cases. Frewer and others showed that the focus of public ethical concern was for those applications involving use of animal or human genetic material.[47] The CSEC study confirm these results, though another ethical dimension was detected as well, namely concern about the environment and possible effects of the technology on the poorer nations of the world, as I outline below.

The responses of those in the CSEC study to experimentation with animals was cautious and in some cases caused concern as to whether the animals would be fairly treated. BSE was cited as an example of unnecessary slaughter of animals. Others were worried that experiments done on animals were the 'thin end of the wedge'. In general this was a weaker theme, but there was a greater sense of respect for animals compared with plants, for example. One group was concerned about introducing genes from animals that were not accepted as food on religious grounds. The MAFF report seemed to think

[46] C. Campbell and R. Deech (Chairs.), *Cloning Issues in Reproduction, Science and Medicine: A Report*, London: Human Genetics Advisory Commission and Human Fertilisation and Embryology Authority, December 1998.
[47] Frewer *et al.*, 'Public Concerns', 100–1.

that as long as an animal *looked* the same it could be considered to be this species and not another. Hence, it should not cause grave problems. However, would this work in practice? How many genes from a pig could be transferred to a sheep before it is no longer a sheep? Are looks alone an adequate guide? If there is distaste for eating even a gene of human origin, the same could be said for those who express distaste over eating pork or cows. The logic might suggest otherwise, but consumers do not necessarily respond to 'logical' analyses.

What was somewhat surprising was a tendency in all groups to look at the wider environmental consequences of genetic modification. The long-term and latent effects of BSE served as an example of how hidden dangers could surface much later. When soap powder was modified, for example, the immediate thought in many minds was: what about the effect on the ecosystems? Furthermore, questions surfaced regularly about the Third World; or possible effects or otherwise on poorer communities. Such global and broad ecological concerns perhaps reflect an implicit green theology that is holistic and integrates human need with the wider interests of the environment.

While the notion of 'sin' was never mentioned, another clear theme was an underlying sense of mistrust of the motives of those involved. Many used strong statements like 'it's all for human greed', 'it's for profit'. BSE again served as an example which reinforced the suspicion that the full story is never really made explicit. One participant commented; 'I think if I'd read that before BSE my thoughts might have been more positive . . . Sometimes we meddle too much . . . You can never be sure, be sure what the effects are going to be at the end of the day.' There was little belief in the underlying values of the organisations, especially supermarkets and the Government. While the former was suspected to encourage such developments for pure self-interest and profit – the 'filthy lucre' – the Government was viewed with suspicion as being out of touch with the needs of ordinary people.

Christian theologians throughout the centuries, drawing on the Augustinian notion of 'original sin', have recognised human weakness on an individual level. A more recent development has been the recognition of sinfulness at a structural and organisational level, through the development of liberation theology. What is of particular interest is the overall sense of powerlessness expressed in the focus groups. There is a feeling of inevitability about the course of events and that such events will benefit a few. While 'oppression' is not a word that is used, at least some of the anxiety comes from this sense of being dominated by negative forces wielded by powerful minority groups such as the Government and multinational companies.

Are there any signs of hope in this somewhat negative assessment? There are certainly signs that hope is still present, but sadly it is not the lot of the Church to be bearers of this hope. One group mentioned the idea that the Church *might* be able to become bearers of moral and ethical values, in other words, somehow act as a 'moral voice'. However, this was undermined by the perception that the Church was also a landowner, which would compromise its impartiality. Groups that did come over very strongly as bearers of an alternative vision were Greenpeace, Friends of the Earth and other non-government consumer organisations such as Watchdog. They were seen as those who could balance the discussion by presenting an alternative view that was unsullied by desire for profit. They are, possibly, bearers of an implicit liberation theology by challenging the *status quo* and speaking out for the people on their behalf. Just as liberation theologians owe a debt to Western theology, so too Greenpeace, for example, uses the tools of science to prove its points.[48]

Overall the public response to the new biotechnology is remarkably sophisticated in its ability to take into account a range of different factors. These include the motivation for the research, the processes involved, the possible outcomes and the long and short-term consequences. The public dissemination of science has tended to take a patronising attitude

[48] D. Parr, *Genetic Engineering: Too Good to Go Wrong?* London: Greenpeace, 1977.

towards lay opinion, framing it in certain ways in order to achieve pre-set goals and ambitions. However, it is clear from the recent debates over genetic engineering that public attitudes are much more sophisticated than is presumed to be the case. It seems to me that if science is to have a future it must take into account public opinion and sensitivities to particular issues. Failure to do so will lead to further hostility towards scientists and ultimately the demise of science itself. Yet given that much of this discussion has been about applications of science, it is worth considering the relationship between science and technology. How might a future for science fair in a technological age? Are the futures of science and technology irrevocably bound together, or are these distinct pursuits that can be subject to different critical analyses?

Technology and the future of science

In order to analyse the possible future of science we need to consider not just different elements of its culture and public perception, but also its relationship to technology. Much of the criticism of the new biology has been over the way it is used for particular commercial purposes. However, it is too simplistic to view technology as simply the application of science, especially in the biosciences. New scientific discoveries, such as the cloning of Dolly the sheep, came about through the deliberate application to certain practical problems faced by the pharmaceutical industry. Hence in order to discover the future of science, the future of technology becomes particularly relevant. This is especially the case in those situations, particularly in biotechnology, where science is driven by commercial goals. It is too lame an excuse to suggest that technology does not need to be subject to as rigorous a critique since it is simply applied science. If we see technology as the simple application of science, then it appears, like science, to be under human control. As free agents we are free to use the science in particular ways for our own particular uses. Such an attitude is commonly associated with a fairly sanguine view of science and technology. Philip Hefner, for example, regards technology as part of nature – it is the nature as defined by human beings.[49] His portrayal of genetic engineering as co-creation speaks for itself; such activities seem to be baptised by theology in the name of humanity fulfilling its vocation to be creators of nature, not simply its subjects.

However, we could arrive at a quite different view of technology and one that looks to its essence, along with that of science. Martin Heidegger attempted such an assessment.[50] He suggested that one of the characteristics of our modern age is that we have become unaware of those things which condition our sense of Being and sense of self. For Heidegger the 'rootedness' of humanity was threatened by technology, not in the sense of traditionalism, but more in the sense that we have lost something in an age dominated by science and technology. Furthermore, this loss is concealed in a language of liberation.[51] All attempts at trying to establish the rootedness on our own are bound to fail – rather we have to recognise what this means by accepting our sense of Being. Heidegger does not try to evaluate science, rather he is concerned to establish its essence and show how human life is inevitably influenced by it. The very description of technology as an application of science betrays the presumption that we can somehow stand outside the technology in which we are all shaped.[52] Any attempt to stand outside this world of science and technology amounts to an affiliation with it. For Heidegger, both science and technology share in the same essence, namely a withdrawal from a grounding of human thought and action. Technology sees the natural world as a vast store of energy, a 'Standing Reserve' to be tapped at our own convenience. Have we, as Heidegger suggests, forced on to nature an 'unreasonable demand' to bring forth fruits that are for human benefit alone? Is such an uncovering really the result

[49] P. Hefner, *The Human Factor: Evolution, Culture and Religion*, Minneapolis: Fortress, 1993, 49.

[50] M. Heidegger, 'The Question Concerning Technology', in W. Lovitt (ed.), *The Question Concerning Technology and Other Essays*, New York: Harper Torchbooks, 1969, 3–35.

[51] J. Sallis, 'Towards the Movement of Reversal: Science, Technology and the Language of Homecoming', in J. Sallis (ed.), *Heidegger and the Path of Thinking*, Pittsburgh: Duquesne University Press, 1970, 141–2.

[52] Sallis, 'Movement', 159–60.

of human decision, or is this a pretence or a way of concealing its true essence? If we use the language of being masters of our own technology, then we have not appreciated adequately that we are mastered by it. Technology forces us to use the language of problem-solving in a way that becomes purely instrumental in character. How has the technology itself challenged our sense of who we are as persons? Has it, as he suggested, led to a sense of withdrawal of any notion of Being, so that the language we use is now one of control? He suggests that if we attempt to master technology this itself will prove futile, since we are still within the boundaries of its essence, namely that we can somehow stand outside it and direct it according to our desires.

Heidegger died in 1976 before biotechnology had really developed as a science in the way we know it today. But his comments still seem to point to something about biotechnology that is particularly relevant, namely the desire to control the natural world for human benefit and a loss of a sense of Being. Before we dismiss Heidegger's view of technology as too pessimistic, it is worth reflecting on the fact that it is in the very act of attempting to control nature that the uncontrollable facets loom into view. The dream of ultimate control betrays a false optimism that has been characteristic of all human technological projects. How far we follow Heidegger and go on to suggest that all attempts at control are simply illusory is a moot point. His concern for a reconnection with our sense of Being in the world, rather than simply masters of it, echoes another theme that has surfaced in twentieth century science, but it is one that comes from the science of ecology, rather than genetics.

Tracing an ecological future

Once we consider environmental science, the language speaks less of a desire to control and more of balance and inter-relationships. At least these are the values highlighted by popular accounts of ecology. They have also been taken up by a range of philosophers and theologians anxious to find a credible basis for viewing the natural world in terms of communion with humanity, rather than domination over it.

Certainly, the fledgling science of ecology derived its name from *oikos* or home.[53] Ecology gave us some understanding of the way different species related to one another in a common home. In the early part of the twentieth century ecology was hailed as a guide to a future motivated by a conservation ethic.[54] This view persists in the public consciousness even today, so that ecology creates a sense of positive regard for the environment. Even those who use ecology for political or philosophical purposes, such as the radical left or the exponents of deep green philosophy such as Arne Naess, still rely on the vision of ecology as a system of stable interconnections. The equation of ecology with equilibrium, stability and order and harmonious interrelationships persists and influences cultural activity outside that of the science itself. Yet on the other hand ideas of harmony and order are reflections of our human culture as much as the science itself.[55]

The view of ecology in the early twentieth century was in terms of a dynamic succession of plant communities appearing one after another until a final stable climax was reached.[56] Yet as ecology progressed after the Second World War, shifts in thinking took place. Ecology now looked to interrelationships between species in terms of energy exchange and flow through thermodynamic systems. The word 'ecosystem' became popular and it was held that all parts within the ecosystem contribute to the dynamic whole.[57] The overall strategy is to produce as large and diverse an organic structure as is possible within the constraints of the system. In the end we arrive at a state of order and equilibrium, where the nutrients stay in circulation

---

[53] See D. Cox, *Charles Elton and the Emergence of Modern Ecology*, PhD thesis, Washington University (USA), 1979; D. Worster, *Nature's Economy: A History of Ecological Ideas*, New York: Cambridge University Press, 1977.

[54] Paul Sears was particularly important in this respect. See P. Sears, *Deserts on the March*, 3rd edn Norman: University of Oklahoma Press, 1959, 162–77.

[55] See in particular Worster, *Nature's Economy*.

[56] Worster suggests that Frederic Clements was particularly influential in establishing this as the dominant view, namely that the scientist can chart the progress of nature's course to a final stable state of equilibrium. *Nature's Economy*, 210.

[57] Eugene P. Odum was a leading figure in promoting the idea of ecosystems. His book, first published in 1953, is still widely used today. E. P Odum, *Fundamentals of Ecology*, Philadelphia: W. B. Saunders, 1971 edn.

instead of leaking out. The implication is that if the ecosystem was interfered with in any way there would be a loss of nutrients and the system as a whole would be damaged. I suggest that a more radical version of this same story is found in Lovelock's global Gaia hypothesis. Both Lovelock and the ecologists would agree that too much human interference would lead to destruction of the life-support system on which we all depend. I could qualify this by adding that such a view could be used to support technological intervention, for as long as we know the threshold of any likely damage, it might seem we could go ahead with impunity. More persistent is the view that delicately balanced ecosystems can be disrupted by wanton human intervention. Such an attitude seems to be behind much of the hostility of environmentalists towards the genetic engineering of crops.

But if we look at the science of ecology today, another very different voice is beginning to make itself heard. Now the science of ecology is not so much about stability, as about chaos.[58] Any view of a final stable state is being challenged – instead of a stable ecosystem we have an erratic shifting mosaic of different species, all competing against each other for survival. Instead of finding balance in nature, there are natural disturbances, among the most prevalent of which are fire, wind, and pests and drought.[59] Instead of an ecosystem, championed by the earlier ecologists, we have a fluid landscape of patches of different environments, loosely assembled together and never staying the same. Is this alternative view simply a result of the growing influence of population biologists, trained to track with mathematical precision the life-histories of individual species? Or is it the resistance to

[58] One of the first articles to appear which opposed the dogma of stability was that of William Drury and Ian Nisbet. See W. H. Drury and I. C. T. Nisbet, 'Succession', *Journal of the Arnold Arboretum*, 54, July 1973, 360. They found some historical precedent for their work in that of Henry Gleason, who suggested that species competed against each other in an individualistic way. His thesis had been largely forgotten with the success of the ecosystems approach to ecology.

[59] M. B. Davis, 'Climatic Instability, Time Lags and Community Disequilibrium', in *Community Ecology*, J. Diamond and T. J. Case (eds), New York: Harper & Row, 1986, 269.

holism with its political overtones and replacement by a new form of social Darwinism? While both possibilities may be partial explanations, a more intriguing one is that this coheres with a wider scientific trend towards a discovery of chaos.[60] The natural world as a perfectly predictable, controllable phenomenon is only one way of describing its reality.

I have argued so far that biotechnology, in its attempt to control the natural world, often yields new, unexpected and unpredictable results. A closer examination of ecology shows that even without human interference we have a patchwork quilt of interrelating species. But whereas human technology aims to control and arrives at disorder, ecology in the most recent accounts contains disorder within it, even though ecological systems are still present. In other words the ordering in ecology is just one level of description – at another level we find disorder. Both human technology and ecology are at the uneasy interface of disorder and order. How might we envision genetic science so that it took more account of such complexity? I suggest that a case study for such a trans-formation comes from the pioneering work of Barbara McClintock.

Seeking wisdom in the future of science

Barbara McClintock: a case study

Barbara McClintock's life spans the dawn of genetic science in the twentieth century (1902–).[61] After a glittering early start to her career in 1942, she put forward the hypothesis that transposable genetic elements could move from place to place in the genome and exert control over the expression of other genes. Her discovery was based on quite simple techniques of cytology, using a particular staining technique and careful

---

[60] I am particularly indebted to Donald Worster for his analysis of the situation. See D. Worster, 'The Ecology of Order and Chaos', *Environmental History Review* 14, 1990, 4–16.

[61] N. Fedoroff and D. Botstein (eds), *The Dynamic Genome: Barbara McClintock's Ideas in the Century of Genetics*, New York: Cold Spring Harbour Laboratory Press, 1992.

observations of maize chromosomes and kernals. The cell cycle that triggered these changes seemed to be related to stress.[62] Her research was met initially with disbelief and even hostility. Her observations were against the background of the discovery of the structure of DNA and the central dogma that the flow of information is always one way, from nucleic acid to protein and not the other way round. She was dismissed as out of touch and obsolete in her research methods. However, her determination undaunted, she continued to conduct research and publish her results in the Carnegie Research Institute's annual reports, in spite of them being rejected by other official scientific journals. Her research was unfashionable for other reasons as well – work on higher organisms was laboriously slow and tedious, compared with the rapid generation time in other organisms popular in genetic research, such as the fruit fly *Drosophila*, bacteria *Escherischia coli* or phage virus. However the story does not end here; eventually transposable elements were discovered in these organisms as well, and slowly it dawned on the scientific community that Barbara McClintock had been correct all along. Eventually her transposable elements were subjected to analysis by the modern genetic toolbox, showing different sequences on a chomosome map.[63] In recognition of her contribution she was given the Nobel Prize for medicine in 1983.[64] The genome could no longer be thought of as a static template, but a dynamic responsive cellular component. In McClintock's work the possibility of environmental influence on genetics surfaces, along with the ghost of Lamarckian theory, long since thought to have been laid to rest by genetic dogma.

What is the secret of her success? She suggests that it depends on a number of factors. One is the close attention to detailed observation and the refusal to dismiss apparently anomalous results: 'The important thing is to develop the capacity to see

---

[62] B. McClintock, *The Discovery and Characterisation of Transposable Elements: Collected Papers of Barbara McClintock*, New York and London: Garland, 1987.

[63] N. Fedoroff, 'Maize Transposable Elements: A Story in Four Parts', in Fedoroff and Botstein (eds), *Dynamic Genome*, 389–415.

[64] Fedoroff and Botstein, 'Introduction', *Dynamic Genome*, 1.

one kernal that is different and make it understandable.'[65] She also finds it hard to pin down verbally how she knows what she knows, except that you have to 'hear what the material has to say to you' and openness to let it 'come to you' and a particular 'feeling for the organism'. She declares, 'I know every plant in the field, I know them intimately and I find it a great pleasure to know them'.[66] For McClintock reason, in the conventional sense of the word, is not adequate to describe the vast complexity of living forms; scientists can at best only partially fathom the life and order of living things. Her biographer believes that the special relationship and sympathetic understanding that McClintock had with the maize plants heightened her powers of discernment, so that 'what for others is interpretation or speculation, is for her a matter of trained and direct perception'.[67]

I suggest that this type of listening and perceiving develops and is fostered by wisdom. McClintock hints at a kind of mystical experience in the act of knowing, a mysticism emerging from the sense of unity with the natural world. While there is some common ground between different religious experiences of mysticism, it is important not to identify wisdom exclusively with mystical experiences. Biblical wisdom is rooted in practical daily reality, rather than esoteric Gnostic experiences. Yet wisdom is not limited to this role, but allows a deeper perception of the limits of the research undertaken and how it fits in with other kinds of knowing. McClintock's work is also significant in that it shows how attempts of geneticists to delineate the process of genetics as a one-way system of control proved to be far too simplistic. Instead, there is a dynamic element to the process that leads to new configurations and new complexity that we could even describe as a form of chaos. While geneticists continue to search out the meaning of such chaos, any attempt to constrict this to pre-set dogmas was bound to fail.

---

[65] E. F. Keller, *A Feeling for the Organism: The Life and Work of Barbara McClintock*, New York: Freeman, 1983, xiii.
[66] Keller, *Feeling*, xiv, 198.
[67] Keller, *Feeling*, xiii, 200.

The liminal face of wisdom

Wisdom, too is a liminal concept in biblical literature – it sits at the interface of the sacred and the secular, order and disorder. Lady Wisdom as portrayed in the book of Proverbs, for example, sits in uneasy tension with her counterpart Folly. The invitation of Proverbs 9 is somewhat fitting in the context of this discussion. After meticulous preparations, Wisdom offers an invitation to 'Come and eat my bread, drink the wine I have prepared'.[68] Those who decide to share in this meal leave the company of the immature, the eventual goal being to 'find life'. Such an offer of life is normally reserved for Yahweh alone. While we might interpret the Wisdom figure in various ways as a cosmic, cultic, prophetic or even domestic figure, it is the sharp contrast with the woman Folly that I would like to develop here. Folly, like wisdom, invites us to a meal of food and drink, but now 'Stolen waters are sweet, and bread tastes better when eaten in secret'. So the drink that she offers is stolen and we are told that it is sweet to the taste. Little preparation has gone into the meal, she merely announces her wares to the fools who are passing by. While Wisdom's offer of food leads to life, Folly's meal unwittingly leads to death.

Wisdom shares in the characteristics of the divine and I suggest is the feminine face of God. This is not meant to imply that God normally is male, but has a feminine aspect. Rather, as I discussed in Chapter 4, our image of God is beyond gender, so our metaphors need to reflect that fact by showing a balanced imagery. Does the role of Folly undermine any elevation of Wisdom as in some sense divine? I suggest that this need not be the case, rather the very ambivalence encountered reflects something experienced as real both in that society then and in a new way in our society as well. As women of that era, both Folly and Wisdom symbolise the marginal status of women: they were on the boundary between the ordered world of men and chaos.[69] Yet while we might wish to redescribe the

---

[68] For further commentary on this text, see J. E. McKinlay, *Gendering the Host: Biblical Invitations to Eat and Drink*, Sheffield: JSOT Sheffield Academic Press, 1996, 48–63.

[69] McKinlay, *Gendering*, 63–4.

role of women in ways that are more appropriate for contemporary society, wisdom's position as intermediary between order and chaos seems to me to be worth exploring further. Wisdom understood in this way is a profoundly suitable metaphor as a description of the changing tapestry of science as we find it in ecology and in biotechnology as well. The future of these sciences, I suggest, rests at this precarious boundary of order and chaos. The possibility of life or death presented by the figure of Wisdom in Proverbs is a reminder of the real risks that need to be faced in developing a future for science, in particular that associated with genetic technology. Such risks include not just threats to human health and the environment, but the future of science itself and its possible demise or flourishing.

Yet wisdom offers practical instruction and so is concerned with ethics as well as theology. For the sage rooted in a life of careful observation of the natural world, true wisdom has to be joined with righteous action and justice between peoples. Wisdom as discernment points to the quality most needed in polarised debates over genetic engineering. The social aspects of the debate can easily become lost if we allow ourselves to become restricted to technological problems and their technological solutions. The government may acknowledge that ethical issues need to be taken into account in the debate, but the way ethics is framed will affect the outcome of ethical deliberations. Appropriate decision-making in complex situations needs to take into account a range of opposing views. In seeking to find a way forward for the new technologies we need to be realistic about the impossibility of ever achieving total control. On the other hand, to reject all new developments as against some preconceived order fails to face the ambiguity already inherent in nature. I suggest that by developing a wisdom ethic a degree of communication can be achieved, one that looks not just to immediate commercial interest, but wider social issues as well. Furthermore, ethics is not just about how particular applications will be acceptable or not, but how science policy might be shaped in the future. I suggest that wider social issues need to be taken into account in such decisions. I am not suggesting that theology, in a spurious way, tries to reclaim its power as queen of the sciences. Rather, given that science has been such a powerful shaper of our culture and continues to shape our culture, then other voices need to be heard as well. The voice that I suggest is the most relevant from a theological perspective is that of wisdom. Furthermore, such a voice responds to the deeply felt public anxiety about the future of biotechnology, the sense that it is a system that is outside our control and one that is leading to a highly ambiguous future. I suggest further that if science is to regain the respect that it once had, then incorporating other voices will only enhance its status in society, rather than diminish it.

Conclusions

I have suggested in this chapter that the future of science is too critical a phenomenon to be left just to the scientists themselves. Rather, science as we know it today is not only embedded in our culture but has also become a shaper of it. The influence of science extends beyond itself and informs all aspects of human life, including the humanities. The way science develops in the future will depend on how far it retains particular claims about itself. One of the claims that has been particularly influential in the past and one that still influences most working scientists is the claim to be objective and thus value-free. However, I have suggested that the reasons for holding on to this claim have as much to do with particular social and political issues as science itself. Fortunately, the new physics shows that any rigid interpretation of objectivity is impossible to retain, given the modern discoveries of quantum physics. Furthermore, the search for truth and the search for wonder offer a richer interpretation of the scientific enterprise than pure cold objectivity.

However, all science has the potential to become scientism, that is a mythology that takes over all other ways of perceiving the world. If science becomes scientism then it claims power over all human activities. Theology needs to resist all forms of scientism. Although scientism is normally aimed at the general public, research has shown that the public is far more discerning towards the practice of science than one might have anticipated. The attitude of the public is important for the future of science, for where there is public hostility, science cannot flourish. The particular case of public attitudes to genetic engineering has uncovered a degree of ethical sensitivity that looks not just at the products, but the goals and motivation for the research, as well as the wider social and environmental consequences. I have suggested that the objection to genetic engineering as 'unnatural' could be retained without committing the so-called 'naturalistic fallacy', as long as this is interpreted in terms of Aquinas's view of natural law.

The relationship of science to technology is also significant in the context of biotechnology and public attitudes to it. Heidegger's critique of technology is particularly apt in this context. While we may not wish to endorse all aspects of his philosophy, his understanding of the alienating effects of modern technology has a remarkable contemporary resonance. He hints at what has become another parallel voice in the biosciences, namely the influence of ecology and ecological wisdom. While holism may be one value identified in ecology, another aspect is beginning to surface, namely an understanding of the world as chaotic. While this has not yet reached public consciousness, it seems to me to be important for the way science will unfold in the future. For science is now at the boundary of order and chaos, not just in physics, but in ecology as well. To presume that we can have complete control amounts to hubris. This brings us back to the idea of wisdom, which seems to me to be vitally important in shaping an adequate future for science. Wisdom need not be divorced from the practice of science, as Barbara McClintock's discoveries indicated. Her battle to have her ideas accepted shows that science can be entrenched in its own dogma as much as any other human enterprise. The figure of Wisdom again offers herself as a liminal concept, at the boundary of order and chaos. In this she echoes something of the future of science. Yet Wisdom also has a practical dimension as well. For she is vital in helping scientists and policy-makers to consider the complexity of the issues that they face in making decisions.

One of the problems of the new biology is that in its very newness it has not yet had time to be tested. From a psychological perspective wisdom is a quality that grows with age and experience. It is the employment of decision strategies that are effective, as they have been learned over time.[70] It involves solving a complex set of questions simultaneously, one that looks in particular to the future in order to consider long-term effects as well as short-term ones. Rather than being one character trait, it is a blend of qualities that come together in a certain way. Hence, even in terms of biological science, wisdom is a good that needs to be fostered. As I have argued throughout this book, from a theological perspective wisdom is an alignment not just with any value or any outcome, but an alignment with the purposes and intentions of God. The way this would work out in practice to develop science in the future relies on dialogue and greater communication between scientists, policy-makers, members of the public, ethicists and theologians. Fortunately there are some signs of a greater appreciation of the importance of such dialogue through the development of committees that are more, rather than less, inclusive. The shift in 1999 of the composition of those elected to be members of the Advisory Commission on Releases into the Environment is a good example of such a change.

The methodology of science makes it hard for scientists themselves to undertake such a broadening of their vision. Where theology retreats into a narrow dogmatism the same criticism would apply. Yet if theology at its best is to offer something to science it is surely this: an affirmation of its values of wonder, beauty, reason, truth and imagination, but at the same time a rejection of arrogance, closed mindedness and irresponsibility, especially in certain applications in technology. In the place of the 'ethical vacuum' left by biological science alone, theology can bring a framework for ethics. However, if nature alone is looked to as a source of ultimate value, it is

---

[70] See J. E. Birren and L. M. Fisher, 'The Elements of Wisdom: Overview and Integration', in R. Sternberg (ed.), *Wisdom: Its Nature, Origins and Development*, Cambridge: Cambridge University Press, 1990, 320–1.

bound to disappoint. The suggestion of Pope John Paul II which I mentioned in the first chapter is relevant again here and is worth repeating. He suggested that scientists need to 'continue their efforts without ever abandoning the sapiential horizon within which scientific and technological achievements are wedded to the philosophical and ethical values which are the distinctive and indelible mark of the human person'.[71]

[71] Pope John Paul II, *Faith and Reason, Encyclical Letter Fides et Ratio*, London: Catholic Truth Society, 1998, 152.

7

Conclusions

I began this book with a brief discussion of issues facing us in
the new biology. While on the one hand genetic engineering
offers a promising new future for humanity, with the potential
to detect and treat genetically inherited diseases, on the other
hand the technology itself poses a potential threat, both to
the environment and human health. Furthermore, any imple-
mentation of genetic engineering raises issues of justice, for
example through the use of patents and the development of
the technology in the poorer nations of the world. The complexity of these issues can lead to both anxiety and ambiguity
towards the new biotechnology. In addition, the ability of
humankind to change the genetic basis for life presents us
with a future that will be very different from any future we
have known in the past. Those who liken the new technology
to an extension of either breeding or use of microbes in, for
example, cheese-making or brewing, fail to take into account
the drastic changes in life-forms that are now possible. For
example, never before has it been possible to introduce genes
from one species to other unrelated species.

At the heart of the dilemma facing us there seems to be a
crisis in knowledge – how do we know that the knowledge we
have gained will be used for good or ill? Classical science was
rooted in philosophy or love of wisdom. Wisdom was
integrated into the search for knowledge, and was understood
as integrated into life itself – very different from our modern
notion of knowledge as just a 'string of information'. Once

science becomes fragmented into specialities containing mere information, as is the case in modernity, it loses touch with its deeper philosophical roots in wisdom. It seems possible that the ambiguity which we experience today in considering the new technology is a child of this distortion of knowledge into fragmented information. There are also other possible dangers of this kind of fragmented mentality, since it has the ability to take over and dominate other ways of reading texts, such as we find in poetry or narrative. Yet, ironically perhaps, the major advances in science have not, in practice, presumed such a truncated view of knowledge. The philosopher of science, Karl Popper, recognised that scientific knowing at its most creative is never simply gathering information, but relies on a tacit understanding and perception that goes beyond the facts themselves. Even more significant perhaps, the turn to the Eastern religions in the new physics, however superficial from a religious perspective, acknowledges that science and religion are not as incompatible as they might appear. In other words within science itself today we see a turn to a greater degree of synthesis than has been possible in the past. Such a shift is not yet obvious in the new biology, relying as it does on a mechanistic view of the natural world.

I have argued throughout this book that the theological motif we need to recover as an appropriate response to the new biology is that of wisdom. Such wisdom is grounded in the Old Testament wisdom literature, which has become the subject of active interest among biblical scholars in recent years. One of the reasons for its dismissal in the past relates to the fact that salvation history is in a minor key in most wisdom literature. Furthermore, it seems to have drawn on images from the surrounding culture in a way that rendered it less distinctive compared with other biblical writings. Wisdom for the sage deals with right relationships with God and between peoples, but it is thoroughly down to earth and grounded in everyday decisions facing humanity. Above all it offers guidance about life based on the practical historical reality stemming from everyday problems and issues. Much of this wisdom shows parallels with those cultures, such as that of ancient Egypt, that were historically and geographically close to ancient Judaism. Yet undergirding the wisdom literature we find that the main tenets of Jewish salvation history are assumed, surfacing at times through a retelling of some of its key events, such as the exodus narrative. Wisdom literature does have its own distinctive narratives, but they are focused on particular people and events. The book of Job is a good example of wisdom in the mode of narrative.

Yet the wisdom tradition also deals with creation themes in a way that is far more pronounced compared with other Old Testament literature. Some might even suggest that the careful and detailed observation of the natural world that was characteristic of the sage even implies a kind of proto-natural science. Creation is not celebrated in order to give evidence for the existence of God in a natural theology, rather creation simply points to the same God who exercises divine providence over human history as well. Wisdom, in particular, is co-creating with God, one who playfully comes alongside God in the beginning. Hence wisdom has a cosmological aspect, showing forth the glory of God in the world. In the later literature wisdom becomes personified in Lady Wisdom, who, in contrast to Folly, offers humanity the path that leads to righteousness and life. Wisdom takes on characteristics of the divinity in such a way that some have argued that she is a hypostasis of God. A more likely explanation in a Jewish context is that she is a personification of the divine, though to relegate her to simply an attribute of God does not really do justice to the strength of the figure who confronts us in the guise of Wisdom.

In an anthropological sense wisdom is learned through education, mainly in the context of the family, but is also a gift from God. A paradox exists whereby only those who seek her find Wisdom, but she cannot be grasped or used for human aggrandisement. Wisdom, humility and justice are all inter-related with each other. While it is probably incorrect to call wisdom political in any specific sense, the underlying assumption in wisdom is that right relationships between God, humanity and the natural world need to be respected. A failure to respect the rights of others through oppression of the poor is a failure in wisdom as well as justice. Furthermore, wisdom

seems to bind all the moral attributes together. Hence wisdom
in the Old Testament has many faces, anthropological, social
and cosmological. The breadth of the roles of wisdom strikes
me as a considerable advantage in developing a theology of
creation, particularly against the background of the challenges
facing us in the new biology. The creation of the world cannot
be divorced from social issues. In this wisdom begins to emerge
as a metaphor for a theology of creation.

It might seem surprising that contemporary theologians have
not so far developed the concept of wisdom in a creation
theology. One of the reasons for this may be the dismissal of
wisdom literature in past scholarship as an appropriate source
for theological reflection. Another is the myopic use of the
first chapters of Genesis to the exclusion of other texts. A
third is the way wisdom becomes developed in the New
Testament so that it includes the wisdom of the cross. However,
it seems to me that the wisdom of the cross is still an essential
ingredient of creation theology if it is to deal adequately with
the issue of suffering in creation. Those creation theologies
that focus simply on the return to a state of blessedness in the
beginning fail to consider in sufficient depth the horror of
creaturely suffering that has become known to us through an
understanding of evolution. One alternative might be simply
to accept such suffering as part of the process, a view common
among those influenced by Hegel and process philosophy.
Yet the cross challenges any such acceptance; rather we are
left with an image of a co-suffering God who identifies with
the victims of such a process, rather than the process itself.
The cross is a reminder that all our images of wisdom pale
before the shock of the wisdom of God presented to us in the
form of the Crucified One. It seems to me this is necessary,
not only in order to take into account the issue of theodicy,
but also to confront the constant temptation to hubris.

The way the New Testament developed a Wisdom
Christology is instructive as it gives us clues as to how to link
the creation-centred wisdom of the Old Testament with the
figure of Christ. How might we perceive salvation history
within a theology of creation? The opposite danger to creation-
centred theology which ignores redemptive themes is a theology

where creation is just relegated to a stage of salvation history. It seems to me that creation-centred theology is responding to the lack of an adequate theology of creation in much contemporary theological writing. Wisdom Christology seems to offer a way out of this dilemma by affirming the importance of the person of Christ, but linking Christ with creation in an integral way such that creation is thoroughly affirmed. It is, in a sense, a way of greening Christology so that wider issues such as the environment come into view in the scope of salvation history. Such an integral link is essential if creation is to become fully affirmed in a manner that is at the heart of any doctrine of the incarnation. The writers of the Synoptic Gospels seemed well aware of the Jewish wisdom literature and pointed to Christ as the teacher of wisdom. In John we find an even more profound identification: Christ the Logos is also the same Sophia, Wisdom, celebrated in Jewish literature. The parallels drawn between the particular texts describing the role of Wisdom in creation and that of the Logos are particularly striking. However, I suggest that John's intention was not to replace Sophia with the Logos, so much as to celebrate the incarnation of Sophia in the person of Christ, using the language of the Logos. Hymns to the cosmic Christ in the letters to the Colossians and Ephesians are more likely to be showing how Christ is the expression of the cosmic activity of Wisdom, rather than a literal description of Christ as co-creator of the world. At the same time John's Gospel points to the pre-incarnate role of the Logos in the beginning. It is possible that the divine Logos and Sophia could be seen as working together in the creation of the world in such a way that the activities of each become almost indistinguishable. Yet some distinction must be maintained if Sophia is to retain her identity apart from the Logos. I suggest that one way this may be possible is through widening the scope of the activity of Sophia beyond that of Christology.

Given that a Wisdom Christology has shown the possibility of linking creation and Christ, how might wisdom be developed in a theology of creation? Here we have some clues from the Eastern Church, where there is little fragmentation of theology into different specialisms in the manner that we find in the traditions of the Western Church today. Furthermore, the early Fathers of the Eastern Church anticipated the theology of Wisdom, or Sophiology, that emerged in the writing of Solovyov, Florensky and Bulgakov. Solovyov developed a philosophical interpretation of Sophia, and identified her with the soul of the world. His visionary, mystical experiences of Sophia seem to take their cues from the figure of the Virgin Mary, who is also identified with Sophia. Any intimation that Sophia is a separate hypostasis or Quarterary in the Godhead was met with condemnation from the official hierarchy. Bulgakov attempted to put Sophiology on a more theologically respectable footing, though his writing was never officially recognised. For Bulgakov Sophia is the intermediary between God and creation, the yearning love of God for creation, the longing of creation in Romans 8. In other words the discovery of the future of creation comes through participation in Sophia. He suggests that Sophia is both divine and creaturely. In her creaturely mode Sophia is visible in the creation, expressed through the love of God. She comes to the fullest expression in the person of the Virgin Mary. Sophia as both divine and creaturely is expressed in the incarnation of Christ, who is perfect human and divine. Sophia is the means through which divine ideas become reality, so that truth as identified with the Logos becomes transparent in beauty, identified with the Spirit. This movement between Divine and creaturely Sophia reflects the glory of God, so that Wisdom signifies the content of the Trinity and glory, the manifestation of the action of the Trinity. In this Bulgakov takes the radical step of locating Sophia in the *ousia* or being of God. While his views were condemned at the time as heretical, it seems to me that his theology does have significance in developing an adequate basis for a theology of creation.

In particular, bringing the feminine Sophia into the heart of the Trinity is particularly suggestive for a feminist theology, which takes into account feminine metaphors for God. Bulgakov's notion of the shadowy side to Sophia allows for the suffering in creation in a way that is missing in Teilhard de Chardin's theology rooted in evolutionary categories. However, Teilhard is interesting in that he acts like a kind of bridge between East and West. His hymn to the Eternal Feminine draws on the wisdom literature, though he never spelt out his Sophiology in a formal sense. Furthermore, his concern seems to have been primarily with the discovery of an appropriate image of the Virgin Mary, rather than Sophia as such. Overall the Sophiology of Bulgakov offers an interpretation of Wisdom that is theologically rich and highlights the power of Wisdom to integrate different strands in theological discourse, including, for example, God and creation, creation and redemption, cross and resurrection, God and humanity, masculine and feminine, present and future, reflection and action, East and West.

In Thomas Aquinas there is an emphasis on practical wisdom and prudence that is somewhat lacking in the theology of Bulgakov. The influence of Aristotle, rather than Plato, contrasts with Bulgakov's approach to wisdom. Aquinas describes the action of prudence in the moral life in terms that echo those of Aristotle. He is significant for our present purposes in that he reminds us to keep wisdom down to earth by addressing practical problems in everyday decision-making. Such decisions must include those that impinge on the relationship between humanity and the natural world, as well as those that affect our relationship with God. The goal of the moral life is towards goodness and prudence, which is the means whereby virtues find their orientation and action. However, his thesis on wisdom becomes specifically theological in his recognition that wisdom is not just learnt, it is also a gift of the Holy Spirit. The gift of the Holy Spirit that is most clearly linked with wisdom is that of charity. This marriage of love and wisdom echoes Bulgakov, though he was concerned with the particular action of God in creation, rather than developing a model for human action in the world, as in Aquinas. In addition, Aquinas suggests that the beatitude that is most relevant for wisdom is that of peacemaking. Love expressed as friendship with God finds expression in the Eucharist. Bulgakov and Aquinas both seem to suggest that love and wisdom come to be expressed liturgically in the Eucharist. Such an insight confirms the suggestion that both the wisdom of the cross and the wisdom of the created world come together in a communal way in the celebration of Holy

Communion. However, it seems to me that the significance of wisdom goes further than this in that it is through the Eucharist that the Christian community finds the resources to develop the moral life, to become icons of wisdom in a broken world.

Such reflections lead naturally to a consideration of the relationship between the Spirit and wisdom. At first sight it might seem strange to connect the wisdom literature with the Spirit, the former is more naturally concerned with the sage rather than the seer. Yet there is a considerable body of Old Testament literature that points to a link between wisdom and the activity of the Spirit. The tendency to confine the activity of the Spirit to the human community reflects an impoverished understanding the work of the Spirit in the world. There is a need to distinguish between the working of the Spirit in creation, as identified with the figure of Wisdom, and the work of the Spirit as wisdom in the human community. At the same time, insofar as humanity is also created from the dust of the earth it must share in the work of the Spirit in creation. The problem is a common one, namely how to affirm humanity as part of the natural realm, but also apart from it. I suggest that one way that this unity and distinction could become clarified is through distinguishing the Spirit of Wisdom in the mode of pneumatology from the Spirit of Wisdom in the mode of Christology. The Spirit of Wisdom in the whole of the created order, including humanity, is a cosmic Spirit. It is that aspect of Wisdom in the mode of creativity and creation. However, there is a sense in which this creation is still unfinished and there is a longing in all creation for redemption, for healing. The groaning of all creation is in the Spirit, but it points to a hope in Christ as redeemer. The Spirit of Wisdom that is the Spirit of Christ begins in the human community. Yet the Spirit of Christ is not confined to the human community, the healing scope of Christ's activity extends to include all of creation in the new creation. In other words the healing work of the Spirit of Christ/Wisdom begins with the human community, so that in this healing humanity becomes an icon for the possible salvation of the whole world. Thus there is a cosmic scope to the work of Wisdom through the Spirit's activity in creation and a cosmic scope to the work of Wisdom through Christ's redemptive activity. Creation and re-creation are in Love, but through Wisdom. While the former is marked by the playful action of the Spirit in the world, the latter is marked with the sign of the cross and resurrection.

The dynamic movement between God and creation takes on a Trinitarian shape in the guise of Wisdom. This Trinitarian understanding of God's action in the world bears some resemblance to the models of God as the social Trinity, such as in the theology of Jürgen Moltmann. However, there are important differences. Augustine suggested a model for Wisdom in the Trinity in essentialist terms, which concurs with the view of Bulgakov that Wisdom is integral to the being or *ousia* of God. Yet on the other hand Wisdom speaks of relatedness, of finding communion between all the persons of the Trinity in Love. Understanding the Trinity in wisdom categories holds in tension both the Unity and Tri-unity of God, without insisting on the priority of one over the other. At the same time the Wisdom of God can never be fully understood or grasped, keeping alive the apophatic tradition in theology. While the shape of the action of wisdom in the world may be best understood in a Trinitarian way, the language of wisdom is important as a way of clarifying the process involved in the dynamic of the relationship between God and creation.

Such language is best understood as metaphorical, hinting at the possibilities in defining such a relationship between God and creation, rather than confining the action of God to either the processes in the world or in detachment from the world. Wisdom in her creative mode is like a whisper to the world in its becoming, perhaps on a different plane of reality to that currently discovered by science. Yet wisdom bears its stamp on the material world in much the same way that humanity can be thought of as made in the image of God. The material creation experiences a freedom of expression that makes itself vulnerable to the possibility of turning away from wisdom. Such a turning away leads to death, while the alternative of finding an echo with wisdom leads to life. God as Spirit of Wisdom is not so much intervening in the world in the traditional sense, as being there alongside, a pansyntheism.

However, there is more to the relationship between God and the world than the pansyntheism that expresses the activity of the Spirit. The future of creation looks to a new creation, one that expresses the *parousia* of Christ. Such a *parousia* highlights the significance of the cross and resurrection. The biblical images of apocalyptic are a stark reminder that this world alone cannot give an adequate basis for interpreting the new creation. How might wisdom be related to apocalyptic? The conjunction between wisdom and apocalyptic sounds strange, yet within the apocalyptic literature we can find appropriation of wisdom sources. This wisdom may be transformed into the particular eschatological view of the writer, but it does show a precedent for using wisdom language in thinking about the future of the earth. To suggest that wisdom is irrelevant for such a task ignores a considerable body of biblical material. Furthermore, the first book of *Enoch* gives some interesting clues as to the way that the wisdom of this world may be related to the next.

Enoch may have been written in language that is strange to contemporary readers, but it does show a deliberate attempt to include the science of the time in reflections on wisdom. For the writer of *Enoch* the full knowledge of the creation of the world is given to those who seek wisdom, but wisdom is withdrawn from all those who are proud, the sin of the fallen angel. The new creation is creation that is healed of sin. Such a model points to a view of history that expresses the eternal present, rather than one that is straining forward in a linear way towards a future. Scientific models of the future of the earth according to physicists depend on whether the universe is a closed or open system. In the former scenario the end will come through a 'big crunch', while in the latter the end comes through a slow heat-death. The language is apocalyptic, but the future is ultimately bleak, rather than full of hope. Such images contrast with the future according to genetic engineers that more often suggests utopia, rather than catastrophe. Theologians who engage with genetic science more often than not seem to reinforce such utopian imagery by identifying the work of humanity in terms of co-creation. The stress on human freedom in this context seems to eclipse more cautious approaches to the ability of humankind to define its own future and that of the earth. The eschatology adopted in this case is one that emerges from the present and, as Moltmann has suggested, a *futurans*, rather than an *adventus*.

I suggest that it is important to retain a sense of the second coming of Christ as a reminder of the final glory that is to come. If eschatology simply emerges from the present world, then what hope is there for a new creation? The tradition of *parousia*, or second coming, is an affront to any assumption that we can find all that we need to know by looking at the past and present. Yet such a past and present is caught up into the new future, rather than being detached from it. A model of eschatology that stresses the *parousia* shows some coherence with wisdom in that both challenge any arrogant assumptions that we can read the 'signs of future' entirely in the 'signs of the times'. However, there are problems with a radical portrayal of eschatology as simply coming from ahead. One of the main difficulties of Moltmann's eschatology as conceived entirely from the future is that it tends to detach itself from the present in a way that leaves behind the language about creation as found in science. This is reinforced still further by his rejection of any form of natural theology as invalid. We are left with a dilemma of how to relate creation and new creation. Hence, an eschatology is needed that can give due weight to an alternative model hinted at in the wisdom apocalyptic writings, one that expresses a sense of integration as well as difference between the present and the future, between earth and heaven. Wisdom, once integrated into an eschatological mode of thought, takes into account the eternal now, that is that signs of this future can be discernible in the present, but also qualifies this by reference to the future. This is not the myth of the 'eternal return' so much as an antici-pation of blessedness in spite of the traumas of the present. Paradoxically, perhaps, apocalyptic literature that draws on wisdom speaks of a healing of this world in order to fit it for the next. In such literature wisdom delineates not just creation, but new creation as well, when all of creation will participate in the Wisdom of God. Christian theology can draw on these images by reflection on the icon of Christ as the Wisdom of

God. The *parousia* is a fundamental reminder that Christ is Lord of time and history. Yet Christ as Wisdom more readily appropriates the spatial dimension in cosmic redemption compared with other temporal descriptions of Christ as Lord of History. Eschatology that is defined in either temporal or spatial categories alone is incomplete, but Wisdom allows for such an integration.

How might these reflections bear on the practical workings of science, in particular the biosciences? What kind of future can we expect in science? I suggest that the way science is likely to be shaped in the future is related to the culture of the sciences. This culture still carries the burden of positivist thought, especially the desire for objectivity and value-neutrality. While there are some signs that science is moving towards a more sensitive approach to the idea of objectivity through the insights of the new physics, traces of this attitude remain. Yet alongside this we find other aspects to the culture of science that cohere with theological goals, such as the search for truth and the search for wonder. Once science claims to be the basis for all knowledge, then it becomes a mythology that is best described as scientism. Such language expressing the supremacy of science is characteristic of the more popular writings of scientists, which have a direct influence on the public. However, public opinion shows itself to be both sensitive and discerning when it comes to consideration of practical issues that affect them, such as genetic engineering. It is unlikely that science will be able to progress without public support, hence public opinion has a direct bearing on the future of science. Focus-group work suggests that in general the public is dismissive of much genetic technology, criticising the motives for the research, the beneficiaries and the likely social consequences. Research into public attitudes shows a far greater degree of sophistication than tends to be parodied by scientists, many of whom believe that the only role of the public is to understand their particular goals, rather than to be critical of such goals.

However, some might argue that the public rejection of genetic engineering is not so much rejection of science, as of technology. The relationship between science and technology is a complex one, but technology certainly cannot be thought of in a simplistic way as just applied science. It is a two way process where the discoveries in biotechnology make a significant contribution to science as such. Martin Heidegger is deeply critical of the influence of technology on humanity, in particular its pretence to show forth means of controlling the natural world for human benefit alone. We need instead to tune into the *telos* of nature. A more theological interpretation of Heidegger would be to suggest that such a *telos* is discoverable through natural law, insofar as it reflects the eternal Wisdom of God.

Nonetheless, the future of science is not as gloomy as this might suggest. There are narratives in the sciences that show a rather different approach is possible, even within genetic science. An alternative model for science practice is epitomised in the story of Barbara McClintock. Her research into maize chromosomes demonstrated clearly the degree of determination combined with perception that is important in moving science forward. I suggest that her approach exemplifies a form of wisdom, though it is one that needs to be critiqued from the perspective of theology. There are other hopeful signs in ecological science as well. Recent research shows that rather than accept the standard image of ecology as an ecosystem, we need to think of the relationships between species in terms of patches of diverse and fluid communities. Furthermore, this tends to portray ecology not as the science of an ordered network of relationships, but as chaos. This move to a greater awareness of the natural world as both ordered and chaotic bears some resemblance to shifts taking place in the new physics.

Yet what is at the boundary of order and chaos in a theological sense? Surely once again the figure of Wisdom comes into view, an intermediary between the ordered world of the masculine and that of chaos. In their search for order genetic engineers have arrived at the possibility of chaos. Yet in the acceptance of order in ecosystems, other surprising chaotic elements come to the surface. The future of genetic engineering needs to take into account this element of the chaotic, the unpredictability inherent in all life systems in their interaction

with each other. Perhaps an element of the chaotic is part of
the risk of creativity, so that all attempts at human control are
doomed to fail. How far we wish to take the chaotic into our
own hands is a matter for serious reflection. Yet as the story
of creation reminds us, ultimately under God an ordering does
come out of chaos. There is some truth in the model of ecosystem, just as there is some truth in Newtonian physics. Such
a discovery of chaos has profound implications not just for a
theology of creation, but also for ecological theology as well.
The use of ecology as a model for interrelationship, community
and order is one that seems to be as deep-seated as the
alternative mechanistic one parodied as that which leads to
the death of nature. Green theologians in particular are apt to
use ecological language as a way of either reinforcing social
models of God or to supporting particular political imperatives.
However, it seems to me that to pose the organic model of the
earth in opposition to the mechanistic one only takes us to a
new set of problems. Both models suggest a fixity of order
that is only part of reality. Instead, holding the complexity of
life through a model of order and chaos is one that is more
consistent with current research. Furthermore, it is one that
offers a more dynamic view of the action of God in creation
in a way that is impossible with either the organic or
mechanistic approach. If we replace a machine with an
organism, there is still a fixity of boundaries, even if the idea
of an organism seems to be more in tune with our understanding of the natural world as alive. Yet the nature of how
this life is expressed is one that seems to draw simply on models
of human egalitarianism in a way that cannot avoid the charge
of anthropocentrism.

The way such a model of creation as the dynamic of order
and chaos through Wisdom is related to the future of creation
can only be hinted at here. I have suggested earlier that the
future is one where all of creation participates in the Wisdom
of God, that in the final Glory the natural world is caught up
in the Wisdom of the Trinity. How far the element of chaos
and order remains in the future of creation is a matter for
speculation. Yet it seems to me that however it comes to be
expressed, the future of creation will be one that is dynamic,

rather than static, expressing the energy and compassion of God as well as showing the scars of suffering Love.

In what way might this impinge on the task of genetic engineering? Just as a theology of creation through Wisdom takes its cues from the issues facing us in the new biology, so a theology of creation can give some hints in shaping a future for genetic engineering. An ethic based on wisdom helps to delineate such a task. According to Aquinas the virtue of wisdom is directed towards a particular goal, a *telos*. However, I suggest that this *telos* is not just emergent from the present, but needs to orientate itself to the eternal Wisdom of God. It is well known that in evolution the unfolding course of nature is presented with a number of possibilities. In as far as humanity expresses the virtue of wisdom the goal of goodness is achieved. In as far as humanity seeks wisdom in a holistic way, rather than simply through information gathering, then this will serve to reflect the future of creation as redeemed. Such a task of careful discernment is one that requires patience and sensitivity.

Ultimately an understanding of creation through Wisdom points theology to a new spirituality, one where all of creation is caught up with humanity in praise and worship of God. Giving the Trinity the garment of Wisdom helps to foster dialogue with other religions, where Wisdom is recognised as a religious symbol, but the Trinity is not. Such a dialogue is one that awaits further development, for the future of humanity is through a joint exploration of common themes. Nonetheless, in the Christian community Wisdom as expressed in the liturgy of the Eucharist is a reminder of the affirmation of the action of God in creation. The gifts of creation are part of the natural world as well as expressions of human creativity. When humanity works with the *telos* of the natural world in as far as it expresses the Wisdom of Christ, then this future is one that bears the seeds of a new future, one that is life giving. This exemplifies not just the idea of flourishing, but also that of beauty, as expressed in the guise of Wisdom as Spirit of beauty.

But where humanity turns away from wisdom and seeks after its own self-interest in detachment from others and the natural world, this leads to death and denial. For a Christian, it is in the Eucharist that strength to walk the way of wisdom is given. In as far as we fail in such a task, the whole creation groans with longing, waiting for redemption. In as far as we try and walk the way of wisdom our responsibility to bear the image of Christ is secured. Such an orientation is one that is both learned, but also a gift. As long as we live in a world broken by sin and disfigured by suffering and rejection, the attainment of wisdom is never complete. Yet with eyes fixed on the Wisdom of God we can begin to discover the meaning of creation. Such a discovery brings with it a sense of home-coming, a reintegration of humanity in the world, while offering humanity a distinctive place in that world. For it is in humanity that Wisdom in the guise of the Spirit of Christ becomes most evident. Yet Wisdom seeks to integrate the anthropological with the cosmological. We find avenues to express such a belief through offering praise to cosmic Wisdom in Hildegard's poem, where the three wings of Wisdom signify the Trinity. In considering the idea of creation through Wisdom it is fitting to give her the final word:

> O power of Wisdom!
> You encompassed the cosmos,
> encircling and embracing all
> in one living orbit
> with your three wings:
> one soars on high,
> one distils the earth's essence,
> and the third hovers everywhere.
> Praise to you, Wisdom, fitting praise![1]

---

[1] B. Newman, *Sister of Wisdom: St Hildegard's Theology of the Feminine*, Berkeley: University of California Press, 1987, 64.

Index of Names

Index of Subjects